DAVID **DAVID** DAVID **DAVID** DAVID **DAVID** DAVID

B E L O V E D DAWGS

DAVID DAVID **DAVID** DAVID **DAVID** DAVID **DAVID**

DAVID **DAVID** DAVID **DAVID** DAVID **DAVID** DAVID

BELOVED DAWGS

DAVID DAVID **DAVID** DAVID **DAVID** DAVID **DAVID**

14 🏈 47

MEMORIES OF THE FOUR MAGICAL YEARS
OF THE DAVIDS AND SOME OF THEIR FRIENDS

BY LORAN SMITH

FOREWORD BY VERNE LUNDQUIST
AFTERWORD BY MARK RICHT

LONGSTREET PRESS
Athens, Georgia

DEDICATION

For Mark Christensen,
a friend and hero of the Richt Dawgs,
and to our grandson, Alex,
may he someday wear silver britches.

LONGSTREET
PRESS

LONGSTREET PRESS, INC.
325 Milledge Avenue
Athens, Georgia 30601
www.longstreetpress.net

Printed in the United States of America
1st printing, 2005

ISBN: 1-56352-749-9

Book photographs by:
Don Contreras, Dan Evans, Bulldawg Illustrated, Terry Stephens, Kay Greene, Kelli Pollack,
University of Georgia Athletic Association

Jacket and book design by Burtch Hunter Design LLC

First of all, to the teammates of The Davids, who helped make this story possible.

To Mark Richt and his capable and cooperative coaching staff.

To Damon Evans, whom I admire, and who I think is going to establish himself as one of the foremost athletic directors in college athletics.

To Rick and Kay Greene and Norm and Kelli Pollack whose support, remembrances, manuscript proofing and generous background information were invaluable.

To my wife, Myrna, for her patience and indefatigable assistance in shepherding the raw copy through her computer.

To George Harwood, a retired English teacher, whose mind, fortunately, has not retired.

To Claude Felton for his advice, support and assistance. Georgia has never had a more valuable public information servant.

To Karen Huff in Claude's office, who is an able assistant and smiles politely and gently when she answers any request.

To Steve Colquitt, who brought his Associated Press style and knowledge of Bulldog facts to this publication.

To Jared Benko, Jordan Posey and Jenny Menkes, student assistants, for assisting with research. They make you realize that there are capable young people out there, who will contribute positively to society.

To Claire Smith for valuable editorial assistance. She edited, organized and managed *Beloved Dawgs* into its final form, before the book reached design status.

To Burtch Hunter, *Beloved Dawgs*' layout and design artist with the right stuff.

To the ultimate Dawg loyalist, Dan Magill, my mentor and Beloved friend. I've tried to follow in his footsteps.

To the passionate Georgia fans, whose love for the Beloved Dawgs is unsurpassed.

To David and Davey: It is nice to be appreciated for your play on the field, but to be beloved for what you stand for—which is how the Bulldog Nation feels about you—should make you cling to the campus of the nation's oldest state chartered university, as long as you live.

DAVID **DAVID** DAVID **DAVID** DAVID **DAVID** DAVID

BELOVED DAWGS

DAVID DAVID **DAVID** DAVID **DAVID** DAVID **DAVID**

CONTENTS

FOREWORD
BY VERNE LUNDQUIST

Under a broiling September sun in Austin, Texas, in 1952, I watched the Notre Dame Fighting Irish and their legendary coach, Frank Leahy, defeat the Texas Longhorns and their not-quite-so-legendary coach, Ed Price, by a score of 14-3.

I was twelve years old. My late father, an ordained Lutheran minister, had accepted a call that faraway summer to become the pastor of Gethsemane Lutheran Church in Austin, and so had moved our family - himself, mom, me and three younger brothers - from his previous parish in Everett, Washington, to the beautiful capitol city of Texas.

On that mid-September afternoon, I was selling soft drinks in the north end zone of Memorial Stadium. A Coke cost a nickel back then. We young capitalists purchased a couple of dozen of them from the vendor for three cents apiece, and then went into the stands and sold each one for two cents profit.

Memorial Stadium was filled beyond capacity. More than sixty thousand fans were stuffed into every available seat, plus some not available. I was dazzled, not only by the players on the field - Notre Dame's Johnny Lattner would go on to win the Heisman Trophy one year later - but was mesmerized by all of the so called "peripheral" activities: the cheerleaders, the card stunts in the student sections (Remember them?), the pre-game and halftime spectacles, and the alma-maters and the fight songs played by the bands. I still perk-up whenever I hear the beginning notes of "Hail, Hail To Old Notre Dame" or "Texas, Fight!"

Notre Dame vs. Texas was the first college football game I ever saw in person. So began a fascination with, and affection for, a wonderful sport that has now exceeded a half a hundred years.

For the past four decades, it's been my good fortune to watch college football from a professional perspective, first as a local television sportscaster in Austin, San Antonio, and Dallas, and, later, as a play-by-play announcer for both ABC and CBS Sports.

Since 2000, Todd Blackledge and I have served as the principal broadcast team for CBS in its coverage of Southeastern Conference football games. That brings me, finally, to the purpose of this foreword.

During the years 2001-2004, we televised more than twenty football games involving the University of Georgia Bulldogs, which means we spent roughly seventy hours perched in broadcast booths at various locations in the southern United States watching David Greene from Snellville, Georgia, perform his magic on one side of the ball, and then David Pollack from Snellville, Georgia, perform his magic on the other side of the ball. We also held countless conversations with them both, almost always together, in preparation for our Saturday afternoon telecasts.

The story of their close friendship, from the mornings of youth league football games as six year olds, to the afternoons of shared stardom wearing the uniforms of the Georgia Bulldogs, became a recurrent theme of our game presentations.

That was because of both of what they did and who they are.

Todd and I were eyewitnesses to two of the most spectacular single plays in their Georgia careers.

David Pollack, then a sophomore, who, against his desires, had been moved from defensive tackle to defensive end, somehow stripped South Carolina quarterback Corey Jenkins of the football in the Gamecock end zone to help secure an early season win in Columbia. Because Pollack jarred the ball loose from Jenkins' grip as he was initiating a throwing motion and then, somehow, grabbed it before it hit the ground, he had created an interception and a Georgia touchdown and secured a Bulldog victory. It became the defining play for Pollack and made his jersey number, 47, the most replicated jersey number in Georgia football history, with the possible exception of Herschel Walker's number 34.

David Greene, also a sophomore, faced a couple of formidable obstacles on a soft November evening in Auburn, Alabama. His team trailed Auburn late in the fourth quarter, and as the Bulldogs broke the huddle, only mildly distracted by the collective screams of 86,063 Auburn fans, they were attempting to convert a fourth down and fifteen from the Tiger nineteen-yard line. Well, there were 75,563

Auburn fans and 10,500 or so wearing the red and black. The old stadium was shaking.

Greene fired a perfect left handed spiral to a leaping Michael Johnson, who had made his way five yards into the left side of the Auburn end zone. Johnson's catch and the subsequent touchdown secured both Georgia's first SEC championship since the days of Herschel and David Greene's legendary status as one of the most beloved Bulldog signal callers of all time. He ended his career as the winningest quarterback in NCAA football history.

Ironically, Todd Blackledge and I missed David Greene's first great comeback as a Georgia quarterback. We were sitting in our broadcast position at Tiger Stadium in Baton Rouge, preparing to do the second game of a doubleheader, and watching on the television monitor when Greene, as a freshman, hit Verron Haynes over the middle for the winning touchdown in front of 107,592 hostiles at Tennessee.

We have, however, heard Larry Munson's memorable radio call of that play, oh, maybe, 300 times. "Broke their nose!" "Hobnail boot!" Larry Munson is, descriptively, in a league all his own.

The Davids will be forever acknowledged for their contributions to the accomplishments of the Georgia football team, but they should be equally remembered for how they represented themselves and their families and their university out of uniform.

They are both good men - affable, responsible, courteous, industrious, ethical, humorous, and loyal. Their values are rock solid. They will contribute to their communities and their country in a multitude of ways in future years, no matter how diverse the paths they follow might become.

David Greene and David Pollack are two of the best ever. And they could play a little football, as well.

INTRODUCTION

David—probably derived from the Hebrew word "dod" meaning "beloved." David was the second and greatest of the kings of Israel, ruling in the 10th Century BC. Several stories, including his defeat of Goliath, a giant Philistine, are told in the Old Testament. Jesus was descended from him. Other famous bearers of this name include the 5th century patron saint of Wales, two kings of Scotland, empiricist philosopher David Hume, and explorer David Livingstone. David is also the name of the hero of Charles Dickens' semiautobiographical novel *David Copperfield*.

— from www.behindthename.com

What is the likelihood of two boys, both named David, one born in an Atlanta hospital and one born in a hospital in New Brunswick, New Jersey, meeting in the first grade, playing youth football together, becoming lifelong friends and ending their college careers as roommates? Both hail from the town of Snellville, incorporated in August, 1923. (Two Londoners, one named Snell, settled the town in the 1870s. In 1885, the first post office was opened and was named, Snell.)

There are contrasts in their lifestyles, but emotionally and spiritually, it is as if they are joined at the hip. While they are the same age, Greene got ahead in school when the hyperactive Pollack was held back for a second tour of kindergarten. The only time they have been apart was in high school, and that had to do with residency and the geography of school districts. Greene attended South Gwinnett and Pollack attended Shiloh, five miles down the road. Otherwise, they were inseparable.

With "The Davids," identity became a problem. Two guys on the same team with the same first name needed distinguishing handles, so Pollack became Davey, which remains his preference. When he joined his friend in Athens, Pollack pretty much became David again, but if you call him on his cell phone and his voice mail answers, you will hear him begin with, "This is Davey…"

Their friendship got underway when they met in the first grade at a youth league football signup. Their fathers became their coaches, and they were dominant, just like the Yankees. They won the championship every year, right on into high school.

Following Greene's redshirt year with the Bulldogs, Pollack cast his lot with Georgia. He came when Mark Richt arrived, a turning point for him and for the University of Georgia Bulldogs. Richt immediately began preaching

The Davids say goodbye to UGA VI in Tampa

family, team and togetherness. No problem with The Davids. That is exactly how they grew up. Preaching team to them was not a new awakening. They had lived it since the introduction at age six.

After teaming up to lead the Shiloh Generals (Gwinnett Football League teams took the name of the nearest local high school.) to that first championship, this was a case of two boys always outside and playing whatever sport was in season. They were good at everything; nothing, however, indicated the accomplishment that was to come. They had competitive savvy; their desire was intense and enduring. Even when they were alone, which was not very often, they were tossing a football, shooting baskets, swinging a bat, playing pitch and catch.

Every waking minute, they were into action. When the summer youth league competition ended, the families vacationed together before

school started up again. When they arrived at North Florida beaches—Destin to Mexico Beach to St. George Island—the boys were out of the car by the time the gearshift was put in park. Before their fathers could unload and their mothers could organize the kitchen, they hit the beach, and that is where they stayed the entire trip. We are talking about early morning until dark. Literally.

Their mothers often catered meals to the beach, so they could continue their games without interruption. They invented games, ran, splashed, and played non-stop until they were summoned to the rental house at nightfall.

Neither ever gave his parents any trouble save Pollack when his hyperactivity troubled his teachers in his early years. But that was not an attitude problem; he simply needed an outlet for all that energy.

School work was never a concern and going to

GEORGIA'S KING DAVIDS

David, the shepherd boy who slew the giant Philistine warrior Goliath with his slingshot, became King of Israel in 1010 B.C.

Nearly 3,000 years later, the University of Georgia's King of Quarterbacks, David Greene, slew 42 opponents during his four year career for an NCAA record, and the King of Sacks, David Pollack, slew countless quarterbacks (36 career sacks) on his way to winning the Lombardi Award, given to the nation's No. 1 defensive player; he also joined Herschel Walker as the only other Bulldog three-time All-American.

If the Georgia Bulldog Nation were to elect a king, there's no doubt that David Greene and David Pollack would be voted co-kings.

Ripley wouldn't believe it, but Georgia's King Davids were born only three days apart (Pollack was born June 19, and Greene was born June 22.). They also started playing Little League football at age six on the same team, became best friends and roomed together in college.

—Dan Magill, the greatest and grandest Bulldog

church they enjoyed. Even today when you ask them the most favorite book they have read, they will say *The Bible.* They got along with their friends; their friends ganged up at their homes where the cooking was tasty and filling; game options were many, and welcome was the order of the day at both the Greene and Pollack households. No kid ever entered the homes of the Greenes and Pollacks and felt uncomfortable. There was no sign over the door which proclaimed, "Our home is your home." It wasn't necessary. It was a way of life for both sets of parents.

We are talking about middle class America. Both parents worked at each household. They were not moneyed; they were not people of privilege; they enjoyed few perks and first class. "First class" was the way they treated everybody. They simply put their kids first and understood, early on, that the most wholesome activity for youngsters growing up was to allow them to pursue athletics for pure enjoyment. At the outset, nobody thought

about athletic scholarships, and certainly there were no expectations of what was to come their way.

These were two families who raised their boys (and their siblings) by supporting and encouraging them the old fashioned way— with love and involvement.

You found neither Rick and Kay Greene nor Norm and Kelli Pollack berating a youth league official. They weren't the type to confront an umpire in Little League baseball. They were advocates of "just let the kids play."

They wanted the best for their kids, and they expected to be involved as parents. And that didn't mean being loud or badly behaved. They were parents who were under control.

When Richt and his coaching staff went to work early in 2001, they were not clairvoyant about the future of The Davids. They saw encouraging signs, however. Attitude and work ethic were prominent in the makeup of the two boys who were to become selfless stars.

The Richt Dawgs of 2004

Nobody could have foreseen or predicted the impact the Snellville sensations would have in 2002 resulting in Georgia's first Southeastern Conference Championship in 20 years.

The Richt staff taught the Bulldogs how to win, expected the team to rise to the occasion, and with big-play playmakers like The Davids in the lineup, almost always achieved their goals.

Georgia showed class. The Dawgs played hard; they fought tenaciously. They were never out of any game during the career of these Snellville stars who refused to act like stars.

In all the years since football was begun in Athens in 1892, there have never been two more beloved players. In 1942, Frank Sinkwich, a senior, and Charley Trippi, a sophomore, were teammates, but for only one year.

Theron Sapp became a beloved player when he broke the drought against Georgia Tech in 1957. Following his pass to Bill Herron to defeat Auburn and claim the SEC title in Sanford Stadium in 1959, Fran Tarkenton, a preacher's kid with widespread rapport with Georgia fans across the state, enjoyed a fling with beloved status.

Herschel Walker hit the scene in 1980, led the Bulldogs to a national championship and became the most popular player ever in Athens. He was beloved, too, and still is for that matter. He represented not only a national title, but three SEC championships as well. He and Terry Hoage engendered great respect, both making it into the College Football Hall of Fame. Herschel and Hoage were two of the most accomplished players in history. Exceptional. They were not, however, inseparable as are The Davids.

There have never been two more beloved players at the same time than David Greene and Davey Pollack, who are recognized as "All American Boys." It is their "good guy" qualities that have endeared them to the Georgia people as much as their adroit playmaking.

How many kids did you see during their college careers wearing Greene and Pollack's jerseys? No. 14 and No. 47 are the two most purchased jerseys ever at Georgia, rivaled only by Herschel's No. 34, which remains in demand. The Davids could speak every night of the week at high schools, churches, and youth organizations. There was no time for that while playing for the Dawgs, but the requests came in nonetheless.

Autographs? Somebody stopped The Davids in the street most days. They were approached at restaurants, on the way to class—wherever they were and wherever they went. It got so out of hand, that the Athletic Association put in a policy that no players could sign autographs when they exited Butts-Mehre, the heartbeat of athletics at Georgia. This was only complying with NCAA rules, in need of strict emphasis. The players were overwhelmed for autographs, especially Greene and Pollack.

The goal of many was eBay—The Davids considered that distasteful; they didn't appreciate the commercialization of their names for profit, but they would sign all day for deserving kids.

At one awards banquet, Pollack was asked to sign a helmet. "Who to?" Pollack inquired. The guy kept insisting, "No name, just a signature." Pollack knew what he was up to, so he wrote "NOT FOR SALE" above his signature.

One of the things about them that humbles my red and black heart is that in their final year on campus, they constantly talked about coming back

Scoring with Greenie

as alumni to tailgate and to watch the Bulldogs play.

Everybody envisions NFL glory for them, but if that doesn't work out, I see them this way: responsible parents—chips off the 'ole block, and good citizens in their community, supporters of school projects, successful in business and sharing with others, enthusiastic alumni, always ready to support causes of their alma mater, and men of altruism and goodwill.

They won't have to win a Super Bowl to be heroes to the Dawg Nation. Let's toast The Davids. Damn good Dawgs. Let's forever be grateful they came our way.

IN THE BEGINNING

BLESSED INTRODUCTION

Norm and Kelli Pollack moved from Edison, New Jersey, to Gwinnett county in 1986 following a visit to see her father, who had relocated his building and decorating company to Stone Mountain. They found a house in nearby Snellville, which seemed to be booming, but the main appeal was that the cost of living was less and housing was about half of what it was in the Garden State.

The other big attraction was that the weather would allow "365 days for Davey (and his older brother, Jason) to be outside." With Jason that was not as much of a requirement as it was with the younger son. Jason enjoyed sports and the outdoors, too, but with Davey, all that pent up energy had to be dealt with. Daily. He had to have an outlet.

The younger Pollack took to football like a jet pilot to a cockpit. But there was a waiting period that almost did him in. The youth league in Gwinnett County required that kids must be six years old before they could participate.

Davey stood on the sideline, agonizing, while Jason played. He couldn't understand the age requirement. He chaffed, complained and fretted. He was vexed. The Pollacks realized that if anx-

iousness were to become a factor for success, their precocious son should turn out to be very competent at football. Little did they know how far that competitive anxiousness would take him.

In a nearby neighborhood, a laid back, young lefthander, who had begun his athletic career playing T-ball at age five, was awaiting the opportunity to join the youth league football team, too. David Greene and his father, Rick, spent a lot of time in their yard playing pitch and catch, one of the normal things fathers and sons do. When Rick was not available, David played by himself. Like Davey Pollack, he took to sports with an intense desire to compete.

Greene was different, however. He had an inner fire that fueled his drive. He would grow up to be a reserved leader. He was not as demonstrative or as expressive as his new-friend-to-be. Their temperaments were ideal for their respective responsibilities. A quarterback needs to be calm under pressure. Disrupting calm is the modus operandi of a defensive end. Greene and Pollack perfectly fit their job descriptions emotionally.

David Greene appreciated his friends and teammates. Kids at age six usually are not egotistical or arrogant, but how many of them go through high school and college and not become affected by the clippings and the rave reviews? David Greene is one who did. "I've never been big on all that cockiness," Greene told me after the 2002 championship season, when he had the entire state of Georgia swooning at his feet.

I'll never forget being in a locker room before a golf pro-am with a group of reporters interviewing comedian Bob Hope. Not sure how the subject came up, but Hope said, "This," tapping one hand softly against the other, "is the greatest drug of all." When the cheering stops for The Davids, I think they will be able to get on with life.

It was only natural, in my view, that Greene would become friends with the Manning family of quarterbacks. I got to know Archie Manning soon after he left Ole Miss and signed to play with the New Orleans Saints. He was never big on all that cockiness either, and he passed this attitude on to his sons, Cooper, Peyton and Eli.

Archie, after the 2002 season, invited Greene to the Manning summer quarterback camp in Hammond, Louisiana. Eli, who signed with Ole

A precocious Greenie under center; Pollack (44) awaits the snap

Miss, and Greene became good friends and competed against each other in two SEC games, Greenie's team winning both times.

When Peyton was at Tennessee, David Greene was learning T. McFerrin's pro-set passing game. Interestingly, I have always thought Eli had emotional feelings for Georgia. Many of his classmates at Newman in New Orleans enrolled in Athens. His best friend, Merrick Egan, matriculated at Georgia.

For the two Tennessee games in Athens, when Peyton was the Volunteers quarterback, the Mannings and their close friends, Patricia and Vernon Brinson, stayed with us. Merrick and Eli slept in our basement. I wanted Georgia to recruit Eli, but if that had worked out, he and Greene would have competed for the quarterback job.

In New York, after the 2002 championship season, Archie came up to me and said, "What a nice young man David Greene is. We are going to invite him to our quarterback camp." Class recognizes class.

In December of '04, Greene made his first trip to New York. He was honored by the National Football Foundation as a scholar athlete. Eli's image as the rookie quarterback of the New York Giants graced a number of billboards across the city. Greene called Eli, getting his recording. "I'm in your town," was the message, "and I love it."

There is a lot of the good guy, laid back qualities in Eli Manning's makeup that you can see in David Greene. It was family first with the Mannings just like it has always been with the Greene family. However, with the first family of New Orleans, it was a high profile growing up.

+ + +

It was a bright, sunny day in the summer of 1988 when The Davids met. Their parents had taken each to Shiloh High School for signups for the summer league competition of the Gwinnett

VINCE DOOLEY ON THE DAVIDS

Vince Dooley, a seasoned football observer, didn't coach The Davids, but his admiration for them, nonetheless, carries the passion he regarded for his two greatest stars, Terry Hoage and Herschel Walker. His words:

David Pollack and David Greene are the most amazing two Georgia athletes to ever wear the red and black. In my more than 40 years at Georgia, there has never been a pair of student athletes as unique, who accomplished more, or represented its institution better on and off of the field, than the Dynamic Davids Duo!

They are, indeed, unique. They were born three days apart and, as one writer said, "To UGA's eternal gratitude, they've been joined at the shoulder pads ever since!"

They started playing youth league football, baseball and basketball together: Greene the calm, brainy quarterback, and Pollack the "wild-man" running back.

Despite the disappointment of not being able to play in the SEC championship game last year, individually, the two Davids broke or tied some of the most significant records in college football.

There is no player that I've ever coached or seen that is more relentless and tireless in his pursuit of the football than "Wild Man" Pollack. Being double-teamed all year, it was his relentless play that enabled him to break Georgia's all-time sack record, ending his career as the first three-time consensus All-American since Herschel Walker.

David Greene's record for quarterbacking his school to the career total record in NCAA competition (42) might last for 100 years.

For all that they've done on the field, there are no two Georgia athletes that have ever represented their institution better than the two Davids. They are both excellent with the media, and they both do very well in the classroom, with Greene being named a National Scholar-Athlete by the Football Hall of Fame.

There is no way to properly articulate how much these two Davids will be missed. The Bulldawg Nation has come to recognize that these two exceptional young men represent what is good about college athletics. Nobody has ever represented Georgia better.

Football League. Norm and Rick introduced themselves. Both were easy going men, Norm, perhaps, a little more reserved in conversation. Rick has a gregarious laugh and an easy way. It was like any other gathering of parents drawn together by their kids. Nothing out of the ordinary, but when they saw an opportunity to work with their sons in an official capacity, the fathers quickly volunteered.

The first year Norm served as trainer for the team, and Rick was the special teams coach. The GFL league is well organized and structured. The kids come first, but officials are serious about the schedule and competition.

The second year Norm expressed an interest in the head coaching position with the Shiloh Generals. "I had no experience, and they seemed a little reticent, but Rick agreed to help me and that is how we got started with our boys. I was also offensive coordinator, and Rick was the defensive coordinator."

This went on for seven years. Norm and Rick took their roles seriously. They studied tape of the games, shot by Kelli. They met regularly and devised plays and systems. They scouted opponents; they even signed up for a couple of local high school clinics. It was fun. They wanted to win, but these were not pushy parents who got out of line. They just put their heart and soul into training the kids, teaching them the importance of teamwork. It was a "just have fun but learn football while you are at it" objective. Norm suggested multiple offensive sets, and an assistant coach volunteered it would be too complicated and complex for kids at that age. Norm's reply: "Have you watched how quickly they master those video games? Give them an opportunity to learn the complexities of the game. Let's teach them to love the game, too."

It was not easy to distinguish between them. That is how Pollack became known as Davey. Everybody around Snellville, Shiloh and in the Pollacks' neighborhood refers to the heralded Georgia defensive end as "Davey."

While the two boys became close friends through the youth league and family vacations, they attended separate schools and the Pollacks decided that it was best to have Davey repeat kindergarten. "The best thing we ever did," Kelli says. "The teachers wanted to put him on Ritalin, but we refused. We felt that would not be good and that we had to work with the teachers and find an outlet for all his energy. He was the kind of kid who would do his assignment right away and then become restless. He had to be doing something. Always." Those of us who know Davey hap-

pen to believe that Novartis Pharmaceuticals, manufacturers of Ritalin, couldn't have produced enough of the drug to quiet No. 47 down.

The Pollacks remain grateful to his third grade teacher, Laron Barron, who found ways to keep their youngster occupied. He was not a bad behavior kid, though he was insatiably mischievous. He was devoid of a sour or poor attitude; he just had twice as much energy as his classmates. "Make that three times as much," Norm says. They were to learn later that while his Georgia teammates seemed drained after a game, Davey was bouncing around like the day was just getting started.

At Georgia, it was like it was at home in Snellville. All their close friends on the team seemed to hang out at The Davids' place. The Bulldog offensive line was always there. Same with the defense. There was a close bond, which is exactly what you want in football. The Pollacks never took any trip or vacation without their kids and never, I mean never, had a babysitter when their kids were growing up. When you saw the Greenes, you usually saw their kids, Leslie and David, too.

While The Davids seem to have been inseparable since they met in the first grade, they did have other interests. With Greenie, football camps were big. He attended them all: Georgia, Georgia Tech, the Bowden Quarterback camp, and Auburn, where he won the Punt, Pass and Kick contest at age eight. His dad enrolled at Auburn, but for only a quarter.

Rick had played football, basketball and golf at Decatur High, where Kay was a cheerleader. She first attended Wesleyan and then Georgia State, but something derailed their route to degrees. Marriage. Most of their friends were Georgia fans, and they were on the way to Jacksonville for the Florida game, Herschel's junior year, when it was confirmed that she was pregnant.

She was confident that she was pregnant when she visited the doctor just before leaving for

WHAT THEY LIKE **WHAT THEY DON'T**

	POLLACK LIKES	POLLACK DISLIKES	GREENE LIKES	GREENE DISLIKES
TUNA	🏈			🏈
VEGETABLES		🏈		🏈
SPINACH		🏈		🏈
GREENS	🏈		🏈	
PIZZA	🏈			🏈
FRIED FOODS		🏈		SOMETIMES
READ BIBLE	🏈		🏈	
VIDEO GAMES	🏈		🏈	
BBQ PORK		🏈	🏈	
CHICKEN	🏈🏈		🏈🏈	
FRIES		🏈	🏈	
RED MEAT	🏈		🏈	
SHRIMP	🏈		🏈	
CRAB LEGS	🏈			🏈
BISCUITS		🏈		🏈
CORNBREAD		🏈		🏈
WATER	🏈🏈		🏈🏈	
KETCHUP		🏈	🏈	
MARINATED FOODS		🏈	A LITTLE	
TOMATOES	🏈			🏈
BREAKFAST	🏈🏈		🏈	
MUSHROOMS		🏈	🏈	
ALL MUSIC	🏈		🏈	
COUNTRY	🏈🏈		🏈🏈	
READ NEWSPAPER		🏈		🏈
WATCH SPORTSCENTER	🏈		🏈	
KIDS	🏈🏈		🏈🏈	
SCOOTER ON CAMPUS	🏈		🏈	
SET GOALS PRESEASON	🏈		🏈	
FIND AFGHANISTAN ON MAP	🏈		🏈	
CLASS	🏈		🏈	
GOLF	🏈		🏈	
COOK	🏈			🏈
PRACTICE	🏈		🏈	
HISTORY	🏈		SOMETIMES	
BE A GOOD ALUMNUS	DEFINITELY		DEFINITELY	
FRIENDS	VERY IMPORTANT		VERY IMPORTANT	
CHURCH	VERY IMPORTANT		VERY IMPORTANT	

Florida, but did not know for sure. The Greene's stopped in McDonough, and she called her doctor who confirmed the pregnancy.

Georgia won the SEC title that year for the third year in a row. Little did Kay Greene realize that she was carrying the embryo of the quarterback to lead the Bulldogs to their next SEC title.

COACH POLLACK AND GREENIE

The attributes Norm Pollack, David Greene's first coach (other than the quarterback's own father), saw in the young lefthander was exactly what his coaches at Georgia were saying as Greenie's career was ending.

"He was," Norm Pollack says, "very eager to learn, very disciplined. He could read defenses; he was a student of the game. He could make plays."

Norm, having grown up in Dover, New Jersey (He remembers being a teenager playing hooky and taking the train out to Coney Island.),

The smile of Georgia's future quarterback

became a passionate New York Giants' fan.

He watched Y.A. Tittle lead the Giants to victory on Sunday afternoons, marveling at the balding quarterback's ability to make things happen for his team.

Even today, when Norm watches games, he tries to figure out what is going on offensively. He takes note of formations and sets and watches more than the ball.

At Georgia, naturally, he gave his greatest attention to a certain defensive end when the Bulldogs' mission was to stop the other team, but when the ball went over to the offense, he had fun observing the play of a young man whom he met a dozen years before that young man enrolled at UGA.

"When we started out with our youth league, we had assistants other than Rick Greene, and they were not sure about using multiple offensive sets, but Rick and I knew we could teach the kids reasonably sophisticated plays. One of the reasons was that I had confidence that David Greene could learn the offense, but the important thing is that he could execute it.

"He would sit and watch our videos and you could tell he wanted to absorb as much as possible. He had a wonderful grasp of our offense.

"Football should be fun for kids, but after watching them play those video games, I felt we could add a few wrinkles and develop multiple sets which would enable them to learn football. Football at that age should be fun, but there's no reason that there shouldn't be fun in learning more about the game. What Rick and I wanted to do was give them an opportunity to learn as much football as possible. We really had fun with those kids, not just our own boys, but the entire team."

GREENE(R) PASTURES

On the way to the Georgia-Florida game in 1981, when Kay Greene got the news that she was pregnant, she was happy to learn the good news.

When she delivered a seven-pound, eight-ounce boy, she was all smiles until she cradled David Norman Greene in her arms for the first time. "Something is wrong," she told the nurse. "He is breathing too hard." The nurse assured her the baby was okay, but Kay persisted. "I know something is not right." Her mother's instinct and persistence may have saved the future Georgia quarterback's life.

He was born with holes in both lungs. It is a condition known as pneumothorax. Tubes were placed in both his lungs, and the holes healed after a couple of days' stay in intensive care. It could have been life threatening without the immediate diagnosis.

"When they came to me with the news of his condition, I was devastated," Kay says. "I was scared to death. When the doctor later told me he would be okay, I still worried for a while. The doctor reassured her saying, "He is going to be okay. You'll be able to watch him play Little League ball."

David Greene was born at 12:31 p.m., right about kickoff time. Georgia would win its third consecutive Southeastern Conference championship with Herschel Walker that year, but it would be 20 long years before the Dawgs would win the title again. The man who would lead them to the championship would be David Greene, who was fighting for his life at Northside Hospital in Atlanta in the summer of Herschel's final year in a Georgia football uniform.

"He still has scars on his chest from the surgery," Kay says. "On his feet, too, where they had to prick his heels." When the doctor told her David was okay, and she would be able to go home, she looked at him incredulously. "You think I'm going home without that boy? You can't be serious."

From that day right on up to the spring of 2005 when he was preparing for the NFL draft, Greene has had a close and affectionate relationship with his mother and his father, Rick. When Mark Richt took over the team and began to sell the family concept to his team, one he didn't need to encourage was his red shirt freshman quarterback. He had been living the family concept all his life.

All his life, too, he had been involved with sports, beginning at age five. "He was fast in T-ball before his feet grew," Kay laughs.

David Greene's best friends are his parents, Rick and Kay

home. His nickname could have been "Easy" because that became the dominant feature in his personality. Generous and accommodating, he had the perfect temperament to play quarterback under pressure.

Even though he made All-State AAAA at South Gwinnett, his parents were not sure that he would be good enough to earn a college scholarship, but they offered limitless support in his pursuit of that goal. He attended football camps that he enjoyed from the beginning. "He just loved the Georgia campus and hit it off with players like Brett Millican and Jon Stinchcomb. He played against Jon in high school, and Jon became his roommate prior to moving in with Davey." Rick points out.

When he left the Bulldog football camp in the summer of 1999, then Georgia coach Jim Donnan had a conference with him, aware that he would be visiting Georgia Tech next. The Bulldog coach asked him to call him when he was finished there. Before he left the Tech campus, Coach George O'Leary had offered him a scholarship.

"We were overwhelmed," Kay says. "Then Coach Donnan told us Georgia would offer him a scholarship, too. We were stunned at what was happening."

It was time to retreat and evaluate his opportunities. His interest in Tech was heightened by the reputation of Ralph Friedgen, the offensive coordinator, who would, a year later, wind up with the head job at Maryland.

His parents wanted him to make the decision on his own, but Rick Greene did underscore two points. He reminded his son that there

Greenie always had a ball in his hand. He was always playing catch, even if it was only by himself. He'd throw a baseball high in the air and run catch it. He would bounce a ball off the garage door and retrieve it. He tossed a football in the fall, shot baskets in his driveway until his fingers bled during the winter months and pursued his best sport at the time—baseball—in the spring.

He was a good kid and never caused any problems. He didn't whine or pout. He just played and played. And played. He made friends easy, and his parents always welcomed his friends into their

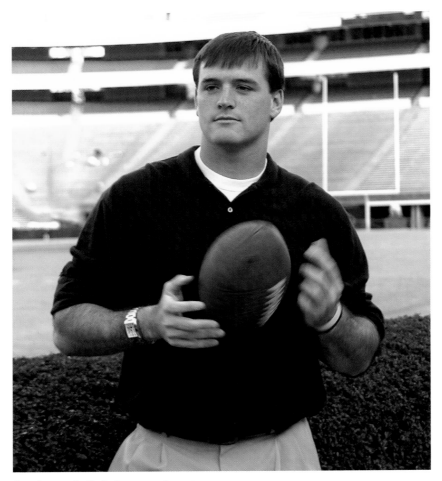

Greenie poses by the hedges as an alumnus

was a big difference between ACC and SEC football. All he said was, "If you want to play with the best, you have to realize that would be in the Southeastern Conference."

Then he pointed out the difference between the capacity of the two stadiums. "You'll play before a lot more people in Athens," Rick advised. They realized, too, that because of the great base of support in the state for Georgia that any stadium expansion was likely to take place above the famous Sanford Stadium hedges. In fact, for the 2003 season, Greenie's junior year, the stadium capacity was extended to 92,058. With the completion of sky suites and boxes for '04, the capacity is now 92,746, and Georgia continues to refund season ticket requests.

In the careers of The Davids, 4,194,794 fans saw them play. Most of the time it was favorable for Georgia—80.7% of the time, in fact.

■■■

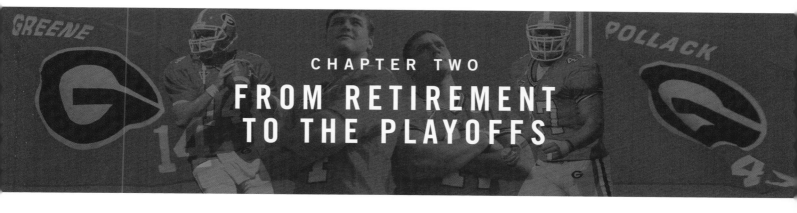

A turning point in David Greene's life came when T.S. McFerrin became head coach at South Gwinnett. The Greene family simply won't discuss what might have been had McFerrin not come out of retirement to coach at South Gwinnett.

"I can't imagine what David's life and football career would have been like without Coach McFerrin taking over at South," says Rick Greene.

T.S. McFerrin's return to coaching almost didn't happen. The man, simply referred to through Georgia high school athletics by his first initial "T," was comfortable in retirement. He had won almost 250 games and more than 10 championships, including a state title. There certainly was not anything at South Gwinnett to excite him other than limitless opportunity. During David Greene's sophomore year, the Comets didn't win a game all season. They won only two when he was a freshman. On top of that, the offensive system was the Wing T, which was not exactly an offense to showcase a quarterback's talent.

When McFerrin met with the team the first time, he informed them that winning had as much to do with attitude as anything. They would be required to work hard, but he promised to make it fun.

McFerrin has had two quarterbacks to play for the Bulldogs. His first, at Peachtree, was Chris Welton, who moved to defense and started at rover for Georgia's National Championship team of 1980. The other, David Greene.

"I'm one who believes," McFerrin says, "that the players who work the hardest are the ones who are the most successful. A lot of positive things have happened for David. He's been honored a lot, but he deserves everything he's gotten. He worked for it. Nobody is more deserving.

"When I first coached him, he was unbelievably mature. He was barely 17 years old when he played his final year of football. He was so coachable and such a leader."

On a sunny December day after the Tech game, David Greene and I met at Chick-fil-A, a preferred restaurant of The Davids. Chicken is a favorite when it comes to mealtime. As we sat and talked, nobody joined in our conversation—nobody took the empty seat at our table—but most everybody who walked by would pause and congratulate him on a successful season. Some would pat him on the shoulder; some would shake his hand. All eyes in the restaurant took note that the starting quarterback of the Bulldogs was in their focus.

Greenie's career begins to take shape

We talked about his career and the highlights—"Not really any bad times," he said—but his musings did embrace regret. "It is tough," he said, "to get to the championship game as a sophomore and win it, but not win it again. Our senior year certainly was not a bad one by any means, but we expected more of ourselves. Being part of the LSU and Florida victories will always be something special to the seniors on the team. To enjoy a 4-0 record against Tech means a lot to us, too. Just a lot of good moments. It has been a good ride, and I appreciate the great support of the Georgia fans. They have made us feel so warm and appreciated for so many afternoons between the hedges."

With that, there was a pause. Something deeply emotional came about as he looked across the parking lot teeming with pre-Christmas shoppers. It was a faraway look, but one which reflected sincere gratefulness. His career seemed to be flashing through his mind in an instant. The 41 wins seemed to be surfacing in his mind's eye as he reflected back on his days as a Dawg.

When he came to Georgia, he was not certain of his future. He was not a highly sought-after quarterback, but there were enough offers to turn his head. All he wanted was to have an opportunity to compete for the job, but was not sure he would ever be good enough to start.

"I was," says T. McFerrin emphatically. "You know when a player is special, and David Greene is special. You never had to tell him anything twice. In all my time as a high school coach, I have never seen a more accurate passer than David, and I am talking about those outstanding quarterbacks on other teams."

When McFerrin became head coach at South Gwinnett, Greene did not know what to expect, but he was soon hearing things that were exciting. He also was learning. He had not been exposed to an offense that included five-receiver sets. He didn't know what a "hot" receiver was. "We didn't throw every snap," McFerrin says, "but we would throw at least 20 times a game."

In McFerrin's first year, South won eight games. The community was ecstatic. It was hungry for a successful program, and the coach and the quarterback would give it to them. As a junior, David took the Comets to the playoffs, losing in the 13th game at Valdosta. The Comet supporters couldn't believe it. Just 12 months prior, everybody was wondering when the school would win a game.

As a senior in 1999, David quarterbacked the team back to the playoffs where they lost in the second round. Disappointing, yes, but the consolation was recalling how far the program had come in such a short period of time. McFerrin generously praises David Greene for being the centerpiece of that turnaround.

Today, McFerrin is grateful that he came out of retirement. "You just don't have an opportunity," he says, "to coach a kid like that."

McFerrin credits Greene with turning around the program at South Gwinnett, which is retiring his jersey. Greene wore No. 15 in high school, but when he got to Georgia, Terreal Bierria had that number, which is why his Bulldog number became No. 14.

In the spring of 2005, when Greene was training for the NFL, McFerrin realized there were skeptics. "The trend is obvious; they are signing athletes as often as possible, like Michael Vick. But I think David will grow on them. He's smart, he doesn't make mistakes, people rally to him and that accurate arm will carry him a long way in football."

On that day at Chick-fil-A, Greene recalled his thoughts when he enrolled in Athens. "When I came, I wasn't sure I would be good enough to start, but if I did, I was resolved to try to put our team in position to win."

There were only a couple of times in his career when that did not happen. The first was in the championship game versus LSU in 2003 when the offensive line was depleted with injuries, and at Auburn, his final season, when the Bulldogs finished their fourth straight road game against an undefeated team on a roll and playing at home.

When the Outback Bowl, Greene's final game as the Bulldog quarterback, was over, he showed up for a victory party with his parents and close friends. Hoyt Stancil, a longtime friend of the Greene family, remembers what Rick Greene told his son after they had embraced. "You got your wish," Rick said. "What is that?" David asked, quizzically. "You said," Rick grinned with the deepest of respect and emotion, "that if you

Posing before the Georgia/Florida High School All-Star Game

became Georgia's quarterback, all you wanted to do was always put the team in position to win. You did that, and we are so proud of you."

FRIDAY NIGHT TALKS

Shannon Jarvis learned to appreciate David Greene's ability as a quarterback when he was an assistant coach at South Gwinnett. When Greenie became of age as Georgia's starting quarterback, his former coach was keenly aware of the monumental significance of the position he played.

"The Georgia quarterback has one of the most high profile positions in the state. I don't think David ever realized that, which is good," Jarvis says. "People live and die by what the Bulldog quarterback does. I know. I am a devoted Georgia fan. My mood in church on Sunday is affected by

Greenie about to initiate a play in a career that was to set the NCAA record for total victories

what the Bulldogs do on Saturday. There is no passion in this state comparable to Georgia football. The quarterback position is one of power. It is extremely important to the people of this state how the Bulldog quarterback performs. David was never affected by all of that. I'm certainly happy for him for the way he handled everything."

In the beginning, following spring practice in 2001, Greenie and Jarvis had detailed conversations. Serious football talk about schemes, coverages, progressions, blitzes, audibles—whatever

took place on the field and in the game. It was mainly a confidence boost for the quarterback talking to someone who knows football, one he could trust and one with whom he was at ease. As time went by, their conversation topics were about anything but football. Late in the fall of his senior year, one conversation, Jarvis remembers, had to do with handicapped children. David had met a handicapped child that week and was emotionally disturbed.

"We talked about how unfortunate that was,"

Greenie enjoying an off day

pay for," Shannon says. "I never got a bill, but I would have paid."

"David proved he could handle any type situation in his college career. As a coach, I can tell you the way he and his family and D.J. Shockley and his family handled the quarterback situation tell you something about the two families. They both showed great class. But to tell you the truth, I would have expected David to handle that situation like he did with everything else. It just comes natural with him.

"I'm proud he is the winningest quarterback in NCAA history—that is a record that will stand a long time—but I'm proudest of the way he has conducted himself as a person and a leader. Praise and tribute never turned his head. All his life he has been a team player. That's why he is a big winner."

Jarvis says. "We both agreed that we were thankful that we were healthy and without complications physically. We got into why these things happened, but agreed that we would never arrive at an answer. You accept certain things, but you always try to be mindful of how fortunate most of us are. That is the way David looked at it. He would always be grateful for good health. David truly cares about others. That is why he has always been such a wonderful leader."

The longest conversion Jarvis had with his former quarterback was the night before the 2001 Tennessee game. Shannon had traveled to Knoxville with David's parents and their good friend, Hoyt Stancil. When David called Shannon after the final team meeting, they talked for almost two hours. Rick Greene kidded Shannon about the length of the call. "After the game, I told Rick that is one call I would gladly

Mike Bobo, son of a coach, aspired to play quarterback and realized, early on, that the best route to a college scholarship, which was his goal, was simple: hard work. He was intuitive and cogent about his situation—he knew hard work was his only hope. Raw talent was not an asset.

While Bobo was not blessed with exceptional natural ability, he knew something about playing the position. His father, George, taught him, pushed him and drilled him until a confrontation ensued.

"I have done everything you have asked me to do," the son said in frustration. "But you are working me harder than anybody else on the team."

Mike's contempt for what he considered an unfair circumstance didn't faze his father, who sounded forth with a challenge that was delivered without the slightest sympathy. "You want to play quarterback, then you have got to work harder than anybody else; if you don't want to play, then you can choose something else to do. If you choose to play the position and you play for me, then you are going to work even harder. Is that understood?"

Bobo accepted the challenge, not overjoyed, however, and there still were times when he didn't understand his father's way of doing things. Like on Saturday morning when everybody else was sleeping in, Mike was up working. "My father worked hard himself, and he wanted me to learn to appreciate the work ethic," Mike says of George Bobo. "He would get up on the weekend and start cutting the grass at daybreak. He would mow right beside my window. He thought I ought to be up working, too. The fact that it was Saturday morning made no difference to him."

Bobo's teammates seldom spent the night with Mike. They knew if they were rousted out of bed and headed off to breakfast with the senior Bobo, they were in trouble. "That meant that he had some chores or a project for us to help with," Mike laughs. "If a buddy spent the night with me and Dad took us to breakfast, that meant they would be working right along with me. Not too many of my teammates wanted to stay overnight. Hanging out at my house was no fun."

One March, all of his friends went off to the beach for spring holidays, but not Mike. He had to help his dad paint the garage. The task began by scraping away the old paint. George worked a power washer while Mike, with elbow grease, used a hand scraper. It was the most boring work Mike had ever experienced in his life, and he was none too pleased. All his father-coach said to comfort

Greenie with quarterbacks coach Mike Bobo who also wore No. 14

him was, "You'll appreciate it someday."

The forecast was accurate, and Mike now looks back on his formative years as not only a learning experience, but also as training that has favorably influenced his attitude and career.

His dad once was an assistant to Ray Lamb, long time coach at Commerce. Lamb enjoyed championship success as a head coach, always winning the region title and advancing deep into the playoffs most years. He won a state championship with the Tigers and two at Warren County. Lamb, a member of the Bulldog's administrative staff, though senior by a number of years, is one of Mike Bobo's best friends.

"Mike is a bright young coach with a great future," Lamb says. "He is an excellent recruiter, and a lot of that has to do with knowing so many coaches in the state. His father not only knows coaches across Georgia, but he has an exceptional rapport with them. That has benefited Mike."

A four-year letterman for the Bulldogs (three under Ray Goff and one with Jim Donnan), Bobo had the finest statistical day of any quarterback in Georgia history against Wisconsin in the Outback Bowl, January 1, 1998, the Dawgs winning 33-6. Bobo completed 26 of 28 passes.

"All I had to do," the modest Bulldog quarterbacks coach says, "was get it to the athletes. We had Hines Ward and Robert Edwards in the backfield. And we also had Olandis Gary and Patrick Pass. Champ Bailey lined up at receiver on that team, too. All I had to do was throw the ball up, and they would catch it. We threw a lot of short and medium-range passes, the high percentage type.

"It was a great day for me because of the athletes I had to throw to. All those guys are still in the

NFL except for Robert Edwards, and he would still be there if he hadn't gotten hurt." The fact remains: no Georgia quarterback has ever had a greater day throwing the ball in a bowl game.

Bobo didn't know much about David Greene when he arrived at Georgia to coach the Bulldog quarterbacks, Mark Richt's first season in 2001. He had worked as a graduate assistant for Jim Donnan in 1998-99, but had no recruiting assignment. In 2000, Greene's redshirt year, Bobo coached the quarterbacks for Jack Crowe at Jacksonville State.

Didn't matter who the quarterbacks were, Bobo's first objective was to land a job at his alma mater. Dating back to the time when he was learning to play quarterback for his hard-driving father, he expected to follow in his dad's footsteps. He knew early in his high school years that he wanted to become a coach.

He had observed the great rapport George had with coaches across the state and took note of the fact that his dad's former players always seemed to enjoy coming back to visit with their old coach.

When Mark Richt was hired, Bobo read a newspaper interview in which the new Bulldog coach said that he wanted to hire a young quarterbacks coach and train him. "How can I be that guy?" Bobo asked himself, but when he went for an interview with Richt, he said aloud as he drove to Athens, "I am NOT going back and work as a graduate assistant. As much as I want to return to Georgia and work for Mark Richt, I am not going to go as a graduate assistant."

When the interview got underway, Bobo was immediately captivated. He quickly concluded, "I WILL be a graduate assistant under this guy if that is what it takes."

An easy rapport has developed with Richt and Bobo. You can see the head coach's confidence level rising in regard to his quarterbacks coach, who is eager to learn, has a near-perfect coaching

Mike Bobo airs it out

temperament with an easy smile, a deep and abiding inner confidence, an excellent rapport with the quarterbacks and a creative knowledge of the passing game.

George Bobo taught his son well, but the son paid attention along the way. He was anxious to acquire knowledge. He was happiest off the field at Georgia as a player when he watched videotape with his first quarterbacks coach, Greg Davis, now the offensive coordinator at Texas. It was like it was with his dad on Saturday morning. He was always on the job. Bobo actually became impatient to study tape, which was far more appealing than cutting the grass and scrubbing old paint off the garage.

When Bobo's young son, Drew, becomes big enough to carry on a conversation, he'll hear his

David Greene airs it out

for the past four years. The only year Bobo wasn't in Greene's vicinity was 2000, during which he spent as an assistant coach at Jacksonville State.

When you watch a young man work every day, when you counsel and conference with him about football, life, degree, golf and any subject which surfaces, you get to know him and what he is made of. How he thinks, anticipates and reacts. Mike Bobo is an expert on David Greene.

Bobo wants Drew to someday play quarterback. He would like for his son to be a leader. He aspires for him to receive his degree, earn the respect of his teammates and lead Georgia to a championship—like David Greene.

"When I review David's career, I find nothing but positives," Bobo says with a distant look in his eye. As he gushes with the greatest of affection and profound respect, he can't hide the regret. "We are going to miss that young man," he said following the Outback Bowl.

Greene's laid-back, egoless style caused him, as a young quarterback, to second guess himself as a leader. Bobo kept reminding Greene that he had earned the respect of the older players with his work ethic and his performance, but it didn't sink in until the comeback at Tennessee in 2001. "He established credibility in that game, and I think that is when he first realized it," the coach says.

In his senior season, Greene showcased his "specialness" in the Florida and Tech games. "In Jacksonville in the second half when the game tightened up, I saw David take a more demonstrative role as the offensive leader," Bobo says. "He gave directions to players, firmly telling them they had to do their job to get us to the end zone. His touchdown pass (15 yards to Fred Gibson to give Georgia a 31-21 lead) in the fourth quarter brought a surge of confidence to our team. That touchdown was critical to our victory.

"In the Tech game, you could feel that same surge of confidence when he went back in the

daddy talk about playing quarterback at Georgia and who he should emulate growing up. "Not just playing the position," Bobo says. "I want him to be like David Greene in every respect."

The Bulldog quarterbacks coach knows Greene better than anybody, except for family. Bobo didn't scout Greene in high school, but he was up close and personal with an athlete he considers the most underrated player in the country lineup after hurting his thumb. You could feel the emotional lift on the field in the huddle, and he made the plays that gave us the field goal and the lead that put Tech in a difficult position. They had to score a touchdown to win.

"In those two games, David showed us all why he is an exceptional player. You don't get to coach players like that too often. When you do, you better enjoy the experience."

Every kid has role models in life, and it is easy to predict who one of Drew Bobo's will be.

THE TEAM COMES FIRST

"The most popular man in a college town is the second-string quarterback."
— **Mack Brown,** University of Texas.

The view here is that Georgia had the best situation possible for a quarterback controversy while David Greene wore the red and black. His understudy, D.J. Shockley, is a terrific athlete and an intelligent quarterback.

Like Greene, he is easy going, laid back and reserved. On top of that, Shockley has the second highest GPA on the team, and Greene got his degree at the end of fall semester. That meant there would be few mental mistakes at the position. In 2002, when the Bulldogs won the SEC championship, both quarterbacks played. Coach Richt had promised D. J. that when the younger quarterback considered transferring, he would give him an opportunity. David Greene understood.

After "Shock" evaluated his options, he chose to stay. He knew his time would come. He enjoys the campus, he loves Georgia, and he relishes the friends he has made.

It didn't become a full-fledged controversy because the two quarterbacks didn't allow it. They honestly like one another. If you don't believe it, ask them.

D. J. Shockley and David Greene wouldn't allow a quarterback controversy

Throughout Shockley's time in Athens, that inevitable question has come up wherever Richt went. "Why don't you put them both in the game at the same time?" The Bulldog coach thought about it, but the view that won out is that you need two quarterbacks who are ready to play. If one goes down and you allow the other to take valuable reps at another position, you not only have put the quarterback at a disadvantage, but you are hurting the team.

Circumstances often create controversy. In the late 50s, when the rules required players to compete on both sides of the ball, many coaches platooned entire teams. Charley Britt and Fran Tarkenton shared the quarterback responsibili-

Mark Richt conferences with D. J. Shockley

ties, and the teams were often referred to as "Britt's team" and "Tarkenton's team."

Coach Wallace Butts usually played Britt's team the first quarter and Tarkenton's the second, and then Britt's the third and Tarkenton's the fourth. There were times when individual substitutions were made, depending on the circumstances. When Georgia claimed a fumble late in the 1959 Auburn game, Tarkenton's team produced the touchdown that won the game and the SEC title. The existing rules prevented a controversy.

When Jeff Pybun and Buck Belue were competing for the job in the late 70s, the fan favorite became Belue, who, as a freshman, directed the comeback to defeat Tech in 1978. Belue's passing reputation coming out of Valdosta probably stimulated the controversy in the beginning. Jeff was sidelined with injury much of the time, but when he was able and ready to play, the fans took sides. With the two boys, it was different.

After finishing at Georgia, Jeff settled in Phoenix, where he lives today. On a trip to his adopted hometown, I invited him to lunch. We talked about his career in Athens.

"Buck and I never had a problem," Jeff said. "We both wanted to play. Fans and sportswriters just don't understand. We never wanted to express ourselves for fear it would be taken the wrong way. If you are a true competitor, don't you want to play? Don't you want to get out there and see what you can do, to lead the team? That is when the coaches should be left alone to decide what is best for the team.

"Recently Buck was out here, and he called me to see if I could join him for lunch. I think in most instances there is not a problem with the two players; it is with the fans and the media."

Nobody would agree more than Mack Brown, the coach at Texas, who went through a draining and downright depressing controversy with Phil Simms and Major Applewhite. "Wouldn't a coach be a fool to play somebody just for spite?" he said. "You want the best for both kids, and you and your coaching staff evaluate it in terms of what is best for the team."

Georgia fans saw Shockley's quick feet; they saw Greene with less movement in his Nikes. If Greene had the slightest off day, they grumbled about more playing time for Shockley. Against Tech in Athens in '04 when the Jackets brought everybody in uniform, blitzing linebackers and defensive backs, upsetting Shockley's rhythm and keeping the pressure on, the critics began to wonder about No. 3.

"What do you expect?" asks Mike Bobo. "We believe in both players. We know what they can do, and we were going to support them and use them with the objective of putting us in a position to win the game. They are different type players with different styles, but we happen to feel we were fortunate to have the two of them together at the same time. We had confidence in Greenie and we have confidence in Shock."

D. J., who has the highest GPA on the team after Ryan Schnetzer, points out that he enjoyed his sincere friendship with Greenie. "We were friends first," Shock says. "When we went on the field, we competed for the job, and we always felt that competition made each of us better. We had great mutual respect. Both of us wanted the team to come first. We often talked about the fact that too many fans and writers just didn't understand. We weren't going to ruin our friendship, and we weren't going to hurt the team if we could help it."

Shockley is quick to underscore that he learned a lot from his quarterback mate. "Before David left in January, we sat down and talked about things. I always admired how calm he was under pressure, how poised he was and how patient. He'll be somewhere else this fall, but he and I will be keeping in contact with one another."

Georgia didn't experience a quarterback controversy because the two principals, the two players themselves, were unselfish, team-oriented and just didn't allow it to happen.

AN APPRAISAL BY JOHN RAUCH

I was very fortunate to receive a football scholarship to the University of Georgia in 1945, and played four years for Coach Wallace Butts, who saw something in me. He let me quarterback the team for 45 games. Playing on Georgia football teams with a legendary coach and great teammates, I was awarded some very high honors.

Recently, I was asked for my impressions of David Greene. Whether he knows it or not, the author bestowed upon me an honor that is as meaningful as any I have previously received. If I were able to put down on paper everything I feel about this young man, it would stretch into a novel. In my view, David Greene is the greatest student-athlete, quarterback and individual, the University has ever seen. He has set records and accumulated statistics so extraordinary they many may never be broken in our lifetime.

Hall of Famer John Rauch at practice with David Greene

We cannot accurately tell what the future will bring, but I'm willing to bet David will be breaking records and raising standards in any endeavor he participates. To me he is the complete human being.

The first thing you recognize about him is his desire to compete. His love of competition is written all over him. He has good size, which is the trend in professional football today. He can see the field.

He has the mental ability to handle stress under pressure and doesn't become unraveled. He needs to improve his footwork, and I think he will be like Peyton Manning who, if you notice, always has his feet bouncing. He is a like a boxer when he drops back, always moving his feet. I am sure

Greenie with Terry Hoage after the '04 Vandy game

David's footwork will improve as he plays football for a living.

My impression is that David is eager to learn. He is very coachable, and that will be important to him. I suspect he will be like his friend Peyton in regard to being a student of the game. Peyton is always into the game, talking to his receivers, reviewing the Polaroid shots on the sideline when his defense is on the field. Because Peyton is such a student of the game and works so hard at learning all there is to know about his opponent, he calls a large percentage of the Colts' plays. David Greene is that type of quarterback, and I see that as an asset for his future.

Assuming that nobody is perfect, David comes as close as anybody I know. He's a left-hander, and left-handers tend to be unpredictable when throwing a football. I think that he will be an

exception. Left-handed or not, David has made the Dawg Nation very proud. We hope that he will always return to Athens for G-Day and attend the Wally's Boys' Reunion Breakfast. We thank him for giving the University of Georgia four years of outstanding football. Coach Mark Richt and Wally's Boys will have an extremely hard time finding another David Greene.

SOMETHING IN COMMON WITH TERRY HOAGE

"David Greene," Terry Hoage smiles, "is the best athlete to wear No. 14 since Andy Johnson."

When Hoage came to town for the Vanderbilt game to promote his new wine, "The Hedge," he dropped by the Bulldog locker room after the game and posed for the above photograph with Greenie. "It was fun," Hoage said, "to see somebody out there doing great things, wearing your old number. The first thing I noticed about him was that he showed a lot of poise, especially under pressure. It was obvious that he is a respected leader and commands respect in the huddle. He showed great command when he walked up to the line of scrimmage. I enjoyed watching him play and was happy to warm up the number for him."

CHAPTER FOUR

BUS RIDE WITH A HAPPY RETURN

Friday, Sept 10, the Bulldog traveling party gathered at the Equestrian Center near the community of Whitehall for its charter bus trip to Columbia to play South Carolina. Players have the option of riding from the Butts-Mehre Building on buses or driving their own cars and leaving them in the parking lot overnight.

The objective is to leave Athens in time to follow a relaxed routine in Columbia for the late afternoon kickoff the next day. By leaving at 2:30 p.m., players could attend classes until noon.

Football players miss less class than any athletes. There never is a time when the team heads out of town before mid-afternoon on Friday. Late kickoffs to accommodate television often make the return trip after a game tense. Coming home from a night game in the Central time zone, like one of the two Mississippi schools, Arkansas or LSU is a real pain. With security requirements as a result of 9/11, this has become more of a problem in recent years.

Georgia takes the bus to as many road sites as possible, including South Carolina, Auburn and Alabama. Georgia Tech is the easiest road trip— an hour and a half by bus to Atlanta.

When the team boards the bus on the way to the first SEC game of the 2004 season, you notice that there are a lot of headsets for listening to music. Some players wear one earring. Some two. Some none. Some have dreadlocks, and some heads are shaved bald. Black kids. White kids. Big kids. Little kids. Smiling kids and some talkers. Quiet kids who nod and seem to want to be by themselves. Tall kids. Short kids. Just college kids who happen to play football.

There is good harmony with the Georgia team. It has been that way for some time. "We really have good kids," Coach Rodney Garner says. "They aren't perfect, but we have good kids. You would have to be around them to appreciate the type of young men that they are."

The offensive bus is usually first in the caravan, followed by the defensive bus and two staff buses. Up front is the State Patrol car driven by Trooper Steve Rushton. Coach Mark Richt and Katharyn usually ride with Steve. A few fans were there to see us off. There was a mood of quiet anticipation throughout the campus on that Friday. Everybody knew the importance of the mission in Columbia.

We take U. S. 78 through Crawford, Lexington, by-pass Washington and pick up I-20 at Thomson. It was a pretty drive with rolling fields and pastures

The stars fall on the Dawgs at Columbia

on each side of the road. There is not a lot of bill-board clutter on this stretch of road, but roadside trash is everywhere. Why do we Americans dese-crate our landscape? Why should someone's litter become everybody else's eyesore?

Coach Richt had given me permission to ride the offensive bus to South Carolina. He is not superstitious, but the thought crossed my mind that we needed to win the game. Lose, and I would be banned from any future bus rides with the offense. Somebody surely would note I was the interloper and needed not to start a streak. It made me wonder what the bus ride home would be like.

Most of the trip was devoted to watching a movie, Rundown, which starred Dwayne Johnson, "The Rock," a former Miami player and a one time professional wrestler. There was a lot of acrobatic violence, unbelievable somersaults and karate, with the star taking out three and four adversaries with physical dexterity that is, in truth, as unlikely as anybody on the bus making a

trip to Mars in the foreseeable future. Nonetheless, it was enjoyable and entertaining. The players got a series of throaty chuckles at some of the clashes that took place on the screen.

When the movie was over, the players engaged in quiet conversation. David Greene stretched out, lying down in the aisle with his headset on, listening to music. Russ Tanner thumbed a paper-back novel. Coach John Eason read a book. Jeremy Thomas slept. Leonard Pope, his head ris-ing higher than the rest, dwarfed the cramped seat in which his 6' 7" body seemed to overflow like an overweight grandmother sitting on a foot stool.

Reggie Brown rocked to the beat of his head-set music. Coach Neil Callaway sat in the front seat, looking straight ahead. He was in the "look-out" seat, but I suspect he was reviewing blocking schemes in his head.

Much of the way, I sat by Dave Johnson, the tight ends coach. He is a professorial type and reviewed his checklists for the game and the reminders he would be discussing with his players at the motel

Davey Pollack in pursuit of another quarterback

Ready, Aim, Fire – another completion in the making for David Greene

Georgia's fans drive to this game if it is played late in the day in order to accommodate a television kickoff.

One of the reasons Richt tired of the Marriott at Southpointe Drive in Jacksonville was that it had become akin to Grand Central Station, with people coming and going all hours of the day and night. The team, he believes, needs to be isolated from people traffic as much as possible.

Visiting teams playing Georgia don't stay in Athens anymore for the same reason. Just too much noise and traffic as the town becomes keyed up for Saturday's big games. The Ramada at Two Notch is exposed to none of that, which is why Coach Richt loves the facility.

As the team moved into its Friday routine, it begins to get its game face on. Damon Evans and I and others in the staff party headed out to a nearby lake home of Hinton Davis, a starting guard on Georgia's SEC championship team of 1959.

Hinton has become a very successful insurance executive and has substantial business throughout the Southeast. He always hosts a big party for his friends on Friday night when Georgia plays in Columbia.

With his business success, he has been generous to his alma mater. Nothing like seeing a lineman, a graduate of the trenches, make it big in business and maintain deep, abiding affection for his school. Hinton Davis is a friend of the Dawgs.

Saturday morning was quiet. The early risers find the lobby for coffee. Neil Callaway is the earliest riser of the coaches. We usually have coffee and talk about the game. He was very basic, saying the obvious, but added a homey twist that might remind you of what a Bear Bryant would say. That would only be natural because Neil played for the Bear.

when it was time to meet in the evening.

The long stretch of interstate from Thomson to Columbia brought on some restlessness. A three-hour-plus bus ride for active young boys, whose physical dimensions are not conducive to relaxing in seats designed for smaller people, has them anxious to stretch by the time we arrive at the Ramada Plaza Hotel on Two Notch Road.

This is not a four-star facility by any means, but is ideal for Coach Richt. The fewer distractions the better, and this hotel is isolated away from any hubbub of social activity. Most of

Dave Van Halanger is an early riser, too. He usually finds a quiet corner of the hotel, either in the lobby or the meeting rooms and reads scripture and has his own devotional. It is the way he starts everyday, and when I see Dave, I always see a man at peace. That has to be comforting and reassuring. He has the friendliest smile of anyone in Athens. It is a smile that suggests, "You are welcome in my presence." That is why he is so popular with the players. They know he wants them to become bigger and stronger for football, but also he seeks for them to develop inner strength, the strength that will take them through troubled times which come their way.

Larry Munson doesn't arise as early as I once remembered, but you can be sure that when he gets to percolating and upright, he is anxious to get to the stadium. If he could, I think he would sleep at the stadium. Some of that is his personality, and some of it is his dating back to the past.

Old timers got to the stadium early and visited with writers, broadcasters and home team officials. They might pick up something of interest. But most of all, it is good neighborly visiting with folks in the trade. You hear the scuttlebutt and the gossip. Munson can hardly wait for kickoff, and when it comes, he is as up and as anxious as the team. The broadcast crew gets to the stadium at least four hours prior to kickoff.

The team awakens leisurely for a late kickoff and tries to stay off its feet as much as possible. Final reviews are followed by more reviews. Checklists are checked and rechecked. The focus is the opposition. In addition to meeting, the team conducts walkthroughs. Players line up in their respective positions and a coach stations the opposition (reserve players) and goes over situational alignment. "If they do this, we do that. If they do that, we do this." If the mind remembers, if the mind is ready and sharp, there is a greater

The two Davids enjoy a light moment prior to the 2004 season

opportunity for the scoreboard to reflect what you came for—victory.

Nothing is worse than losing on the road and having to take that long bus ride back. It was a happy scene for Georgia during this game. The Davids made two trips to Columbia and had pleasant bus rides home.

On the return, I rode on the defensive bus. I wanted to rehash the game with the coaches, but nobody was interested. Too drained to talk. Another movie was played on the bus video system. Coaches and players pretty much slept. Brian

VanGorder took a walk down the aisle offering congratulations to each player. At the end of the trip, he took the in-house microphone and reminded the players of the weekend routine.

Sunday is an off day, but any player needing treatment is reminded to check in with the training room. "If you need treatment men, be sure and do what you are supposed to do," the Bulldog defensive coordinator reminded them. "We need every man to be at his best for the next game."

By the time the bus reached the outskirts of Athens, the players were into light and flippant conversation, kidding and cajoling. They were ready for their own beds. They could sleep late. They could enjoy Sunday afternoon, knowing that they had won another big conference game. Their weekend was successful.

The Davids would be in church Sunday morning. They would relax in the afternoon. There would be phone calls to family and friends. Then it would be Monday and the preparation beat would go on. It is not exactly a grind, but it is intense—which is why winning is so much fun.

College football—as much as possible—is kept simplified. Terminology with the offense has changed noticeably in recent years with as many codes and colors utilized as numbers.

Anybody who has ever played football at any level probably remembers when his coach numbered the holes between the linemen on both sides of the ball. Holes to the right, most often, were assigned even numbers and to the left, odd numbers.

Backs were usually numbered as follows: The quarterback was No. 1, the fullback No. 2 and the tailback No. 3. If the quarterback called play No. 36, it meant that the tailback took a handoff and ran between the right tackle and end.

While the Bulldogs' use of numbers is much less than is traditional, numbers still are used: even for plays to the tight formation and odd to the split formation.

At Georgia, Richt, Bobo and Neil Callaway, along with John Eason and Dave Johnson, choose the names for plays, but they also allow the quarterbacks to get in on the name game. "Sometimes in [pre-practice] meetings, we will show them a play and tell the quarterbacks to give it a name by the time we take the practice field. Joe Tereshinski, III has been particularly clever with names," Bobo explains.

During the '04 season, while watching University of Alabama Birmingham versus Cincinnati in '03, (the offensive coordinator at Cincinnati had moved on to Marshall and the staff was reviewing Cincinnati's offense for tendencies they might expect from Marshall when the Thundering Herd had the ball), the offensive coaches were impressed with a post route utilized by UAB. They put the play into the Dawgs' playbook and named it, "Birmingham."

For the Florida game in '04, the coaches designed a new flag route for Leonard Pope. They already had a play in the playbook called "Y-flag." No need for confusion, so at a meeting, Bobo drew up the play and asked if the quarterbacks knew who Betsy Ross was. He gave them a quick history lesson about the great American who sewed the first flag for our country. Since the play was to the split side, he named it "43 Betsy." Pope ran his route efficiently and effectively, and Greene hit him on a 27-yard pass for a touchdown.

When they put in a quarterback draw for David Greene, they simply named it, "Norman." That is his middle name. "He was going to get the ball," Bobo says, "so using his middle name made it simple."

Clay Walker (left) flashes personnel information to the defense

"P-44 Haynes" was the pass from Greene to Verron Haynes to beat Tennessee in 2001. "P" indicates the protection; 44 Haynes refers to the route of the tailback. This play works when the defensive coverage is aligned with two safeties instead of one. In order for the play to succeed, Verron's main assignment, other than catching the ball, was to avoid the Mike (middle) linebacker. He had to "slip" the linebacker (avoid contact and get open). If Tennessee had lined up with a single safety, the plan was for Greene to throw the ball away, allowing Richt to call another play. A single safety would have a better chance to stop the play in that situation. If the defense recognizes the formation and reacts accordingly, it is unlikely that the play will work. Calling it at the right time created scoring opportunity. It connected for a touchdown with J.T. Wall versus Florida in 2002 and Alabama in 2003 with Jamario Smith. Verron Haynes is playing with the Pittsburgh Steelers, but "P-44 Haynes" is still in the playbook. Likely you will see it again.

When Tyson Browning sprinted 93 yards with a screen pass against LSU in Baton Rouge in 2003, the play was called, "Snake Crack." Names for plays to the split side begin with S. To the tight side, the names begin with T.

The play that won the Auburn game and the SEC East championship in '02 was "70X Takeoff." The play got a lot of attention, widespread newspaper coverage. "If it had failed," Richt said later, "nobody would have asked what the play was called."

✛ ✛ ✛

Other noteworthy plays in the Richt era and their names and results:

"Flatback rooskie" was a play used in the Auburn game. It was fourth and two, and Greene hit Terrence Edwards for a 56-yard touchdown. This play works best in short yardage and the offense SELLS the run. Flatback means that the offensive linemen keep their backs flat as if a run is coming. On pass plays, linemen usually take a step back and are more upright to protect the passer. When they come off their block "flatback," their blocking stance indicates run. The wide receiver must also demonstrate that it is a run, overselling his intent to block the safety. The quarterback takes a nonchalant move backward faking the run, keeping the ball on his hip. Against Auburn, Terrence was wide open. The play also produced a touchdown versus Vandy in 2002. Against Tech in 2003,

Sideline huddle, Greene and Richt usually figured out how to best opposing defenses

it was completed for a 46-yard gain to set up a touchdown which jumpstarted the offense.

"Rooskie" is a term used throughout college football referring to trick plays. In the 1988 Orange Bowl, Miami defeated Oklahoma 20-14, but the Sooners tightened the score with "fumblerooskie," a play in which the quarterback takes the snap, puts the ball on the ground, and a lineman, most often the guard, picks it up and runs for big yardage. Many times it has resulted in a touchdown. After the game, Barry Switzer, the OU coach, went up to his old friend, Jimmy Johnson of Miami, and said. "I got you on the 'fumblerooskie,' didn't I?" There wasn't much else for Switzer to talk about. It was the Hurricanes' night.

When Nebraska was down to Miami in the National Championship game of 1984 in the Orange Bowl, the Cornhuskers called "fumblerooskie," and All-American guard Dean Steinkhuler not only made it into the end zone for a touchdown, he ran over Willie Martinez, now Georgia's defensive coordinator. "I can't get away from that play," Martinez laughs. "Everybody kids me about that play today, but I always remind them we won the game and the National Championship."

When Richt was at Florida State, the Seminoles utilized a play they called "puntrooskie" one year to beat Clemson. On this play, the snap goes to the upback, who puts the ball between the legs of a protector. The wing blocker

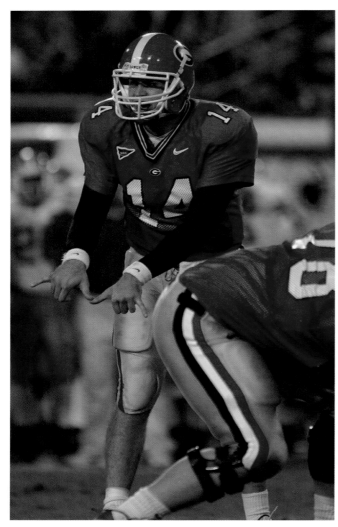

Master of Georgia's audibles

comes around, takes the ball from the protector and sets sail—if you catch the punt return team napping as FSU did in 1988. FSU's LeRoy Butler ran the fake punt 78 yards to the Clemson one-yard line, which set up the winning field goal.

"Unitas" was a play designed for David Greene to run the ball. Here is how it worked in the Auburn game in '02 and against Tech in '03. In the second half at Auburn, Greene ran "Unitas" as it was drawn up, but was hit and fumbled at the goal line. Not to worry, because his roommate, Jon

Stinchcomb, fell on the ball in the end zone for a touchdown. Against Tech, same results. Greene fumbled at the goal line, but Nick Jones recovered for a touchdown. "Greenie," Bobo laughs, "holds the 'all-time' record for quarterback fumbles recovered for touchdowns." It gets its name from its play number, which is 19. Normally the tailback gets the ball on a handoff on 19, but since the variation calling for the quarterback to run the ball, another name was needed. The great Colt quarterback John Unitas, wore 19, hence the play "Unitas" was coined when Richt wanted the quarterback to run the ball.

2003

The following was put in for Alabama Birmingham. After watching tape of the Blazers, he felt the opponent's defense was susceptible to a deep post route. After considerable review and discussion with the coaches, and subsequently, the quarterbacks, they became so convinced of the play's potential, they suggested "Touchdown." They were so convinced it would work for a score that they lobbied successfully for the name. Receivers coach John Eason, a sage and seasoned veteran, however, advised against it. Bryan McClendon was wide open but dropped the ball. With a firm and stoic look, Eason remarked, "That is why you don't call a play 'Touchdown.'"

2004

Against South Carolina at Columbia, the Greene pass for a touchdown to Reggie Brown that won the game was named "Colt-Patriot." It works when the safeties are aligned for run support. The receiver's responsibility is to show block to the safety, but "slips" him vertically. As he is running his route, the quarterback is faking the run. When the safety feels pressure indicating a block and is poised to support the run, the receiver often is open in a flash. That was the case in Columbia and Greene hit Reggie for 22 yards and victory. "Colt" is the protection on this play; "Patriot" is the route of the receiver. When the offensive coaches reviewed the play with the quarterbacks, the quarterbacks remembered the Patriots scoring on a very similar play in the Super Bowl, so they suggested, "Patriot." Not only easy to remember, but graphic in the mind's eye.

"44 flatback seam" is the play that sealed the game in Jacksonville with a touchdown pass to Fred Gibson to advance the Bulldogs' lead to 31-21. The line sells the run, like "flatbackrooskie." Greene takes a five-step drop and Fred angles to the post. "It is a deep slant and basically a play in which the receiver simply must go get the ball," Bobo says. "The quarterback needs perfect timing. That play had been good to us three or four times already in the game. Fred simply made a terrific play, which we had to have. He just went and got the ball. He was not going to be denied."

+ + +

Names in football bring about curiosity and intrigue, if they work. "If we had beaten Auburn in 2001, 'flatbackrooskie' to Terrence Edwards would have been a talked about play for a long time," Richt says. "But since we didn't win the game, that play lost a lot of its importance."

Georgia fans clamored throughout Greene's career for Richt to put Greene and D.J. Shockley in the game at the same time. He did—in the Outback Bowl. Greene lined up to his left in a trips formation (three receivers to the same side of the field). Shockley was to fire a sideline pass to Greene who was to turn and throw back to Shockley. The play, "crocodile," didn't work.

Greene's pass fell to the ground in futility, making everybody aware that by whatever name you call a play, it will be remembered for its execution or lack thereof.

The Bulldogs put in play "R47" a couple of years ago, a tailback toss to the split side. Pollack's number is 47, and because of his constant clowning around, ribbing and cajoling everybody, Richt renamed it "Joker."

Fans often see offensive players entering the game flopping their arms in the fashion of a flying bird. This is to alert those in the offensive huddle that the plan is to run an eagle set which means the coaches are calling for a "3" personnel set (three wide receivers). You sometimes see personnel substitution situations with players entering the game with clenched fists over their shoulders in Charles Atlas fashion. This means jumbo set or two tight ends.

All of this is to let everybody on the field know as much as possible in the shortest period of time. It also helps with communicating what the plan is and to expedite the process within the short period of time allowed between snaps.

When General Robert Neyland coached at Tennessee, he used a term "Oskee-wow-wow," an Indian name, for the defense to use when there was an interception by the Volunteers. That meant that all defenders became aware that Tennessee had the ball and they must immediately become blockers. To this day, Tennessee coaches practice "Oskee" drills. Oskee-wow-wow could be heard in coaching clinics around the country as Neyland disciples populated the coaching ranks.

Neyland got the name from Illinois. The great Illini coach, Bob Zuppke, who coached the immortal Red Grange, used it. Cheerleaders, who were imitating the war cry of the Indians who had settled the area, originally used it.

Football can be inventive, imaginative and

creative. There, too, is adaptation and recycling of ideas. Some of the most original plays have been outlawed. Like the sleeper play where a receiver would hide out on the sideline and dash down field for a long pass for a touchdown.

The popularity of the pro style passing game has reduced use of the option, but in all likelihood, the option will never go away. The man credited with inventing the option was Don Faurot of Missouri. I once called him to talk to him about the option, and he told me he would be taking a golfing vacation to Ponte Vedra in the spring. I made an appointment with him and videotaped our interview about the Split T. I still have the tape.

Faurot played and coached basketball at one time. He remembered how it was with a player with the ball driving to the basket.

If the defender gave him the lane, he drove for the basket and attempted a layup. If the defender moved to block the ball handler's path, he would pass off to a teammate who made the move to the basket.

Faurot took that concept and invented the Split T option, which became the rage of college football in the 50s. Vince Dooley was a Split T option quarterback at Auburn. Faurot taught his quarterbacks to move down the line of scrimmage and take the most attractive option available. If there were a hole in the defense at any point, he would run into the hole. If holes were clogged up or stalemated, he would pitch to a trailing back. The Split T option became the preferred offense for most schools in the 50s. Bud Wilkinson, at Oklahoma, won 47 consecutive games with this offensive formation. Wilkinson learned the Split T option from Faurot in World War II, when they were coaching at the Jacksonville Naval Air Station. John Donaldson learned the formation while playing for Faurot in the Navy at Jacksonville and ran the option at Jesup when he became a high school head coach.

The wishbone and veer options were later developed off this concept, confirming once again, there is nothing new under the sun.

∎

CHAPTER SIX

GREENIE'S SIGNATURE PLAYS

In 2001, David Greene convinced Mike Bobo that he had special quarterback qualities. "He could take constructive criticism without getting his feelings hurt. He knew what he had to work on and actually asked for critiques. In the Tennessee game, he handled that winning drive like a seasoned pro. We could not have been more pleased. In the pocket with bodies flying all around him, he was so poised. He played like he had been there many times before, and we are in Knoxville with over 100,000 fans. Unbelievable."

Bobo can remember the plays like the game was yesterday. "I don't think I'll ever forget," he smiles. Here are the sequence and results:

Freedom Top: Georgia starting at the Bulldog's 41. Greene hit Damien Gary (at running back)— an option route that produced a first down.

Smoke: An incomplete pass to the wide receiver, running two flag route.

560 Switch: A pass completion over the middle to Randy McMichael for 26 yards.

44 Demon: Inside post to McMichael for 14 yards to the six yard line.

P-44 Haynes: TD pass to Verron Haynes.

In the Auburn game, Greenie made the pass of a lifetime. The Dawgs gained possession for a last opportunity late in the fourth quarter at the Georgia 41.

In the huddle at the start of the drive, quarterback David Greene only spoke the words that everybody in the stadium wearing red and black knew. "Men, this is it," he said. "Our season is on the line."

On the 41 yard pass to the Auburn 14 from Greene to Fred Gibson, Fred was not the primary receiver. "In fact, he was not in my read at all when we lined up for the snap." Greene says. But the quarterback noted that Gibson was facing one-on-one coverage. In that case Greene realized that more often than not, it is advantage Georgia. "So I just took it," Greene said of the opportunity. "I knew the odds were in Fred's favor." He was right, but that play was now in the past. The urgency to produce a score still remained.

An incomplete pass was followed by a false start. It became 2nd and 5. Then two incomplete passes left the Dogs with a 4th and 15 challenge. It appeared that the advantage was all Auburn's. The last yards of the red zone are always the toughest place to succeed. The field becomes smaller; there is less room with which to work

Verron Haynes – aftershocks in Knoxville

and less room for error.

In the huddle, Greene called the play that Richt had sent in. No encouragement. No comment otherwise by the quarterback. "We all knew what was at stake," Greene says. "70 X takeoff," he firmly informed his teammates. Then he added, "On first bob." Everyone knew that meant Greene would line up in the shotgun formation. On the initial lift of his left foot (first bob) center Ian Knight would snap the ball.

When the team lined up, Greene called out the defense which is standard. "Stack," he barked. Then he repeated his call. "Stack." Everybody knew what the situation was. All that was needed at this juncture was execution.

The players were confident in the play sent in by the head coach. Richt knew that if it were a jump ball, the man most physically equipped for the job was Michael Johnson, an Oklahoman with good size and excellent jumping ability. As the play developed, he knew that the right call had been made.

Fred Gibson had lined up wide to the right, and it was important for Greene to freeze the free safety. If he paused just enough before coming over to help out on coverage of Johnson, the one-on-one matchup that the Bulldogs needed would take place.

This meant that Greene had to sell the play with a pump fake to Gibson. When the snap settled into his hands he immediately looked right in Gibson's direction. It worked. The free safety hesitated just enough.

Greene then pivoted and lofted a pass to his left. Johnson had run his route perfectly. He was in position to make the catch. The ball was airborne and thrown just right. Johnson is now in the air, too. He is up over the defender, and the ball settles into his waiting arms for the score.

Touchdown! Glory! SEC East championship!

Michael Johnson's winning catch at Auburn

CHAPTER SEVEN

CONVERSATION WITH GREENIE

Early in the '04 season, David Greene and I met at Chick-fil-A. A guy who asked him to sign several schedule cards interrupted our lunch. Greenie, ever the accommodating nice guy, obliged with a smile.

"What about the Heisman?" the nervous fan asked. "I just want to win," Greenie said. He picked up a to-go order for Davey Pollack when we finished, and as he was walking out the door, a couple of people stopped him for his autograph.

During lunch, it also happened, but for those who weren't bold enough to interrupt, you could see that all eyes in the restaurant were focused in his direction. They knew who he was. He seemed oblivious and unaffected as he spoke:

It doesn't bother me that people want my autograph. Sometimes, you just have to go. You have a schedule. Sometimes you want to be alone, but it is not possible in this town in the fall. I take it as a compliment that they want my autograph. Also, I realize that it has to do with the fact that I am playing for Georgia. People all over this state are crazy about the Dawgs, and we are aware of that. It is nice to be with a team that is so popular and well appreciated.

Couldn't imagine what it would be like to play for a school which had trouble winning year after year. It happened to me in high school before T. McFerrin took over our program. That was very frustrating, and I certainly don't want to go through anything like that again. Fortunately, it has been a consistency of success at Georgia. That is because we have good players and good coaching. Everything seems to fit with Coach Richt's program.

On the road, I room with P. [Pollack]. We room together for home games at Lake Lanier Islands, and we room together for all road games. He is always the same, except as we get closer to Saturday, he becomes more serious. He is deeply serious when it counts. His way of doing things and his style keeps us loose. He always says something that cracks me up—even if we are just watching television.

We both enjoy watching tape. You say film? We grew up in the era of tape, but I heard my coaches many times say film. It has always been interesting to hear older coaches talk about how the game has changed. Both Davey and I carry tape

DawgWalk Tribute

pared, he can't expect the rest of the team to do their job.

This fall has been a very enjoyable one. Friday, I have class from 9:00 to 11:00. I usually get a massage and then the rest of the day is free. You need to feel relaxed going into the weekend.

I always lose my voice by the end of the game. Lose it on Saturday and get it back by Monday, usually after a good night's sleep.

Saturday games between the hedges are so exciting and such a wonderful experience. If you win, it is simply the best. After we get to the locker room in the Butts-Mehre Building, we shower and then head over to the RV camper parking lot. My parents and Davey's parents park across from each other, and sometimes it looks like everybody left the stadium and came over to the RV lot.

People bring their own food and refreshment, and have a good time rehashing the game. It is a time, too, to relax, and we do that by kicking back and watching whatever game is on TV. It is always interesting when we watch some team we will be playing down the road. We both like to keep up.

Sometimes there will be two teams playing, and we will have to play them later on. You just don't know who to pull for. You try to figure which result will help our team the most. One of the things I like about playing in the Southeastern Conference is that we play the best. It is never easy in this league. Put Oklahoma or Southern Cal in our league, and I bet they wouldn't win 'em all.

P. and I never lock our doors. We have never had anything stolen [His father Rick chimes in, "Easy to understand that. Nobody could find anything in that mess!"].

On Fridays we gather at the Butts-Mehre Building and hear from a speaker. Often it is a former player,

home during the week to study. Before practice, I often watch tape in Coach Bobo's office. He'll have it ready for me when I walk in the door. During the week, I spend about six hours with the coaches. Later on, if I am not sure about something or have something on my mind, I pop a tape in the machine and check it out. The amount of time I watch depends on the complexity of the game plan or if we are playing a team that does a lot of different things. After you see it several times, you gain confidence that you know what you will be up against on Saturday.

The thing you expect of yourself as a quarterback is to be prepared. If the quarterback isn't pre-

The beloved Larry Munson with the Beloved Dawgs

and that is always interesting. One of the most interesting speakers we have had was Fran Tarkenton. I pay close attention when somebody with his success talks. He has a good insight into football, and he has had such a great experience. I am amazed. He is not a big guy, and he started for 18 years in the National Football League. That suggests that it is not all physical. We usually arrive at Emerald Pointe in time for dinner about 7:00. There is a team meeting at 7:30, we have snacks around 9:00 and then lights out at 11:00. If it is a CBS game, we get to sleep as late as 9:30.

The best game of the season for us was LSU. We had such rhythm. It is like golf. You get into a groove, and you can't explain it. After the LSU game, a writer asked me why I threw it so well, and I laughed and said, 'If I had an answer, don't

you think I would be doing it every week?' I am a rhythm passer but sometimes the defense takes your rhythm away.

Sometimes, when there is a timeout on the field or some type of delay, like measuring for a first down, you have more time to talk between the plays. Coach Richt doesn't like it if there is any foolishness going on. He considers the huddle our office, and we need to keep our minds on business. Sometimes somebody will wisecrack and loosen us up. Reggie [Brown] and Fred [Gibson] always remind me that we should go deep. "I'll catch it," they will say. They believe they can catch it anywhere on the field. I have confidence in them, too. How could you not have confidence as a quarterback with those two guys on your side of the field?

A LETTER FROM GREENIE'S MOTHER

Dear David,

It seems like yesterday that we brought you home from the hospital. I just can't believe that almost 23 years have gone by. I can tell you that you have truly blessed our lives. To me you are still the same little boy that I loved watching play T-ball. You have always done everything with such enthusiasm (as long as it had something to do with a ball!). I laugh when I think about you growing up, your non-stop motion! We used to have to play the "time-out" game all the time just so you would settle down and let someone else talk.

Your honesty, your faith in God, and your love for your family and friends make you so special. I really don't know that I have ever heard you talk ugly about anyone. You have always seen the good in everyone. I admire you so, for that is a wonderful trait. Over the last two years you have really grown into a wonderful young man. I look at you and Leslie and know that God has truly blessed me. You have been a wonderful son, brother, grandson, and cousin. You make everyone around you feel loved and special.

I will never forget when we had to put Granny in the nursing home. The closeness and the love you felt from her I believe helped shape you into the person you are today. She had lived with us during the most important time in your life. The first 17 years of your life that she was with us were truly wonderful, and she, as well as your Dad and I, showed you what true unconditional love was all about. When she was getting sick, the tenderness and care you showed her did not go unnoticed.

I often watch you with the small children who want your autograph. You get down on their level. You make them feel like they made your day for asking for your autograph. Little do you know how you have made them feel so special. I read this little saying somewhere, I don't remember where, but I have always remembered the message. It reminds me of how your Dad and I feel:

You don't raise heroes, you raise sons. And if you treat them like sons,
they'll turn out to be heroes, even it if it's just in your own eyes.

Thank you for all the thousands of memories that you have given us over the years. Your hard work has definitely paid off for you. You have been a wonderful leader and role model for many. You never looked to tomorrow to see what it might bring – you always looked at today and made that day the best it could be. You are truly a hero in my eyes and I love you so very much. You are a terrific athlete, but more important you are a wonderful friend and son. Just don't ever forget where you get all your talent, FROM YOUR MOM'S SIDE!!! HAHAHA! Just kidding. You knew I would have to throw that in.

Keep up the hard work. Trust your instincts and always know that Dad and I are always here for you whatever your future brings. I love you Sweetie and may God always be there to guide you and comfort you.

Love always,
Mom

As a quarterback, you enjoy throwing the ball. If you are fortunate to throw touchdown passes, that is about as big as it gets, but you have to keep your perspective. You are aware that you need a good running game to be successful. That is why I enjoyed our young running backs, Danny Ware and Thomas Brown. They are very good, and I enjoy handing the ball off and watch them hit a hole and move us down the field. You can hear the crowd buzz when Thomas gets the ball. He really has a lot of pop. He's dynamite, always moving forward. He always keeps his feet moving.

Many of us have scooters that we ride to class. Kevin Breedlove, one of our offensive linemen, was the first to own one. Mine had over 650 miles on it in the middle of the fall. It is great with parking being so restricted. We can park it in the bike racks. Nobody bothers it. None of us take it on Loop 10; we just ride them for convenience.

[After the Tech game] Looking back we didn't achieve our goals, and that is a big disappointment. Not a bad season, but we expected more of ourselves.

Beating LSU and Florida gave us great satisfaction. I didn't want to leave Georgia without a win in Jacksonville. That meant so much to our seniors. And to have a 4-0 record against Georgia Tech—that is special. There were a lot of good moments. We felt we could win every time we went out. I am happy that is the situation at Georgia now, and I am sure I will enjoy Bulldog football for years to come.

Another thing I am proud of is getting my degree. When I enrolled, I set that as a goal. I don't think that is anything out of the ordinary. It is something that I expected of myself. That is the reason you go to college. I wanted to play football and

play on successful teams. You never know if you will win a championship, but I am grateful for that experience. We played in four bowls and we won three of them. That is nice, too.

The Georgia people have been great to us. I have enjoyed seeing the unbelievable enthusiasm. When you go through the DawgWalk and see all those kids wearing your number, you feel so humbled. I will always be grateful that I became a Bulldog. The memories will last forever. Fortunately for us, they have been good memories.

BIG SISTER'S BIG LOYALTY: WEARING RED AND BLACK IN THE AUBURN STUDENT SECTION
BY LESLIE MATHIS

When my parents told me that I was going to be a big sister, they said I was so excited and couldn't wait to have someone to play with. I was 22 months old when David was born. When he came home from the hospital, I bit him!

David and I were not kids who stayed inside and watched TV; we played outside all day long, everyday. We played every sport imaginable and a ton of games that we made up ourselves. If it was football season, we played football. If it was baseball season, we played baseball. Basketball season, basketball, etc. Since our dad was the coach for David's teams, there was always equipment in the garage. I remember dressing up in full catcher's attire and letting David pitch to me in the front yard. When we would play football, I would always play quarterback and David would play receiver. He would make me throw him passes that were almost out of bounds so that he could make the diving catch! My mom claims that he gets all of his talent from her, but I did teach him how to punt the football. He was actually the punter in high school as well as the quarterback!

14 47

David loves to scare me. I am a pretty big chicken, so I guess it's not very hard to do! My bed was pretty tall, and if I was in my room watching TV, David would crawl into my room and sneak under my bed. He would wait until I got up, and as soon as my feet would hit the floor, he would stick his hands out and grab my ankles! He always got such a kick out of that! The time that he scared me the most was one night when I was coming home from a friend's house. David was hiding in the woods beside the driveway. I got out of my car, thinking that everything was ok; my dad was outside on the porch waiting for me with all the lights on. I got out of my car and as soon as I shut and locked the doors, David jumped out of the woods screaming! I didn't know who to be mad at—David or Dad, who let him do this while he watched and laughed hysterically from the porch! I did get David back plenty of times though! We would each be lying in bed in our rooms, which were next to each other, and I would start yelling, "David, David, come quick, you have to see this!" He would jump out of bed and come rushing into my room and I would say to him, "Can you turn my fan off?" He fell for it every time.

I have always been so protective of David and threatened all of my guy friends when David was going through "initiation" for varsity football and baseball! I told them that they better not do anything to him or I would kill them! Even my freshman and sophomore years at Auburn when David was playing a big game, I would drive home on Friday nights to see his games. I always knew that he was a good quarterback, but it still amazes me when I think of all the things that he has accomplished over his career.

The first collegiate football game that David played was against Arkansas State. When he walked into Sanford Stadium for the first time, I had chills all over, and I just burst into tears. I just couldn't believe that he was able to achieve something that he had dreamed of since he was a little boy.

Everyone always says to me, "So what are you going to do at the Georgia-Auburn game?" or "Is it hard for you?" It seems so crazy to me that people even ask that question because it wasn't hard at all. I wanted David to win no matter who he is playing. Of course I was going to pull for Georgia. And the truth is that I really didn't even want Auburn to have a good game because it just made it more nervewracking for us! (Still not sure where he gets his calmness from!) When he signed with UGA, I promised him that as long as he was there, I was a Georgia fan! I actually cried when Georgia lost to Auburn his freshman year because I wanted him to win so badly! Now that he has graduated, I can return to being an Auburn fan.

A lot of people consider my brother a hero. Let me assure you. He is his sister's hero.

UP FRONT WITH RUSS TANNER

For the most part, my on-field memories of David Greene (in the huddle, we call him Greenie) are of his overall leadership and composure. I do not recall a single game in which he was rattled to the point that his performance was rattled. Looking back on my three years with him, I cannot remember a huddle in which he was not in control and was not commanding the attention of all ten other guys.

His command of the huddle was unique to me, however. Ninety-nine percent of the time he was very cool, calm, and collected. He did not yell, scream, or chastise any of us. Greenie was the most calming influence I have ever been around since the time I was playing peewee football. Guys paid attention to him because they knew that if he told them something, they could take it to the bank. No matter if you had just fumbled, missed an assignment, or in my case, were flagged for holding. He would only yell at you if you got down on yourself. Greenie was great at making a guy believe that he was at the University of Georgia for a reason, and that he believed you could get the job done. To have a guy who is in charge of your huddle and respected by everyone tell you he has confidence in you, that you will get it done, means a whole heck of a lot. That is what he did best.

Aside from being the biggest morale boost most of us got during a game, David also took it upon himself to make sure that we were staying loose and enjoying the game we had been playing since the time we were old enough to strap on a helmet. He truly enjoyed wearing the Red and Black and playing in Sanford Stadium. Greenie is an inspiring leader who is very mature, but that does not mean that he is not a big kid having the time of his life throwing a football around. Whenever we start talking about games and things guys have said during games, talking about our laid-back quarterback always cracks me up.

I will never forget the Clemson game in 2003. It was opening day and we were all extremely pumped up about playing. We were at Death Valley, and the temperature was about 120°, or so we thought. By the time kickoff rolled around, we were about to bust to hit somebody other than our defense. I can only speak for the O-line, but I know that we were all nervous and very anxious to get going. For most of us it was our first start. We were all a little uptight and unsure about what we were getting into. David was just as fired up as we were, but he knew that we needed something to make us relax and repeat the things we had been practicing for over a month. The first couple of plays are still a blur to me, but when we came back the huddle after the third play, David cracked a one liner that made us all laugh and ultimately relax. All I remember is that it was a pass play, and he threw a

Russ Tanner appreciated Greenie's appreciation for his lineman

deep out. He was laughing when he came back to the huddle. He looked directly at us and in his "aw shucks" style said, "Boys, I just threw the hell out of that ball," and then he called the next play. I remember coming up to the line, looking at Bartley Miller and Josh Brock and asking "did David just say he 'threw the hell out of that ball?'"

It was one of those situations you really had to be there to fully appreciate but that off-the-cuff lighthearted comment, to me, summed up what David Greene was all about. We were in a hostile environment, in sweltering heat, and the O-line had a combined total of one start, and our leader was joking about how good of an arm he had. David is probably the most humble and calm guy

Kevin Breedlove, letterman 99-02, figured out how to solve parking-on-campus, initiating a scooter craze for the Richt Dawgs

I know, but we all knew that he was having a great time and seemed to know that we were going to win that game and many more.

We all looked to Greenie to see how we were supposed to handle ourselves, and he set a great example. If you were down, he tried to pick you up. If you were in a daze, he tried to snap you out of it. If you were lacking confidence or thought you lacked the ability, he made you believe that you had plenty of both. I heard one time that "Confidence based on fact is not arrogance." The facts about David Greene reveal why he was so confident. He is going to be sorely missed around the University of Georgia and not just for 42 wins. He is going to be missed because of the way he treated guys and how he made them feel like they were born to wear Silver Britches.

THE WHIRRING DERVISH
COMES TO TOWN

If you are past 50 and you are aware that time flies, consider that it was 25 years ago this year that Herschel Walker, as a freshman, led the Georgia Bulldogs to an undefeated season and the national championship.

Herschel would become Georgia's first three-time All America selection. If he had stayed with the Bulldogs, he could have been the first four time All American.

When Herschel left, it disheartened the Bulldog Nation. They understood, with the millions that were involved, but they, nonetheless, felt like the fan who said to Shoeless Joe Jackson after the old Black Sox scandal in baseball: "Say it ain't so, Joe?"

That is how we felt when Herschel left. Were we being fair? Were we being selfish? What would we have done if we had been in his moccasins?

For a fan, football is never a business. It is heart and soul and alma mater and emotion. We don't think about paydays and endorsements. We think emotionally about the welfare of our school. We believe everything should be neatly wrapped in red and black.

Perhaps, that is why we learned to love The Davids so much. They made us feel that they feel like we feel. In Pollack's case, he could have turned pro a year early. That he didn't may have had something to do with why the fans clamored to reach out and touch the hem of his garment. Maybe that is why he enjoyed exalted status for a lineman. It wasn't just the kids; it was grown men and ladies in their senior years, donning No. 47.

If he had left, I don't think he would have been as revered as he is. We thrilled to his play, his arresting attitude and pure hustle, his spiritual preachments and his unadulterated love of alma mater, and a game he mastered in Bulldog clothing.

It was the same with his accomplished roommate, the quarterback we call Greenie.

Charley Trippi could have, because of his military time, turned pro after the '45 season. He didn't, and while there was not the hoopla surrounding the game then as now, it was, nonetheless, a great day for Georgia that a man every bit as good as, or better than, Herschel Walker chose to stay home and play his senior year. Many years after that decision, I appreciate Charley Trippi, whom I never saw play.

I was in the room when Pollack said, "No," to the NFL in the spring of '04. While I had no inkling of his choice, I sat in the back of the room—a row behind Katharyn Richt—and

COMPLICATIONS

Complications at birth were frightening for Davey Pollack's mother, too. Kelli, like Kay Greene, was very alarmed. "When I went into labor, I was rushed into emergency C-Section delivery," Kelli Pollack says. "The umbilical cord was wrapped around his neck three times. He was in intensive care for two days. He was blue for almost that long."

She could have added that was the last time No. 47 was blue. His cheerful personality would suggest that he emerged from his emergency state into a ball of energy that confirms, even with risk at birth, there was no way to keep this young man down.

"Kay and I have talked for years about the unusual complications of their births," Kelli smiles.

thought to myself. "I really like this kid, and if he goes, I'll understand, but surely he won't! He's different. He has the right values, the maturity and the wisdom to stay." I looked over at Greenie. "Does he know?" I thought. "Why won't he wink and tip us all off?"

The reason I wanted Pollack to stay was that I believe in the college system. I know there is financial gain for kids who opt for the NFL, but no matter how you figure it—for most of them it is short-term gain. A degree still has limitless value.

As a society we have let our values become skewed. The bottom line is a tail that wags the dog. We need somebody to speak up for the college game in the traditional sense. Davey did.

Spend your time on campus for love of your alma mater. Don't stop short of that pursuit of a sheepskin. When Davey Pollack said to an anxious press conference gathering in the team meeting room at the Butts Mehre Building "I think I'll take one more year," every red-blooded Bulldog sang his everlasting praises.

That may have been his biggest accomplishment, more than all the awards. He convinced me that he stayed because he had feelings for Georgia and college football.

As an alumnus, I will always be grateful for that choice. He was the first lineman to make All-America three times. He won the Lombardi, the Bednarik, and the Lott Trophy all in 2004. That's good. I like all that, but most of all, he made me feel that he feels like all us passionate Bulldogs feel.

Now on with his story.

CHAPTER NINE

A FABULOUS RELATIONSHIP

It was a chilly December morning before the Outback Bowl when I met Jon Fabris for breakfast at the Mayflower Restaurant on Broad Street across from the Georgia campus. The town was dead, the students having departed for the holidays, but one of Athens' most traditional and popular institutions was filled with hungry morning-after diners.

When I told our waitress, Lisa Vaughn, I wanted grits with my eggs and country ham, Jon Fabris noted that I was ordering Georgia ice cream. He knows about grits, having been born and raised in the South, but he is not big on breakfast.

If you look closely as his long, lean and lithe physique, you easily conclude that he probably skips as many meals as he eats. His body fat is probably as low as some of the players he coaches. An intense and energized man, "Fab," as everybody associated with Georgia football calls him, was born to coach.

His father, Frank, after winning several region championships in football at Vidalia and a state championship at Rossville, coached in college at Brigham Young, Vanderbilt and Mississippi State. Jon and his older brother, Robert, finished high school in Starkville, but State showed no interest

in Robert. They had the recruiting advantage, but missed out on a pair of overachievers. At the last minute, Ole Miss offered a scholarship to Robert. Jon followed him to Oxford.

By the time Jon finished high school, his father had taken a job with the Georgia Center for Continuing Education in Athens, where he worked as an Associate Director until retirement.

While at Ole Miss, Jon spent part of his summers in Athens and became acquainted with and worked out with Georgia players. He played one year of football at Cedar Shoals. Danny Rogers was on the team. Rogers signed with Georgia and told Fab that Erk Russell, whom Fab has always admired, had a habit of making Bulldog defenders "play better than we were."

Fabris began to observe the Erk Russell approach to coaching. He concluded there was an undercurrent that brought pulsating results. You didn't see it, but those results frequently demonstrated that heart and effort, along with limitless intangibles, often made Georgia the underdog that finished on top. The Bulldog defensive coordinator didn't always field the most talented team, but somehow or other, his players seemed to be able to get the job done, no matter the competition.

Coach Jon Fabris (Fab) says it was the work ethic and intangibles that made Davey Pollack (right) a three time All-American

Hustle, fight, gang tackling, reacting to the ball and putting as much emphasis on heart and attitude as talent seemed to characterize Erk Russell teams. Big "T E A M," little "me."

He remembers Rusty Russell, Erk's oldest son, telling him about a tattered piece of paper that was stuck in the back of his dad's locker, a set of reminders that Erk lived by:

If you don't, they won't.
If you don't work, they won't.
If you don't care, they won't.
If you don't compete, they won't.

Once he read a clinic speech by Erk Russell and has never forgotten Erk's 4F reminders about coaching philosophy:

+ Fundamentally sound
+ Firm
+ Fair
+ Fun

You have to be firm in your approach to discipline, you discipline with fairness and above all, football has to be fun. Fab would be the first to point out that fun begins and ends with winning.

Today, you will find Fabris trading in slogans, preachments and inspirational homilies that are created to remind players that to succeed, to win—it all starts with attitude and commitment.

When the Mark Richt program got underway, Fabris (who had been around—coaching stops at Georgia Tech, Washington State, Iowa State, Kansas State, Notre Dame, South Carolina and

Pollack and Coach Fab after the Georgia Tech victory in 2004

the Cleveland Browns) just like Erk, became the Dogs' slogan aficionado.

If you fail to prepare, you prepare to fail.

Hard work beats talent when talent doesn't work hard.

A good plan violently executed is better than the perfect plan executed too late.

The only thing worse than believing you can't win is believing you can't lose.

Fab's grinding intensity is often a topic of conversation, and he admits that "Some folks think I am a little crazy," but respect is there. He also admits to being a "little high strung, which probably comes

from my mother's father." People, particularly the defensive ends, know that he cares. When he announced to the team in the locker room after the Tennessee game in Knoxville in '03 that, at last, his wife, Marcy, was pregnant, he was literally mobbed by all the players. It was evidence that the team cares about a man, who took overachievement from the playing field to coaching.

Fab cares about winning, he cares about his players and he cares about the University of Georgia. He knows Georgia's history better than many who played for the Bulldogs. It's like he played for the Dawgs and went to work in the

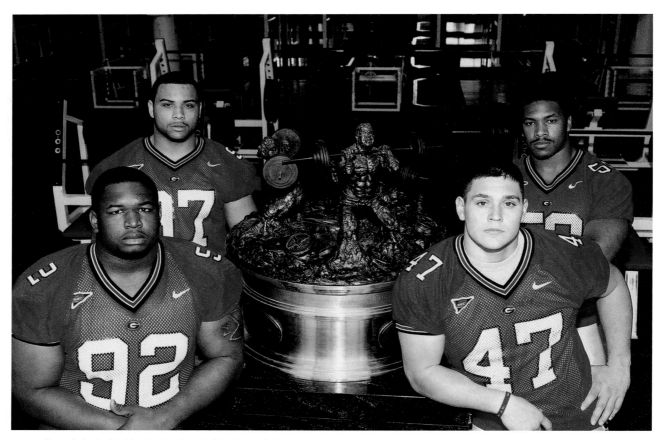

Davey Pollack with his daunting Dawg D-line, from left: Gerald Anderson, Kedric Golston and Will Thompson

sports information office.

Like Erk Russell, he believes that defense is a state of mind. Erk always said that half the battle is believing that you can stop the other guy. Fabris concurs, which is why for every game there is something in the way of a slogan posted on the wall or printed on the worksheets handed to the players each week.

An ongoing exercise, he tries to instill pride in his players. "Players must care more about what's on the side of their helmet than the guy across the line of scrimmage cares about what is on the side of his helmet," he says, referring to team decals.

For Fab there is a fine line between winning and losing. To maintain the edge from week to week is an eternal challenge. That search that might be the difference in a game is, for him, a

drill forever unfinished.

Jon's dad has always espoused deep affection for the University of Georgia. He played at South Georgia Junior College for Wyatt Posey, who played and coached for Wallace Butts. "My dad always referred to Georgia as 'the promised land.' It didn't work out for him to coach at Georgia, but he wound up finishing out his career with the University. I have always felt comfortable here."

Richt is all about family, and Fab knows plenty about that. When he was a senior in high school in Starkville, his father would drive from Athens on Friday to Starkville to see him play and then return home on Sunday. When he and his brother were at Ole Miss, the senior Fabris and his wife, Bettye, never missed a game, which meant that some weekends it was a shorter drive to where Ole Miss played than when the Rebels were at home in Oxford. Didn't matter, the Fabrises were in attendance to see their sons play. They never missed an Ole Miss game for seven straight seasons. His parents even drove to College Station, Texas, for a game.

The Fabrises were about discipline, too. How well does Fab remember when he and Robert wanted new baseball spikes as kids? The deal was that they bring home a report card with all A's. Robert did and got a new pair of spikes. Fab had one B. "I got no spikes," he laughs. It left a lasting impression, however. It sunk in that he should always be motivated to be the best he could be. His father knew Fab was capable of all A's.

Fabris was the first to believe in Pollack—he saw something singular in his raw makeup. The Snellville native arrived as a fullback but lettered as a tackle his freshman year before experimenting at defensive end. After only four on-the-field sessions in the spring of 02, the consensus was that Pollack didn't appear to have found a home at defensive end. The lone voice of dissent came from Fabris, who lobbied for more time for the whirring dervish to find himself.

When the coaches took their spring cruise to the Caribbean and reviewed personnel with the doting alumni who made the trip, nobody, believe it or not, had ever heard of Pollack.

"Keep your eye on No. 47," Fabris said, a comment that failed to arouse curiosity or heighten interest. Even other coaches on the staff, who appreciated Pollack's zeal for the game, saw more problem than progress.

Fabris, too, realized Pollack's limitations, but he is a coach who first seeks intangibles. Heart and character count the most. The work ethic is given near equal importance. Intelligence and competitive savvy are on his preferred list. If you find a player with an abundance of speed, size and quickness that's nice—but only if he possesses a

Receiving The Bednarik Award for the nation's most outstanding defensive player

few intangibles. Pollack's intense commitment turned Fabris' head.

Pollack was quick enough, and he developed exceptional strength, but the fact remained that throughout his college career he played against bigger and stronger men, many with equal or superior physical gifts, but none with his cup-runneth-over-intangibles.

From the end of spring practice, his sophomore year, until the fall, Fabris saw Pollack MAKE himself into a football player. There were only 15 days of spring drills, but there were at least l00 days before fall practice that Pollack could devote to improvement. He turned every weakness into a strength. If pure work ethic can take a player to the top, Pollack is Exhibit A. "I've never seen such improvement in a player in such a short period of time. He was better because he wanted to be better and was willing to work overtime to get there," Fabris says.

"Pollack," Fabris says, "lifts weights after weight lifting is over." He was the only player with his own key to the weight room. It was not uncommon to find him there late in the evening when the campus was out partying full throttle. He watches tape of opponents after tape watching sessions have ended. Prior to the Auburn game, two years ago, on a Thursday when the week was finally offering a breather to a beleaguered coaching staff, Fabris got a call from a chipper and upbeat Pollack who rousted his coach from a fatigue induced nap on the sofa at home.

"Coach," Pollack said excitedly, "I have watched seven of Auburn's game tapes, but I haven't seen that eighth tape. Can you let me in the building so I can watch that eighth tape?"

There are many similar examples of Pollack's dedicated initiative in his Bulldog career, and Fabris laments, more than any, the end of the Pollack era.

No more will we see adults clamoring for Pollack's autograph, pushing and shoving to move into his presence. And little kids! So many children are wearing his number!

When Pollack was doubled-teamed, as was often the case, the offensive objective was for the tackle and the tight end to force him back into the linebacker's lap, taking both defenders out of the play. That seldom happened, so when Pollack stalemated the two blockers and the linebacker had a free and clear path to the ball carrier or quarterback, the statisticians credited the linebacker with a tackle or a sack or a hurry. Pollack didn't get an assist, and that happened often after

his sensational sophomore season.

That is what Fabris will miss, those assists. Also, he'll miss Pollack's enthusiasm, his energy, his competitiveness, his intelligence, his leadership, his indomitable spirit, his remarkable morality and his class. He calls the Snellville Sacker—a fun loving, caustic needler—"a character with character." What an apt summation! He also notes that this God-fearing young man is New Testament off the field, good and kind to everybody. On the field, he is Old Testament to the hilt, eye-for-an-eye and tooth-for-a-tooth.

For four years, Fabris had sweet dreams of No. 47 making big plays dancing through his head. Outback Bowl week became difficult for him, as he realized with Pollack's departure, those dreams now turn into nightmares.

■|■

Eddie Shaddix joined Charlie Jordan's staff in Davey Pollack's sophomore year and coached him for two seasons.

Early on there was a problem. Davey came to a crossroads with Coach Shaddix. "We told him, he had to do it our way, he had to manage himself and his emotions better. He certainly was not a bad kid, but he had to learn the meaning of 'no.' Davey was growing and developing, and he was in that stage of life where he was inclined to challenge people. We told him he had to do better in school. It wasn't that he wasn't capable—he needed to make a commitment there like he did in football.

"He had so much energy. When older kids challenged him, he didn't back down. He wasn't scared of anybody. He finally bought into our concept; he made a conscious choice to do it our way and he became a pleasure to coach. He understood the message that you are the sum of your choices. On the field, he went all out every play. There was no time when he ever gave up. His teammates began to appreciate that he was a special player and that his motivation to succeed was exceptional."

The Davids and Diana DeGarmo, of American Idol fame, are all from Snellville. Shaddix often thinks how wonderful all that national television coverage of the three of them is for Snellville. "They have made us proud," he says. "You hear so much bad, but with all three of these kids, it was good. They have represented Snellville well."

On an open date for the Bulldogs, Davey went to watch Shiloh play at Central Gwinnett. Shaddix, now athletic director at Shiloh, and Pollack tried to watch the game from the field. "I don't think he saw a single play. He signed autographs all night, but he didn't complain. I think he knows that there is a warm feeling from all that. His hometown is proud of him," Shaddix says.

"During his time at Georgia, we talked every couple of weeks. Occasionally, my family and I would drive up to have dinner with him. He was always patient with my six year old kid, playing video games with him. I appreciate how far he has come, and he deserves everything that has come his way. Once he became focused, and I am proud to have tried to help, there was no holding him back. His record is proof of that.

"Think about all the negative developments in our society, today. That is why it is so wonderful to know a kid like Davey and what he represents. To have had an opportunity to have coached him, to

We know who this mischevious smile belongs to

running off, took up time with him. They looked after him, making sure he avoided any complications like a weight falling on his foot. They were amused and intrigued that a kid that young had that kind of interest and motivation. The coaches made sure, too, that he didn't exert himself unwisely, like lifting too much for his age and weight.

He was there in the sixth grade and the seventh. Each year he seemed more intense. His interest and anxiousness gained momentum in the seventh and eight grades. He was growing and becoming stronger, asking questions and talking football insatiably. He was always asking older players about situations on the field, and Coach Jordan could tell back then that he had special qualities. "You just knew that he was going to be a football player," Jordan said.

"He was the most self driven kid I was ever around. He started at defensive tackle as a sophomore. There is nothing a coach enjoys more than seeing an overachiever with parents who support him without getting in the way."

know that I spent time with him in his formative years means so much to me. He is an inspiration. He makes me proud."

No. 47 has humbled many adults in his career, and the beat goes on.

"WHO'S THE KID HANGING AROUND THE WEIGHT ROOM?"

The first coach Davey Pollack had in high school was Charlie Jordan, who couldn't shoo the precocious youngster out of the weight room when he was in elementary school.

In the fifth grade, Davey was hanging around, asking questions, fiddling with weights. Actually, he was getting in the way, but he was so eager and polite, the varsity coaches, rather than brusquely

"RIPLEY WOULDN'T BELIEVE IT!"

Bob Krieger coached Davey Pollack his last year of high school, and Shiloh accomplished a Ripley's feat. Due to a rainout, Shiloh had to play three games in eight days his senior year. They won all three games, and as you might expect, Davey led the way to victory.

The Generals defeated Berkmar on Friday, Duluth on Monday and Dacula the following Friday. The last game went to overtime, and Pollack, in Ozark-Ike fashion, ran the ball up the gut from his fullback position. He simply wouldn't go down. Opposing players were hanging all over him, but he kept pounding away to move his team in scoring position. He set up what turned out to be the winning score by breaking to the sideline. As he charged downfield, opposing

CAUGHT WITH HIS PANTS DOWN

When the Shiloh Generals lined up on defense, they got their signals and instructions from Rick Greene, the father of David. Rick was Davey's first coach, just like Norm Pollack was Greenie's first coach. Greene also played middle linebacker, and Pollack lined up in the backfield on offense.

"Davey was just like he was at Georgia," Rick says. "His energy was unbelievable. He was tough as nails, and you couldn't break his spirit. He was very smart, very aggressive. He was never reluctant to mix it up. One day before a game, when he was eight years old, he and another assistant coach's kid were out in the middle of the field fighting over the spray paint cans that were used to paint the field. He never backed away from anybody.

"We played a base 60 defense, and Davey lined up at end, but he was more like an outside linebacker. We never worried about anybody getting around his end. He made big plays all the time. On offense he enjoyed running the ball. Once, I remember we were playing a game, and a couple of kids were on his back, but he kept going, dragging them to the end zone. They pulled his pants halfway down, but he kept going to score. He was a joy to watch and a pleasure to coach."

Sound familiar?

defenders were riding on his back.

Now it was Dacula's turn. It was a tense battle, but Davey Pollack was the difference. On fourth down, a back swept wide, but Davey bulled past the offensive interference and chased the running back to the sideline, forcing him out of bounds short of the first down. Game over.

"It was a brutal week for us," Krieger said, "but nobody complained. Mainly because Davey was such a leader, he caused the team to focus on our mission. We couldn't change anything; we just had to deal with our compacted schedule. We just had to tough it out, and he led the way."

In pre-season practice that year, Krieger learned right away that he could make the regimen tough on all the kids but one. He discovered he simply could not wear Davey out. "We increased both the distance and sprint work. He seemed to be as fresh at the end as he did when he started. I have never seen any player like him, not

before I coached him during his senior year, and I doubt that I will ever see another one like him."

ALMOND'S TWO-WAY JOY

John Almond coached Davey Pollack in the ninth, tenth and eleventh grades. "I coached him as he was making his big transition physically," Almond says. "When I talked to his parents about putting him at fullback, they were pleased and Davey was over the top. He liked the idea of running the ball. He wanted to be on the field every snap. We opened with South Gwinnett his sophomore year, and I noticed how strong he was. We would run the isolation play, and I saw him lifting linebackers off the ground. Like so many others, I always marveled at his strength. He worked every day, every year to become stronger. I thought he would be an excellent college player, but I had not idea he would be as great as he was. I'll tell you one thing

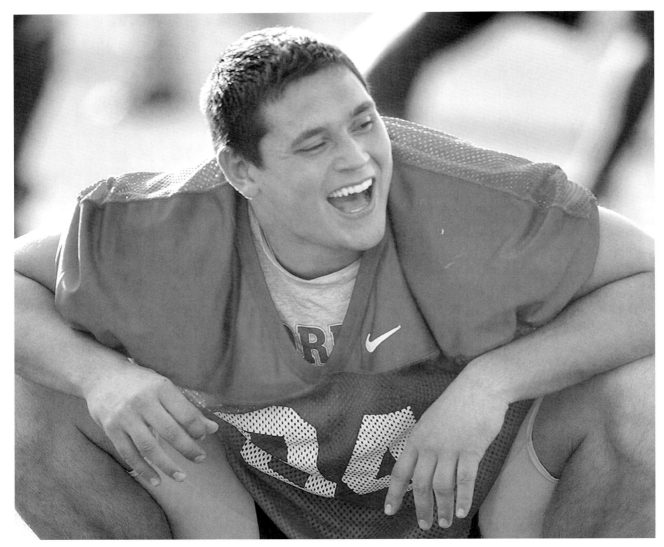

Never serious until the ball is snapped

about that—I certainly was not surprised."

"Davey really got a big boost under Coach Almond," says Norm Pollack, "If it had not been for Coach Almond, I don't know what would have happened in Davey's career. It could have been that nobody would have heard of Davey. You can't imagine how pleased he was when Coach Almond told him he could play offense as well as defense. Davey enjoyed playing running back because he wanted to contribute to the team as much as possible. He wanted to play on both sides of the ball,

and when Coach Almond got him in on offense, it was a great boost to his attitude and career. Kelli and I will always be indebted to Coach Almond. His decisions and his giving Davey an opportunity, motivated him to become a better football player. Without that opportunity, I don't know what would have happened."

CHAPTER ELEVEN

POLLACK'S SIGNATURE PLAYS

In my memory bank, there are many outstanding plays in Georgia football that I, like other passionate alumni, savor with the passing of time.

When I am riding down the road, I often see great plays in my mind's eye. When I recall defensive gems, I flashback to Bill Stanfill's clotheslining, yanking with one arm, a quarterback to the ground and Jake Scott's one hand stab on an interception. I'll never forget Terry Hoage's fingertip deflection of a pass that would have won the game for Vandy in Nashville. What an effort! Nor will I forget Scott Woerner's fielding a punt against Tech, getting knocked unconscious yet holding onto the ball.

Throughout college football and in the NFL, you observe defensive players making a conscious effort to rip the ball from an offensive back or end as they make a tackle.

I don't know who should get credit for that technique, but the first at Georgia, in my recollection, was Bill Krug, who lettered in 1975-77. I can see him vividly chasing a ball carrier down the sideline, grabbing him over the shoulder with his right arm, reaching around with his left and ripping the ball out. Krug often pulled that off in his Georgia career.

Take-aways are a standard objective in football today. It is taught on all levels, but when Davey Pollack's career is recalled many years from now, most who saw him play during his time in Athens will likely point to his signature plays, the ones he made at Columbia as a sophomore and the last play of his career in the Outback bowl.

Whenever he maneuvered to the quarterback, Pollack wanted to do more than collar him for a sack. He sought to strip the ball away. Cause a fumble. Give his team the advantage and momentum with possession.

His remarkable agility, sense of presence and big-play-thought-process enabled Pollack to become the sack-and-steal master for the Bulldogs.

At South Carolina, where Georgia didn't score an offensive touchdown, Pollack's play was the difference in the game. When his Bulldog career is recalled, we will see, in our mind's eye, his leap upwards on the Gamecock quarterback's throwing side, making contact under control to impede the throwing motion, gathering the ball off the quarterback's hand, cradling it to his stomach and falling to the ground for a touchdown.

The Georgia players knew what had happened. They began cheering before the crowd became aware the Bulldogs had scored. Then everybody saw

referee Steve Shaw's upraised arms. Touchdown!

Replays for those watching on television confirmed to a national audience what a stunned sell-out crowd was unsure of. Even a couple of people on the sideline asked, "What happened?"

When the game was over, I waited for Coach Richt to enter the bedlam of the locker room. "Who do you want for POWERade-Player-of-the-Game?" I asked. We recognize a player-of-the-game each week, and I knew he was going to pick a defensive player and anticipated it would be Pollack.

"Can you believe that play?" Richt said without ever mentioning Pollack's name. I didn't know the kid too well at that point, but when I invited him over to be interviewed, he was all smiles. He looked innocent. He didn't appear to be an All-American in waiting. Didn't know it then, but later when I reflected back, that was an extension of the life of a kid who had grown up playing a game he loved for the pure enjoyment of playing.

It was difficult to interview him with players and coaches roaming by and slapping him on the back and extending congratulations. His teammates and coaches will remember that one. And so will his classmates, those who will continue to follow Georgia football and evolve into passionate and loyal alumni.

The historians will often focus on the play, too, and it will go down in history as one of the great plays in Bulldog football. In an earlier day, that wouldn't be the case. There would have been no television to document the feat. If anybody's defensive worth was ever enhanced by television replay, it was Davey Pollack's.

In the Outback bowl he did it again. He grabbed the quarterback—a sack-in-the-making, but like always, maneuvered for greater opportunity. That was always the Pollack objective. After collaring the Badger quarterback, he reached around and forced the ball from the offensive player's grasp and transferred it to his own. Again,

Deja vu in Tampa – stealing the ball from the Wisconsin quarterback

the referee was in position to make the call.

Pollack, predictably, was chosen for POWERade-Player-of-the-Game honors. It would be the last time I would interview him on the Georgia radio network. He was more seasoned and introspective than he was that first time in Columbia. He thanked God, and he was also thankful that the referee was in position to make the call.

Now, my memory bank will include those two plays as long as I live and my memory holds out. That is why I am hoping passionately for a cure for Alzheimer's disease. No Bulldawg who watched Davey Pollack play should ever forget.

BRIAN VANGORDER,
GONE BUT NOT FORGOTTEN

It didn't make sense at first, that Brian VanGorder would leave his coordinator's position at Georgia for the linebacking job with the Jacksonville Jaguars.

A trend of thought has surfaced in recent years that may shed light on the former Bulldog defensive coordinator's thinking. With Pete Carroll coming out of the NFL to produce national championships at Southern Cal and Nick Saban winning one at LSU, many coaches believe,

Life was good at UGA for Brian VanGorder

that it is best to add professional experience to their resume—in their quest for head jobs. For sure Derek Dooley, son of Vince, who followed Saban to the Miami Dolphins, feels that way.

There is constant turnover in the coaching ranks today with the emphasis on the bottom line and winning inextricably tied together. Most established head coaches are now anchored by buyout clauses in their $1.5 million to $2 million coaching contracts. Makes it hard to leave when the grass appears greener.

When one does leave, like Saban, or is fired

like Ron Zook at Florida, the new breed athletic directors feel pressure to hire someone with a proven record. As attractive as the LSU job is, the head coach pickings were slim when Saban left. That is why officials at Arkansas took a dim view of Coach Houston Nutt's interest in interviewing in Baton Rouge. It was like, "Hey, we fixed your contract last year when Nebraska made a run at you. What are you up to?" All we know it that the Arkansas coach quickly declined to interview for the vacancy at LSU.

If there are not many options out there for hiring A.D.s in a given year, then the most attractive assistant coach needs varied experience to showcase prospective employers.

Brian VanGorder certainly has all the qualities you want in a head coach: acute teaching instinct; intelligence; Family man; good habits; good recruiter; indefatigable worker; experienced; and knowledgeable. It is a fact, however, that more often than not, those doing the hiring are attracted to offensive coordinators.

Something about VanGorder that I always got a kick out of was his penchant for country music. Whenever I was in his work place, the defensive staff conference room on the second floor of the Northwest corner of the Butts-Mehre Building, I paused and reflected on my past.

I, too, listened to country music while I worked back on a farm in Middle Georgia. This often led me to point out that my work was not as much fun as VanGorder's, who put every defensive game plan together with popular country tunes playing softly on radio in the background.

"Hot sun and back bending manual labor like chopping and picking cotton," I would say to him about my past. "You sit here in air-conditioned comfort watching video tape and reading statistics. That ain't work."

Without looking up, he would say, "Coaching ball is the hardest work I know. Sometimes I had rather be outside digging a ditch. Sometimes when we don't get execution, it looks like I've been digging ditches instead of coaching."

VanGorder is a teacher. He is exhilarated by his work, which consumes him. The only time he is not consumed by defensive strategizing, opponent scouting and worrying about defensive personal deficiencies, is when he is with his family.

He did not plan to become a football coach. He prepared for a career in criminal justice. Today, the criminals in his life remain quarterbacks, running backs and wide receivers. It was that way at Georgia, and the same can be expected in Jacksonville.

Nothing excites him more than to find a tendency in an opponent's offense, a flaw, or an alignment, which can be exploited. All the while, his favorite country music performer, George Strait, is singing about lost love on the radio.

Always a student of the game, VanGorder, when he went off to college at Wayne State, found time to volunteer as an assistant at his old high school. "We had a linebacker," he remembers, "to make all-district. I saw him improve significantly and felt that I helped him. That was where the seeds were sown; that is what whetted my appetite for coaching."

Somebody else would have to bring criminals to justice. This man became a coaching enthusiast who would sink his teeth into the profession and never look back.

He operates with a very basic concept. "It is not how many correct plays you make but how few bad plays you make." The team making the fewest mistakes is often the team that wins football games. To achieve your objective, you underscore preparation and teaching.

Personnel situations are the staple of coaching preparation. When VanGorder was at Georgia, his staff was given to detailed tape study. Willie Martinez, Rodney Garner and Jon Fabris and the

A rare football player, Davey Pollack enjoyed practice

coordinator were in lockstep.

The week of preparation began with the graduate assistants breaking down the opponent's tape, some of it prior to Sunday morning, when the new week rolled around in the fall.

By game day, the defensive staff had studied every offensive performance of the season of the upcoming opponent. Game day, the only thing left was execution.

Most of the time, VanGorder's defensive teams get it, but 2004 was one of the most difficult seasons ever for the genial Michigan native. He could have composed that familiar tune, "It takes a worried man to sing a worried song." VanGorder, never a whiner, nonetheless sang the blues, beginning with the opening day of practice in August. Some of his thoughts:

+ Too few seniors to provide experience and leadership.
+ Never gained the mental edge to develop the chemistry needed.
+ Losing Tony Taylor hurt significantly. "He would have been able to verbalize his competitiveness."

When he went into a game, VanGorder wore an "apron," a laminated 6 x 8 sheet, on which he has the list of defensive formations and personnel situations for each game. "It is our best guess on what will work, depending on down and distance."

VanGorder's headset was hooked up with Rodney Garner and Jon Fabris on the sideline and Willie Martinez in the press box. Martinez monitored the offensive personnel on the field, including substitutions. He revealed the personnel situation, Rodney Garner signaled it to the players on the field.

For example, if Garner holds up a single finger on each hand, it means the opposition has one back and one tight end plus three wide receivers. Two fingers on left hand and one on the right means two backs, one tight end, two wide outs. One finger on one hand means a running back, four wide outs. In all cases, there are five eligible receivers other than the quarterback.

Standing beside Garner is Clay Walker, who flashes cards with the numbers corresponding to Garner's fingers so the players first know the personnel situation.

Then, VanGorder signals the defense. It might be Under 4, check Zorro. "Under" is the defensive front four down lineman, a walk up linebacker on the line of scrimmage and two set linebackers. "Four" and "Zorro" are coverage calls. Alignment and movement are then predicated by the offensive formation.

After signaling the defense, VanGorder first focuses on secondary "to make sure they are okay." Then his eyes transfer to the offense to see if it is run or pass. "Then my eyes transfer to the second level, the linebackers, to see what our fits are. If it is a pass play, my eyes go back to the secondary."

If the offense clicks, he always tried to determine where there is a breakdown and then tried to make an instant analysis to determine what had to be done to correct it immediately.

I'll always remember his pre-game locker room focus. Somebody sometimes cracked a smile, even wisecracked, but VanGorder was always straight faced. Mum. He never sat; he paced slowly, mentally transfixed on forthcoming game action. He was always mentally reviewing down and distance. Like a golfer imagining pulling off the correct shot, he imagined his defense coming up with the play that stops a drive.

Life was good for him at Georgia, because there was an abundance of three and outs. Perhaps, that trend will continue in Jacksonville. Perhaps, too, it will aid and abet his quest for a head coaching job.

∎∎∎

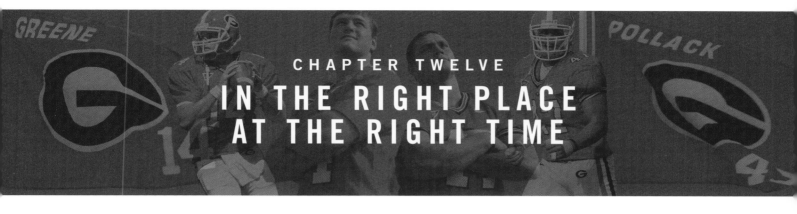

Steve Shaw, the referee at Columbia, South Carolina, couldn't believe his eyes in the rain-delayed Georgia-South Carolina game played on September 14, 2002. His eyes confirmed to him that he had just seen the most remarkable play in his officiating career.

The highly regarded referee observed the Gamecock quarterback start forward with his right arm, and, in an instant, he saw Davey Pollack, in a perfectly timed leaping movement, grab the quarterback's arm, take the ball away, cradle it in his stomach and fall to the ground in the end zone for a TD.

Immediately, Shaw signaled touchdown. Everybody on the Georgia sidelines realized what had happened and went over the top in celebration. In close plays in a championship season, somebody will usually make a big play. This was one of the many big plays Pollack made in his career, and is, without doubt, his most sensational.

Sunday morning after the game, the coaches realized just how great Pollack's effort was, but were quick to point out that it would have been for naught if the referee had not been in position to make the call.

Jimmy Harper, former Georgia quarterback, who was an SEC referee for 33 years (Harper was inducted into the College Hall of Fame as a referee) and remains an SEC observer, says poignantly that SEC officiating mechanics put Shaw in position to correctly make the call.

"We have always felt that the referee should position himself two yards behind the deepest back and six to eight yards away from where the ball is snapped and to the quarterback's throwing side. This gives him a better opportunity to see the play, to best determine if a quarterback's arm is moving forward when there is defensive contact. (The NFL mechanics call for the referee to stand 12-15 yards behind the line of scrimmage. He moves backward as the pocket moves back.) Steve made the right call, but the important thing is that he was in position to make the call." Shaw laughs and says, "I was where Jimmy would want me to be."

Steve recalled more about the play:

"It was the most athletic play I've ever seen a defensive lineman make. It was unbelievable. At the moment of contact, you want to be in position to determine if the quarterback's arm is moving forward. When there is contact, you want to make sure the hit was legal. When the quarterback's arm started forward, you could see Pollack going up in

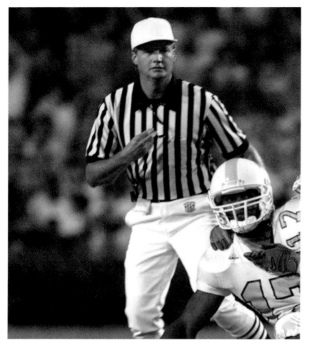

Referee Steve Shaw, in SEC action, saw the "most athletic play ever" at Columbia

the air. He literally took the ball off the quarterback's hand and maintained possession. The look on the quarterback's face was incredible. He couldn't believe it, and I'm sure many others felt the same way.

"With a play like that, you obviously have to be in position to make the call, and I was confident that I made the right call. However, you know plays like that are being discussed in the TV network booth, and you want to be sure. At the next timeout, I asked the clock operator to ask what they had upstairs. He smiled and said, 'Good call. They got a great angle on the play and say there is no question that Pollack had possession and that it was a touchdown.'

"That call has generated the most comment of any call I've ever made. I've gotten calls from all over the country. The week after the game, my phone rang off the hook. Seems that everybody saw the play on television and wanted to talk about it."

Shaw appreciated something else about Pollack, other than his exceptional playing ability. He saw him as a leader who could settle things down when emotions became intense or rattled. "If a teammate got out of line, you could count on him giving you an assist. If you felt a player needed calming, you could rely on Pollack to keep a negative or bad situation from escalating. I was always impressed with him as a leader."

SMARTING FROM THE GREENE TOUCH

When Kirby Smart walked on the field for warmups at Sanford Stadium on October 2, 2004, he had to chastise himself for letting his mind wander. He couldn't help but reminisce about his own playing experience between the hedges. He had deep, emotional feelings for the University of Georgia, but this time, he was in the enemy camp. It was weird and disjointing.

All his Georgia friends were in the stands, pulling against him. He understood and hoped that they would appreciate his burning pride to victoriously leave town. If Georgia won, he didn't want to face his old teammate, Mike Bobo.

His friendship with Bobo is rock solid, but they are like brothers who love one another but would never throw in the towel in any skirmish. Brothers fight a lot of the time and still remain friends. That is the way it would be this time out. Kirby would have given his right arm to have won the game.

He regained his focus by kickoff, but left town smarting from defeat, having no idea there would be the possibility that he would join the Bulldog staff in a little more than three months later.

It was Georgia's offense that stung his pride. The Bulldogs had an efficient game plan, and David Greene was at his all-time best executing the plan. The touchdown passes he threw were over Kirby Smart's defensive backs. His nerves were frayed; his spirits were punctured when he returned to Baton Rouge.

What Georgia did was take full measure of LSU's defense. Former Tiger head coach, Nick Saban, takes extreme pride in defense. He works more with the defense than the offense. He expected better execution and had hoped that there would be some doubt in the minds of the Georgia players after losing twice to the Tigers in 2003.

"We were a feast-or-famine defense. Georgia simply out-executed us," Kirby says. He can pinpoint the difference between the two teams from one year to the next. In 2003, Georgia completed only two of 10 deep balls. "A deep ball," Kirby explains, "is one of more than 20 yards in the air. A back catching a swing pass and running more than 20 yards doesn't count.

"In our game in October, Georgia completed seven passes of over 20 yards, and that was the difference in the game," he explains. "There was a highly intense chess game between our staff and Coach Richt and his offensive coaches. It became frustrating." He then repeated himself by underscoring that the Bulldogs' execution was superb.

The architect of the offensive success was David Greene, for whom Smart has the greatest respect. "We knew he was a quarterback who was excellent at recognizing your defensive plan. He knew when the blitz was coming. We would line up and show blitz and check off. Twice Georgia picked up our blitz, and David threw for touchdowns. That is what you want from your quarterback.

"Once a quarterback recognizes your defensive scheme and what you are going to do, it is still throw and catch. Georgia did that as well as you could want, and we were a pretty good defensive team. We just got beat by a good plan and outstanding execution.

"Coach Saban loved Thomas Davis. He was upset with our backs fumbling a couple of

Kirby Smart: in 2004 this Bulldog wore Tiger colors

times, but after reviewing the game tapes Sunday morning, he told the offensive staff, 'Those were CAUSED fumbles.' Then he paid Thomas the highest tribute by saying, 'Men, that No. 10 may be the best defensive player we will play against.' If defense is your game, and defense is big with Nick Saban, you couldn't receive a greater compliment.

"Of course all the defensive coaches were concerned about Pollack. We came into the game with the plan to chip him as much as possible [a tackle blocks Pollack and a back chips him with a shoulder or forearm as he attempts to maneuver to the passer]. He is very tough to block. Not

The DawgWalk gets everybody pumped, including players, band and fans

DAWGWALK

The DawgWalk, as we know it today, began in 2001 at the beginning of the Richt era. It has become a gameday highlight for both players and fans.

"When you get off the bus and see little kids wearing your jersey and lined up to give you a low five with big smiles on their faces, it puts you in the most positive frame of mind imaginable," says David Pollack. "You want to win for Georgia any time you go out on the field. You want to make all the hard work and effort bring victory on Saturday afternoon, but you have the greatest desire to win for those fans.

"When you walk from Lumpkin Street down to the stadium, your body tingles with feeling and excitement. There is love in that atmosphere, and because we feel those people love us so much, we feel we owe it to them to play our hearts out."

The DawgWalk actually replaced the unofficial Railroad Track Club at the east end of Sanford Stadium. Before the east stands were added for the 1981 season the players disembarked from their buses, entered the stadium proper, walked down the steps to the dressing rooms on ground level. On the railroad tracks, awaiting the team's arrival, were a collection of wild-eyed students, misfits, beer drinkers, rebels and campus castoffs who either couldn't afford a ticket or couldn't find one. Many of them camped out overnight for a vantage point come kickoff.

Their passion reminded me of those Masters fans, who on Sunday for the final round of play, would enter the grounds of the Augusta National Golf Club as early as 8:00 a.m. to grab a spot right behind the ropes of the 18th hole. Great position for the final putt, which might determine the winner, but they had to wait over nine hours for that to come to pass. It would be five hours or more before the first group finished their round at the final hole. To those passionate Masters' fans it was

many can block him one on one, and we were always shaking our head when we watched tape of Georgia games at the great plays he made. When the opposition respects a player around the league like they did Pollack—that should tell you something about him. He gave a lot of offensive coaches a lot of headaches."

TRACY WOLFSON

Tracy Wolfson, the pretty face working the Georgia sideline for CBS, is much more than that. She is insightful, informative, competent and compelling with her well-presented reports for the network. We like it that she finds Athens and Georgia football exciting and alluring, too. Her thoughts after spending time in Athens:

I spent four years at the Big House thinking there was no better place for college football. Well, I was wrong. I hate to admit it, but SEC football is something else. It's a religion down South. Every day of the week is game day. And no school displayed that more than Athens. Maybe it was the hedges at Sanford Stadium; maybe it was the Saturday DawgWalk; maybe it was that they had two of the most personable football players I have worked with in David Greene and David Pollack. Not to mention the talent they had. The effect they had on the game, the fans, the school was unbelievable. And it didn't take me long to learn why. Three games to be exact.

Take Greene for example, Georgia-Georgia Tech, final regular-season game of his career, out with a hurt thumb. Standing on the sidelines, I witnessed his disappointment after the injury, then his support for D.J. Shockley who took over, then the frustration as the game started slipping away, then his resilience as he threw his bandage off his thumb and picked up a football and started throwing along the sidelines, then his insistence that Coach Richt take a look at him so he could go back in and save the game, capping off an illustrious career at Georgia. What a way to go out.

Another story from that final game comes to mind. I took a visit to David Pollack's parents' tailgate party before the game. There in a packed parking lot, donning the red and black, was the

Pollacks' weekend home that is a trailer sporting No.47. Right across from them was the Greenes' humble abode with a No. 14 flag flying from it. They had been doing this together since the boys were freshmen, even earlier since they played youth leagues together. The emotion that spilled over that day though was what really got me. When I asked their feelings on this final Saturday of football in Athens, a teary eyed Mrs. Pollack couldn't speak. The lump in her throat was too big. No need for an answer though. In just the few games I had covered that year, I understood why they were going to miss that place so much.

worth it. Some on the railroad tracks had the same perspective. It was worth the overnight wait to see the Dawgs in action.

Erk Russell had not accepted the head-coaching job at Georgia Southern when the east stands were under construction. He was deeply worried

about the team taking that walk down the steps without the track crazies yelling and whoopin' it up for the Dawgs.

"We are going to lose emotion when they build those new end zone seats," Erk said. "There is no way to replace that." Believe it or not, many of those fans still gathered on the tracks for a couple of years and listened to Larry Munson on the radio.

In Richt's first year, he wondered aloud in a staff meeting what could be done to get the players revved up for a game? Steve Greer commented that a previous staff, under Ray Goff, had tried the walk but without success. Richt is not afraid to take something which has been in place and make it work for his program. The idea sounded good to him. He said, "Let's go with it."

What has happened is that this fan-friendly happening involves kids as well as adults. The adults have developed a routine of letting kids work their way to the front. There is an aisle about three feet wide which allows the players to walk through the cheering throng which stretches about 200 yards from Lumpkin Street to the hedges.

It reminds me of that narrow path you see on television when the cameras follow the Tour de France through small villages in France and fans commingle with the bicyclists.

"Reach out and touch someone?" You can do that at the DawgWalk. Fans pat the players on the back. The players give low fives to the kids. The lusty cheers remind the team that the fans will be there when they take the field to bring glory to ole Georgia.

Mark Richt has brought something special to Bulldog football. He has underscored a blend of the old and the new. The DawgWalk is a tradition that goes beyond loyal fan appreciation; it has gained national recognition.

CHAPTER THIRTEEN

TAKING THE BOYS FROM THE BAYOU TO THE WOODSHED

LAGNIAPPE (LAHN-yap)—In Cajun, it means a "little something extra."

You get it with Cajun cooking and Georgia got it in Sanford Stadium when the Tigers came to town in October 2004. It became Georgia's national championship game. The Bulldogs didn't like it that LSU won twice in '03. You always look at things from your own perspective, and the Bulldogs believed that if they had won in Baton Rouge, things could have been better in the junior year of The Davids. The "if" game, however, has been played since Rutgers and Princeton started this game of football competition in 1869 in New Brunswick, New Jersey, the birthplace of Davey Pollack.

Mistakes are part of football; the game is not an exact science. If anything is predictable, it is the unpredictable. A pass that is just inches away from a receiver's fingers, or a fumble at the goal line, is hard to predict. A tackle is assured, but a runner steps away and goes the distance. Good things happen for you; they can also happen against you.

Many longtime football observers believe that the breaks even out over time. Win a lot of close games one year, and you are likely to be done in by close encounters the next.

In Baton Rouge, September 9, 2003, Georgia lost a game the players felt they should have won.

Then, with a chance to play the Tigers again in the SEC championship game in the role of underdog, there was confidence that things would be better. The Bulldogs entered that game in the Georgia Dome with ambition, resolve and commitment. They believed.

But things didn't go well, on either side of the ball. LSU clearly had improved, and while Georgia might have been better—if it had executed more effectively—in Baton Rouge earlier in the season, improvement and health for the playoff game favored the boys from the Bayou state. By November, Georgia's offensive line seldom practiced as a unit, players were out or hobbled nearly all season and LSU took advantage, dominating the game 34-13.

The players and the coaches burned. They were mad. They wanted revenge. All spring and all summer they worked for it. There were other games to play and they could not lose sight of the capability of their early opponents, mainly South Carolina in Columbia. But revenge on the Tigers was always on Georgia's mind.

The Bulldogs got it on October 2nd.

The populace was anxious but also worried and edgy when LSU hit town. I felt good listening

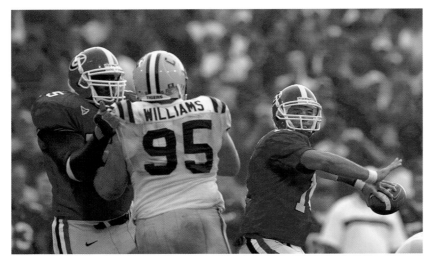

Greenie was never more on target than against LSU in '04

to the coaches and players who enjoyed a week off between Marshall and LSU. How important is an open date? Coaches may say one thing publicly, but I've never heard one admit privately that an open date is not an advantage.

The week of the open date was a good one. The practices were intense and much was accomplished. You never know if that is a good sign. Coaches often say that they have seen teams practice well and play poorly. Practice poorly and play lights out on Saturday. It is like a player who has the reputation of being a "gamer," meaning that no matter how he practices, he is always "on" come Saturday. You get that with some players, but with the team overall, you want sharp execution, up tempo, game-like practices.

Usually, if a team practices well, you can expect it to play well. It means the players are concentrating, that they are focused and heading to a mental peak which is needed to win big games.

On Wednesday, I again met David Greene for lunch. "We are so close to getting it right," he said of the Bulldog offense. "It is a matter of just one player making a mistake, one breakdown. Little stuff is the key, like putting your hat on the right side of the defender, making your cut just right.

I've been off the mark at times throwing the ball. We haven't been playing bad; we just have not gotten it together. We will." He didn't suggest that as a forecast for LSU, just that he had faith in the offense and he could see what others couldn't.

"Against Marshall, we didn't establish the run. When you don't do that, they play Cover 2 against you and make it difficult to throw the ball. To win big games, you must be balanced. Most people who know the game realize that the defense is going to do its best to take away something. They obviously would like to stop your running and passing game both, but they are going to find a way to stop something."

In the next breath, he complimented the defense. "It was a hard-hitting game, but our defense wasn't going to let them do anything." Because of Georgia's defensive superiority, the Thundering Herd had no thunder. Greene recalled one amusing incident when the Marshall quarterback ran near the Georgia bench and got pounded especially hard by two Bulldog defenders in a collision at the sideline. A Georgia player yelled to him, "You better get off the field; you are going to get racked." The quarterback said out of the side of his mouth as he headed back to the huddle, "No s——."

Greene's scouting report of LSU: "They really have outstanding players on defense, and they know what they are doing. Hard to tell what you'll get from them. Can't figure a rhyme or reason for some of the things they do. They don't show a lot of tendencies like a lot of teams and they bring every blitz imaginable. We moved the ball on them a lot last year, but didn't make enough plays. Against a team like LSU you've got to make plays.

"Defensive linemen drop off a lot in football today which tells you how good the athletes are, and LSU has a lot of very good players. I'd like to see a rule to where you are not allowed to drop off the line of scrimmage once you put your hand on the ground [laughing].

"It is hard to see where all 11 of their players are sometimes. Each play takes about 2½ seconds, so you have to process everything quickly. We have had a good week of practice, and I feel good.

"There are so many demands on your time. There is more hype, more requests. You just have to focus on the game, but it is hard. I just refuse to watch television or read the newspapers. It is hard enough as it is, so it is better not to listen to what somebody else says about the game or what you have done in the past."

Greenie on his toes; this usually meant the Dawgs were clicking on offense

When I met with Pollack on Thursday, he was somewhat nonchalant. He can be flippant, rife with boundless energy, caustic—even playfully insulting. He had gone to a concert the night before. He spent the evening kibitzing with his friends and fellow students, grabbing a camera and taking photographs. "Sometimes you get in a cranky mood, and I really don't care what people think. You live your life the way you want to live it. Sometimes people are pushy, and I don't like that. But I can't say no to a kid. You just can't be rude to kids.

"I know I will miss Georgia. I realize this is the best time of my life. I'll move on, but I'll never move away in my heart. This place means so much to me. It has been so much more than I ever expected or dreamed, although I always dream big."

One day, I bumped into Vince Dooley at practice, and he remarked, "I think Pollack is the best since Herschel at being quoted." "Humble Herschel" the coaches always called the native of Wrightsville. Herschel deferred to his teammates; he put them first, he said the right thing and he never sought the spotlight.

It came to him, however. It came to The Davids, too, and like Herschel they seemed to deflect it. If you drink it all in, you will likely encounter problems, but how many can resist? Human nature, for most of us, would cause us to at least take a few sips.

"I can tell," Pollack said, "when the writers are trying to get you to say things. I can see through a lot of the questions. I can be politically correct and all that. I want to accommodate them, but you can't let them know too much. How do you know you can trust them?" Then he stared in my direction as if I was a quarterback with a cocked arm—"You write anything bad about me, and I'll kill you."

On the field during games he doesn't talk much. "I'm not a trash talker. Sometimes we talk about God. There are a lot of spiritual guys in football. I like that."

He will retort, however, if an opponent verbally threatens him. As a sophomore when the game with South Carolina began at Columbia, the offensive tackle started in on him. "Hey, 47, I don't remember you from last year. You gonna be my bitch [meaning dog] all game." By the second quarter, as Pollack kept beating the Gamecock and kept getting by him, Davey couldn't contain himself. "Hey, if I'm your bitch, I'm lovin' it."

When the conversation turned to LSU, he said, with no reluctance, "We're a better team than LSU. The defenses are about even, but our offense is better, which is why we should win."

Tuesday before the LSU game, defensive backfield coach Willie Martinez was perusing a sheet of statistics before practice. He was comparing the two Tiger quarterbacks, Marcus Randall and Jamarcus Russell, a talented redshirt freshman. "I remember seeing Jarmarcus warm up in the SEC championship game. He will be very, very, very good but he is playing like a freshman. Then he has those good running backs around him," Willie added.

Coaches usually are guarded about upcoming games. They know not to say too much in advance or after the game. Mark has an intense desire to win, but he never predicts success nor gloats afterward. On the latter point he would never rub it in. He is just too nice of a guy. But there is a more practical reason. Coaches, like politicians, have long memories. Something said after a game could be used against you—even years later. You don't want your comments to come back to haunt you.

Athletes have pride. One boasting or denigrating remark can be used to fuel ambition. Coaches expect their players to "hate" their opponents. Not literally, but figuratively. The word is used all the time internally. You want to slash and burn on the field, but then help all the little old ladies across the street when the game is over.

Sometimes you gain a sense of things to be by simply hanging around and reading body language. While there was nothing to suggest that Mark Richt was expecting a licking, worthy of

"Lefty" left all Dawgs smiling after victory over LSU between the hedges

14 🏈 47

THE GAME PLAN

When Mark Richt heads out on Friday afternoon, he is accompanied by his play chart. It is a laminated board on which there are detailed references, based on a week of tape study and review, of the Saturday game plan.

Among the categories is "Barnyard Plays." It is a ready reference for something the team has not shown in games to date or something that might catch the opposition off guard.

There is a list of two point plays for consideration.

There is a checklist for 4th down plays, 3rd down plays and "win the game" plays.

Favorite passes are categorized.

The best plays to call when anticipating the blitz.

He even outlines plays for the first half dozen offensive series. A game plan is well researched. At kickoff, all that is needed is execution, which is enhanced by the quality of players who are motivated and focused.

Offensive play calling is predicated on what the defense is doing or what the play caller anticipates the defense is up to. If you get it right or if you catch the defense when it is vulnerable, then big plays result, games are won and praises sung.

But if the defense makes a play and your opponent figures out what you are up to and its execution is better than the offensive production, then, second guessing permeates coffee clubs and talk shows the next week.

Football is not an exact science, but sometimes Monday morning critics suggest it should be.

woodshed ranking against LSU, I concluded that he quietly believed his game plan could be dominating. He anticipated a peak performance. His body language confirmed as much. He didn't reveal publicly that he was going to challenge LSU's exceptional man-to-man coverage and challenge it often. That was, however, his plan.

All he said was, "We've got to make big plays. Greenie's got to be right on the money." That is when I began to sense he was confident his quarterback could successfully challenge the seasoned Tiger cornerbacks. In my time following the Dawgs, I have never seen more precise throwing and catching. When I saw Wallace Butts' teams play, one-platoon football inhibited his creative passing genius. Vince Dooley showed me how to run off tackle, which seasoned coaches believed

was the key to moving the ball.

There are many features to the current Bulldog head coach's personality that I find reassuring and admirable. He is not cocky. He is not an egotist. He has pride, yet he is not ego driven. Make no mistake about it; he is a born competitor.

I suspect he gained a measure of extra satisfaction by defeating LSU. After all, the Tigers whipped his team twice the year prior, convincingly in the SEC championship game. That was a game when he felt that he got outcoached. Nick Saban's personality would never allow such admission. The former Tiger coach seems loath to give credit. He is hard-edged whereas Richt is soft-spoken. It is a well traveled story that when Saban took over at LSU, leaving Michigan State, he sent a plane to East Lansing to pick up any Spartan

GEORGIA VS. LSU

OCTOBER 1ST – OCTOBER 4TH 2004 ITINERARY

FIRDAY OCTOBER 1

3:00-3:30	Seniors pick up jerseys
3:45	Senior picture (In front of Butts-Mehre)
	(Wear Jersey and Khaki pants, hand in jerseys immediately after photo)
4:00-5:30	Segment meetings
5:30	Guest Speaker John Paul Holmes
5:40	Depart Butts Mehre for Emerald Pointe
6:50	Arrive Emerald Pointe
6:55	Team Dinner (Conf. Room 3/4/5)
7:30	Team Meeting (Conf. Room 3/4/5)
9:10	Snacks (Outside meeting room)
9:15	Devotion—OPTIONAL—conf. Rm. 3/4/5
11:00	LIGHTS OUT AND QUIET!!

SATURDAY OCTOBER 2

8:00	Breakfast (optional)
9:30	Wake Up Knock
10:00	Pride Meetings (Salon 1)
10:15	House Meetings
10:30	Team Meal (conference rooms 3/4/5)
11:00	Buses depart hotel for Butts-Mehre
11:20	Non-Travel players begin taping
12:10	Arrive Butts-Mehre; start taping immediately
	K.O., P.R., & B meetings (team room) immediately upon arrival
1:15	Kickers/Snappers depart (A. Bailey, Jordan, L. Jackson, Coutu, B. Wilson, Wolf)
1:20	Chapel – weight room (optional)
1:30	Motivational Video (team room)
1:45	Depart for stadium
1:50	Arrive for DawgWalk
2:00	Arrive in locker room
3:35	Kickoff… BEAT LSU!!! (Buses will return after the game)

SUNDAY OCTOBER 3

2:00	Treatment
7:15-8 pm	Study Hall (freshmen)/All assigned tutor sessions

MONDAY OCTOBER 4

Weightlifting	2:30- Frosh. Char Ed./ 3:00-Off/3:30-Def
4:00	Kicking meetings
4:45	Defense Scouting Reports
4:45-6:00	Dinner at Butts-Mehre
5:45	Offense Scouting Reports

coach who wanted a job at LSU. The plane returned to Baton Rouge empty. "The flipside of that," says Georgia running backs coach Kirby Smart, "is that you learn a lot of football if you work for him."

Richt's even-tempered style permeates throughout the Bulldog staff. Against LSU, Georgia EXPECTED to run the ball, and when lining up on defense, the Dawgs EXPECTED to stop the run. Both missions were accomplished. But the big bonus was big plays, throwing and catching.

When I asked defensive backs coach, Willie Martinez, early in the week, "Can you stop the run?" He nodded his head affirmatively and said softly with a firmly set jaw, "Yes." Then responding like a corner reacting to smother a receiver on a deep route, he exclaimed, "You print that and I'll kill you." Nothing is taken for granted by this staff.

When the team moved from pre-game warm-ups into the locker room, there was that tense mood that settles in before a big game. Brian VanGorder spent extra time with the defense going over reminders. "Expect this, watch for that" kind of talk. I don't think he has ever coached harder. Even with the lead growing in the second half, he didn't let up, huddling with his players every time they came off the field. He burned intensely when LSU dominated in Atlanta in the SEC playoff game. It was payback time. He knew every LSU tendency. He discussed those tendencies with his staff, ticking off their situational habits as they awaited kickoff. When it was over, his eyes were keenly focused on one statistic: Total LSU rushing yards, 67.

I've never seen Richt as loose before a big game. "What do you think?" he said to me in the locker room. "I believe in you, Coach," I answered eagerly. "You better believe in Greenie," he cracked.

Richt eventually let his guard down. He revealed, among other things that:

+ Not many people have sustained drives on them. We must do that today.
+ The way they play defense, we've got to make big plays.
+ Greene needs time to see what they are doing, and our receivers have to make big plays.
+ Do everything right, and you can move the ball on them.
+ We need a couple of home-run balls.

Now we know that he had it figured out, but afterwards he began referring to the long season ahead. While coaches savor any victory, sometimes you sense they savor those payback victories most of all.

███

From Sinkwich to Trippi to Sapp, from Tarkenton and Dye to Stanfill to Herschel and Hoage and, more recently, Pollack and Greene, perhaps the most unique Bulldog is Richard Tardits, the Basque rugby aficionado who showed up as a freshman at Georgia in the fall of 1985. His knowledge of American football was limited to ESPN reruns and football instructional books from the university library.

That this precocious and enterprising man—even with superior intelligence and the heart of a lion—could learn the nuances and rudiments of a foreign sport well enough to earn a scholarship and become a seasoned star is remarkable. It is almost incomprehensible that he would learn the game well enough and play it well enough to become Georgia's all-time sack leader.

His one liability, chronically troubled ankles, shortened his National Football League career, but unlike many college players, who today suffer from chronic myopia, Richard aspired to be more than an accomplished athlete—he had equal passion for scholarship.

The 11th Georgia football player to be awarded an NCAA post graduate scholarship, Tardits is a classic exhibit of how perspective, motivation and responsibility can bring about a degree ahead of schedule.

The language barrier never held him back, and his ambition intensified annually as his curiosity led him to complete degree requirements prior to the start of his last year of eligibility. Current athletes can learn more from this man than how to put the quarterback on the seat of his pants.

With the scholarship aid that came from the NCAA stipend, he used a portion of it to learn to fly and today is a licensed pilot in France. Enterprise has always been his modus operandi. No opportunity with him has ever been squandered.

He and his charming English wife, Joanna, who passionately enjoys cooking, including vegetables from their own garden, have three young children: Charlotte, Samuel, and Elodie. They speak French at school, but only English at home.

When he is not busy with his business—a golf course development at the foot of the Pyrenees—Richard spends time improving his golf game. He also maintains a playing position with his father Maurice's old Rugby team, the Archiballs. Often, he rides his bicycle, accompanied by his surfboard, down to the sea for a fulfilling exercise in the azure waters of the Atlantic.

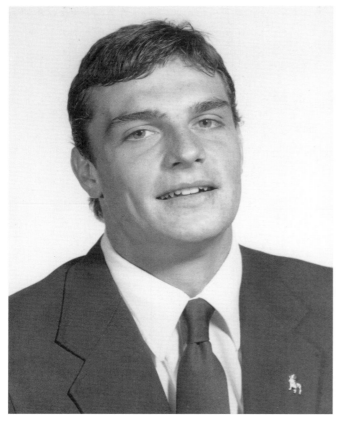

Richard Tardits, the greatest Frenchman ever to play for the Dawgs

"Le Sack" was something of a renaissance man at Georgia, and the beat goes on. If there has ever been a more well-rounded Bulldog letterman, I'd be at a loss to come up with a name—unless it would be Terry Hoage.

Biarritz is a picturesque coastal resort which I have visited often, having made my first stop there as the guest of Denis LaLanne. I met Denis before Richard enrolled at Georgia. The No. 1 sports columnist in France, Denis wrote for L'Equipe, the French sports daily, covering rugby, tennis and golf. A magazine editor at France Golf asked if I could assist with Denis' interest in covering The Masters. After LaLanne was officially credentialed, we spent a lot of time together. A warm friendship ensued. He has visited Myrna and me in Athens, and I have often

journeyed to Biarritz, where I became acquainted with Richard's parents, Crique and Maurice. The Tardits' daughter, Geri, owns a hotel on the Atlantic and one summer hired our daughter, Camille, to manage the front desk.

There have been many get-togethers in the homes of Denis and his wife, Colette, the Tarditses and their friends. We promoted Franco-Georgia Day in Athens in the fall of 1988. With the good assistance of Delta and Coca-Cola, we were able to bring a number of sports officials and dignitaries from Biarritz and Paris to Athens for this very successful outing.

I flew to Paris to meet with U.S. Ambassador Joe Rogers, who helped us organize the event. We asked friends to host couples and individuals in the traveling party, taking them into our homes and extending Southern hospitality. We gave second effort on our attempt to entertain the French delegation, including our kitchen best, when they came to Athens—but as you would expect, when Franco-Georgia day took place the next summer in Biarritz, French chefs overwhelmed us.

On all my trips to Biarritz, the LaLannes and the Tarditses set forth the most appetizing and fulfilling meals, usually in their homes, where the hospitality is as outstanding as the wines for which the French are best known.

"Welcome to your second home," Richard said to me in the summer of 2004 when I arrived for dinner at his beautiful 80-year-old home on a hill. That is exactly how I have come to feel. Because of the hospitality of the Tarditses and the LaLannes, I've always felt very much at home in Biarritz.

Last summer, on that visit to Biarritz, Richard, much to my surprise, delayed his trip to England with Joanna, to host a dinner for his family, the LaLannes' and a visitor from his adopted home-town of Athens.

As dinner got underway, he asked, "Is my

Pollack with Tardits' good friends from left: Earl Leonard, Jeff Lewis and Frank Ros; they adore the Frenchman but delight in castigating Le Sack

record [for career sacks] in jeopardy?" My response was that based on Pollack's intensely competitive and ambitious style, barring injury, he would likely surpass Le Sack's career record of 29 by mid-season. You didn't have to be blessed with genius to make that assumption, although it took longer than many thought and for one reason. Pollack was probably the most double-teamed defensive end in America in '04.

He tied the record versus Arkansas, and broke it the next week at Florida. He finished his career with 36, breaking Tardit's mark by seven. I think that Richard realized it was inevitable that his record would be broken, and while he did not pull against Pollack, he did appreciate that the record was his graphic tie with the University of Georgia Bulldogs.

Pollack would likely admit he had one significant advantage. He started playing organized football before he was 10 years old. Richard

Tardits played in the first game he ever saw. Initially, football was as foreign to him as French would have been to Pollack.

Pollack even carries the Basque colors of "Le Sack." The dark hues of Cortes, hair black as the inside of a chimney, the "Snellville Sacker" has a love of competition that characterizes the style and commitment with which Tardits played the game.

When I arrived at the Tardits' address for dinner, he appeared the same as he did when he peeled off his jersey for the last time, following Vince Dooley's final game as a coach in the Mazda Gator Bowl in 1988. Suave, svelte, bronze, barefoot and fit, Tardits is the picture of health, with muscled masculinity, honed by athletic competition and a passion for the outdoors.

Pollack and Tardits exchanged emails during the season, and each regrets he didn't meet during the '04 season as planned.

NOTHING LIKE IRREVERENT FRIENDS

Earl Leonard, longtime executive of the Coca-Cola Co., has befriended many Bulldog football players following their graduation. For example, he introduced Frank Ros, captain of the 1980 National Champions, to the Coke officials who hired Ros.

Now Assistant Vice President for Corporate Latin Affairs, Ros developed a friendship with Richard Tardits when the Frenchman settled into business in Atlanta prior to returning to his native Biarritz. Leonard was a friend and advisor to Tardits and brought together the two of them and former Georgia center Mark Lewis and Jeff Lewis (no relation), who was a Bulldog linebacker, 1975-77. The fivesome enjoyed many social occasions before Tardits bolted for France and Mark Lewis settled in Salt Lake City.

This group, led by Leonard, their business and professional mentor, is big with Gridiron, the University's renowned Secret Society, which inducted David Greene as a student, his junior year.

Lewis, an articulate and irreverent type, took particular pleasure in 2004 harassing Tardits, a Mr. Big Bull tactic, as Pollack advanced on the Georgia career sack record established by the Frenchman.

Leonard was making plans for a reunion for the Tennessee game, which was Gridiron weekend. Tardits originally had planned to come to Athens for the game, but had to cancel because of a business meeting:

After Tardits declined to travel to Athens for the Tennessee game, his Atlanta friends, led by Jeff Lewis, rode him hard, suggesting he would not be able to handle the news when his record was inevitably broken.

"Richard: So sorry to hear that you will not be able to attend, but I understand your therapist warned you against the shock of seeing your last defensive record broken by David Pollack, clearly the greatest athlete to ever play that position at Georgia. Well, not to worry. With that record goes any memory of your having ever played here, so at least the Bulldog Nation will forget the fact that your teams never won an SEC championship, either. Just keep taking that Prozac until you feel better. Or was it perhaps the fear that Frank and I would take you back to Bull Mountain for another mountain bike ass-whipping that is keeping you away? No need for embarrassment, just keep riding that tricycle along the sidewalk there in France. Maybe play some checkers in the park. Don't exert yourself too much. Jeff."

— Jeff Lewis to Tardits upon hearing the Frenchman would remain in Biarritz for the Tennessee weekend.

Jeff Lewis, Bulldog linebacker and articulate author of friendly insults

AN ALL-AMERICAN IN AWE

During games, especially when Georgia is on defense, I often watch Steve Greer. Many times during a game, I will go up to him and ask what he sees. His expertise on defense as a Bulldog lineman brought him All America honors. At his playing weight of 195 pounds, he probably wouldn't see much game action today, unless he could make it at another position. You'd have to say his heart and his passion, similar to Davey Pollack's, would mean that he would play somewhere, even into today's game of advancing heft.

Greer was a player who was all heart. He was full speed every snap. He got by on competitive instinct, plus quickness and an insatiable desire to succeed. With his speed and quickness, he was frequently in opponent's backfield.

"It was funny," says Mike Cavan, quarterback and running mate off the field. "He got in there so quick that a lot of people thought he lined up in the offensive backfield."

Those of us who saw both Greer and Pollack play see similar characteristics in these two Bulldog All-Americans. No former defensive lineman admired Pollack more than Steve Greer, director of football operations.

"I have always been impressed with David Pollack's attitude and style," Greer says. "I really have enjoyed watching him play, but I like the way our entire line has gone about business. Our interior line, led by Gerald Anderson, is a joy to behold. They come off the ball with great effort and commitment. They benefit from good coaching from Rodney Garner, but they have the desire and commitment to play well.

"You can't help but notice Pollack. It is easier to spot the guy on the end of the line. He is expected to make big plays, and he has more options being out on the flank. I don't think I have ever seen anybody who got in on more plays than David. You get excited when you are on the field and see him beat two guys and get to the quarterback. I don't think he has ever had a bad series. He is about as good as I have ever seen anywhere, and I played alongside Bill Stanfill. All you have to do is look at his record to see how great he was. Same with Pollack. His record was such that it will be a long time before Georgia will line up a greater defensive end, if ever."

And the reply was:

"My Dear Friends: I hate to think how many sacks I could have had if I had played a down lineman position like David Pollack. Being a linebacker and having so many responsibilities on the field didn't allow me to fully concentrate on sacking the quarterbacks!!! I hope the true specialists of the sport will understand that, and I am not too concerned about what some leather-helmet wearing lawyer from the 60's thinks about my past performances….Sorry for not being able to make it for the Tennessee weekend. Unfortunately, it is a long way away, and I can't leave on the Wednesday as I had originally planned. I feel that flying 20 hours round trip for a 24-hour weekend may not be worth it even though seeing you guys would have been rejuvenating. My best to all. A bientot. Richard."

The Rotary Lombardi Award goes to David Pollack; Coach Richt extends congratulations

This good-natured castigating of Tardits continued through the holidays and the Outback Bowl. The Atlanta Dawgs, in fact, adore "Pepe le Pew." They won't let him know it, however. Castigation takes precedent over tribute. Prior to the Outback Bowl, Leonard, Lewis and Tardits journeyed to Athens for a photo with Pollack, holding a miniature 47 jersey which they had Pollack autograph to Tardits.

Alas, the quintessential prankster waxed reluctant. Pollack retreated. "You guys are going to make him [Tardits] mad at me. I'm not here to belittle him. He set the record. I didn't see him play, but I respect him for what he did. Leave me out of all this," Pollack pleaded.

As much as lawyer Jeff enjoys denigrating his French friend, he also has a warm and sensitive regard for the man from Biarritz. When the season was over, and Pollack had claimed the career sack title, Jeffrey Y. Lewis, defensive co-captain of the 1976 SEC Champions, compared the two players.

"My thoughts on these two great Bulldog football players: Physically, they are about the same height, but in college, Richard played at about 220 pounds; Pollack at 265 pounds. David is stronger; Richard was faster. Both were great pass rushers, with unusual quickness off the ball, around or through blockers, and onto the quarterback. Richard's speed allowed him to drop into pass coverages occasionally, thus reducing his sack total. Both Richard and David gave ulcers to offensive coordinators, I am sure.

"Richard's successful career in the NFL was cut short by a knee injury. We are hopeful, of course, for better luck for David. David is a 'Creator of Chaos' and a 'Maker of Mayhem' for offenses, like Dwight Freeney of the Indianapolis Colts, who was allegedly too short and light, at 6'1" and 268 pounds, to play defensive end in the NFL, and was nevertheless, the top NFL pass rusher in 2004, with 40 sacks over three years, and

a consecutive Pro-Bowl selection.

"David, the former fullback, also has great 'Ball-Sense' as shown in his infamous thefts from the quarterbacks from South Carolina in 2002 and Wisconsin in the 2005 Outback Bowl. As an alumnus, am I ever proud these two guys wore red and black. They were unique Bulldogs."

LE SACK SAYS

After Davey Pollack claimed the sack record, Richard Tardits extended congratulations prior to the Outback Bowl and subsequently summed up his feelings.

"It has been sixteen years since I last stepped on the field in Sanford Stadium. A lifetime for some, and it seems to me that it was only yesterday that I said goodbye to the fans, and left behind the magical feeling of wearing the red and black and playing between the hedges.

"The phone calls and all the e-mails received throughout the fall asking me how I felt about David Pollack erasing my name from the total sack column of the record book caused me to reflect back.

"Was this sack record the only thing that connected me to the University of Georgia? Living now more than 2500 miles away in a country that doesn't know the slightest thing about American football, the game and, more importantly, its tradition, would make it easy to forget the four unforgettable years spent in Athens. Being involved in a business that has nothing to do with the University, interacting with employees or clients that could care less if the Dawgs will win the SEC or not, could facilitate the dismissal of all the things Coach Dooley taught us, on and off the football field.

"More than ever, I realize that the four years spent at the University were much more that just playing football. Football is a lot more than a game for young men just leaving their teenage years; it lays the foundations that we build on for the rest of our life. Commitment, discipline, hard work, humility, excitement, never quit attitude— those are qualities that we use all the time in our everyday lives and that we have learned while having fun playing a game.

"I am sure the sack record in itself meant very little for David Pollack when compared to the goals that the 2004 squad had set for itself. I am sure if you ask David to choose between the record and another SEC title or a shot at the National Championship, he would be quick to tell you that the record is meaningless in the grand picture of a football season.

"Breaking the sack record was not even among my fondest memories of my years as a Georgia Bulldog. Moments like my first Clemson game and being hit on the head by Dog biscuit thrown by a belligerent Clemson fan, going down to LSU and beating them in Baton Rouge, losing to LSU in Athens the next year when the refs had to call for a time out because Sanford Stadium was too loud. Those and many more memorable souvenirs take precedent before any record. I am sure David Pollack feels the same way.

"When somebody calls him in a few years to tell him that his sack record is in jeopardy, it will remind him of all these wonderful memories of being a Bulldawg in Sanford Stadium on a Saturday afternoon."

CHAPTER FIFTEEN

CONVERSATION WITH DAVEY

During the fall, Davey Pollack and I had a number of conversations at his favorite spot, Chick-fil-A. He and the spotted cow are in agreement: "Eat More Chikin."

We also made a lunch stop at Longhorn Steakhouse, but the most entertaining meal was at the apartment of his girlfriend, Lindsey, who was at class. ("We eat here; I don't have to do the dishes.")

The conversation touched on a number of topics, and it rambled as conversations with him are prone to do. He is forever entertaining and introspective as he speaks:

A healthy diet is important to me. I may need more weight for the NFL, but I want to put on good weight. I don't ever want to be flabby. My body fat is a lot less than it used to be. You don't look all that healthy to me, so I'm feeding you a bagel, egg whites, turkey bacon, heated oatmeal. How about a glass of OJ and milk? Every day, I cook a healthy breakfast [pauses to return thanks]. Sometimes I eat steak, but not often. I eat tons of chicken. I go for chicken at least once a day. If you are an athlete you can't go on the Atkins diet. On game day I am so hungry by the end of the game, I could eat my socks. Those orange sections they

put out at the halftime, I bet I eat a sack full sometimes. Those power bars. I eat a couple and take a couple to the field for the second half. Just can't wait to catch up with my parents at their RV after the game. My mamma is the best cook you will ever see. My mamma and my girlfriend do all my grocery shopping. I'm so spoiled.

I WILL come back for my degree. You can put that down. Only need about a semester. You know why I will get my degree? How can I tell my kids they should go to school and get a degree if I don't have one?

[Singing] 'She's the woman.' I like most all kinds of music, including Country. My dad likes Elvis. You look like you are old enough to remember Elvis. Hey, you know I'm never serious until I need to be.

The guys on our defense are great to me. I love them. Football is the most integrated thing there is. Big Will [Thompson], he's the man. He comes by my apartment every week. We don't talk football; we just talk about life and things we enjoy. Like our teammates and our friends. Kedric

CHASING DAVEY

Chase Tyson of Thomaston turned nine on November 27, 2004. He was the beneficiary of a wonderful birthday gift to his parents from a friend and was, understandably, overjoyed when he learned how he would celebrate his birthday.

David Piper of WGTA, the local radio station which has carried the Bulldogs' broadcast for years, called his parents, Lori and Wendell, and told them that he was giving them tickets to the Georgia Tech game for Chase's birthday.

Already a David Pollack fan, Chase wondered if there was a chance that he could meet his Bulldog hero. "Sorta hard to do," his mother explained, but Chase had a plan. He would put on his 47 jersey and arrive early for the DawgWalk with a sign. The sign read, "All I want for my birthday is to meet David Pollack."

When the defensive bus came to a stop on Lumpkin Street at the entrance to the Tate Center parking lot, who first should come bounding off the bus but the free-spirited Pollack. By this time, considerate adults had allowed kids to maneuver their way to the front. Pollack spotted Chase and his sign, walked over and said, "Hey, man, I really like your jersey," leaned over and hugged him.

Chase was overwhelmed, but the good news became bad when Lori realized that the photographs she hurriedly took did not turn out, and the sign was done in by the downpour that soon followed.

Then the family took a vacation trip to the Outback Bowl, and Chase and his parents spent time at the Wyndham Hotel, team headquarters. They never got to see Pollack. Chase was unable to secure his favorite Bulldog's autograph. He was fortunate to gain the signature of most Bulldog players but not No. 47.

Disappointed, Chase remained resolved to accomplish his goal. "Mama," he said, "I'll just follow him into the pros until I get it."

On Monday after the game, Lori got a call asking her if she and Chase could come to Athens the next day for a photo session with Pollack and Greene. She was overwhelmed, and the happy ending took place when the family drove to Athens the next day. Chase got to meet Pollack, ask a few questions and have his picture made with his hero.

"You cannot imagine how thrilled our family was to have that opportunity," Lori gushed afterward. "It will be a memory that will last forever for our family. We are humbled by the experience."

Interestingly, the Chase Tyson story is not an exclusive. Since the SEC championship of 2002, David Greene and David Pollack have made countless Georgia fans happy—just like they did Chase.

Golston is always with me, too. He's a man of character. I love my teammates because they would do anything for me. I think they know I would do anything for them. You can't believe how close we are. We all agree that the greatest thing about Georgia has been the togetherness. We just wish society could bond like our team. It shouldn't be all that hard, should it?

Scrapbooks? Yes, I have them, but I don't look at them. My mom and my girlfriend keep everything. I may read them someday. It is obvious why you shouldn't read the paper. Everybody tells you how great you are and you make a bad play and they get down on you.

Sometimes it is hard to make plays. They run away from you, they chip you and they double-team you. Sometimes the other guy does a good job. When that happens, I tell him, "Nice job." You have to give credit or you should, in my opinion. Sometimes the officials miss some things, but I don't complain. I will needle them a little, however. Against Kentucky, I caught a guy's facemask. The ref made the right call, but I kidded the guy. 'Hey ref you call that after all the things they do to me?' I think officials sometimes worry too much about a call affecting the outcome of the game instead of doing their job. I think they do a good job, but they can't see everything. I can't tell you how many times my facemask has been grabbed in my career as I rushed the passer.

Fran Tarkenton autographed a photo for me. He said, "You would never have caught me." I like that. He must be a great guy. When I buy a house, I am going to have a Bulldog room with photos from great players like Fran. The first sports hero I had was L.T. [Giants' Lawrence Taylor]. He wasn't a good example, and I think about that a lot. I wouldn't want some kid seeing me doing some-

Wisconsin quarterback is collared by Davey Pollack

thing bad or wrong and thinking that it would be okay. You can't let other people control your life, and I don't really care what anybody thinks about me. But kids, I love 'em. When I first saw kids wearing my jersey, I was so overwhelmed. It still gets to me when I see them wearing it now. It is cool for a defensive end's number to be requested. Before long I'll be gone, those kids will be grown and the kids after them will wear somebody else's jersey. That's life, wouldn't you say?

When I first came to Georgia, I could always spot my girlfriend in the stands. She wore my No. 47. The next year so many people were wearing my number, I couldn't find her!

The reason I came back for my final year was to enjoy the campus and my friends. Being with my

A LETTER FROM DAVEY'S MOTHER

Dear Davey,

I will always think of you with so much love and pride, for the boy you once were and the man you have become.

When you were a little boy, I wondered daily what kind of man you would be and what you would do with your life. Our journey together has been one that has been rewarding yet very challenging. Everyday was an adventure with you as well as a learning experience. You had an amount of energy that was immeasurable and one words just can't describe.

Every morning when I dropped you off at school and you reached over to kiss my cheek, I wondered if I would make it through that day without a phone call from the school. Looking back, it was always something, for instance cutting the hair of other students, talking uncontrollably, never being able to keep your hands to yourself, having a hard time understanding you only talk when it is your turn, sitting still at your desk, eating in the lunchroom and not throwing your food, and on and on. Every night when I would tuck you in, your kind heart and sweetness was beyond words, as you would assure me that you would be better the next day, you promised. I will never forget that toothless smile you had for four years because you knocked your front baby teeth out at age four, and we had to wait for the permanent ones to arrive. Remember the happy hearts? Remember the special notes in your lunches? Remember the counting for spankings, which you never got? It didn't take long to figure out that keeping your energy channeled would be the key to your success. Sacrificing any free time we had to keep you and your brother busy with sports. Extra activities were the key to your success.

Your accomplishments are beyond my wildest expectations, but I am most proud of the man you are. Your love for life is an inspiration to us all and infectious to anyone who is blessed to cross your path. When I was raising you, I never thought I would become a better person by learning from you. Your daily phone calls just to say "I love you" bring a smile to my face and remind me of just how lucky I am. I have always believed that the good in all humankind can't help but spill over from one another. Davey, keep allowing your goodness to spill over. You'll never really know the lives you have touched and influenced. I am so proud that you continue to keep GOD first in your life but thankful that you continue to keep your family who loves you very much there as well.

Now I await only the next pleasure of my life that has come full circle. As I gently ease around the corner into my golden years, I stand in a special place. I can see the gold at the end of my rainbow-it is a family firmly cemented together with a respect and love of one another. What more could a mother ask for?

I love you beyond words, and I hope these thoughts will let you know just how very treasured you are in my heart.

Love,
Mama

teammates and friends and having fun that one last time. It has been great, no regrets. Lord no. It was the best adult decision I ever made.

I'm not sure if professional football will be as much fun as college. Playing in college is so much fun, but I look forward to the challenge. I've dreamed about the NFL all my life. I can't quite grasp that I'll be dressing with some of those guys I've been watching on television. A player I really like is Brett Favre. I put a premium on people who are tough and those who love. I hate to be around negative people.

Davey relaxes with (from left) Lindsey, Kelli and Norm

One thing is for sure. I will miss UGA.

The college atmosphere, I love it. I'll miss Sanford Stadium. Oh what a beautiful place! I'll miss the coaches, the DawgWalk, and the fans. I'll miss putting on those silver britches and that red helmet. I WILL be a tailgater. I will want a house in Athens. I'll probably want an RV and travel to the games like my parents and Greenie's parents.

The thing I am proudest of is being part of teams that brought Georgia back to where it should be.

LOOKING UP TO LITTLE BROTHER
BY JASON POLLACK

There were many late nights for Davey and me, staying up playing video games—either playing against each other or teaming up and trying to beat a certain level or even a whole game. He would usually be the one that would end up beating it, but I had a lot of fun trying to help. I remember when we got our first Zelda game. We stayed up night after night after night until we beat that game.

Davey and I were part of many teams. Because he went to readiness, we were always in different leagues, which meant we were not on the same team. That is until his first year of Pony League baseball. Not only were we on the same team but our dad also coached us. This was the most fun season of any sport that I participated in. Being able to play with my little brother and have my dad coach made it the most fun season.

When we were growing up, we spent a lot of time with our friends. We had a lot of family friends. Our parents had friends who had a kid either my age or Davey's age, sometimes both or close enough. Those friendships included the Greenes and others. We are still very close to those families.

Watching Davey and David Greene over the last 16 years has been a treat and an honor. It is awesome for me to have been able to look back and remember them playing in the yard at the age of six and then go on to be record-breaking players at the University of Georgia. I am so looking forward to watching them both make careers in

For each passing birthday, the energy level intensified for Davey

the NFL doing what they love to do most, play the game of football.

It is not very often that athletes make it all the way to the professional level, much less two best friends who have played together for such a long time. For me to have been able to be a part of their love for each other and the game of football is very special.

There was no doubt in my mind that Davey would have a very successful career because I know how hard he works, not just at football but at everything he does in life. However, never in my wildest dreams could I have imagined that when it was all over only Davey would be in the same company as Hershel Walker as Georgia's only three time All-America selections.

Other than my parents, there is no one more proud of Davey and what he has accomplished but more importantly what he stands for. I wore his No. 47 jersey to every game and am very proud to be able to say No. 47 is my brother. He is an inspiration to me and I love him with all my heart and soul.

When we were little boys growing up, our parents always kept us busy in sports. It was awesome because they were involved in everything we did as well. We are both so blessed to have such wonderful parents who have devoted their

lives to our happiness, and boy, have we caused them to have gray hair!

Our house had a basketball court in the driveway and one of our favorite uses of extra time was shooting baskets. I bet we broke the windows on those garage doors at least a half dozen times. Of course, it was never our fault because the ball just always bounced in ways that we could never explain. Dad was always awesome about it and always just put in a new window without complaining.

Everyone always hung out at our house, usually because Mom had the kitchen producing goodies all the time. Eating was the only thing for which ever we stopped playing. Davey usually didn't even stop to do that.

We spent almost every night from the time I was seven through eighth grade at the ballpark. Dad coached Davey's football team and Mom was the team mom for all my teams. When it wasn't football season, we were at the baseball park or in the gym.

Davey has always been a ball of energy. He is 21 months younger than I, and I can remember in school when he would get the same teachers I had, they would say, "Is that really your brother?" I didn't have quite the energy that Davey has, and still don't.

May 21, 2005 was a big day for our family. That was the day of Lindsey and Davey's wedding. She is a very special girl, and I look forward to gaining a sister, especially since I have never had one. I know their life together will be a special one and filled with a lot of love. I am honored to be a part of both of their lives.

I am confident he will make it as a professional player. Just like at Georgia, he will work harder than anybody to succeed at the game he loves.

The other end during much of Davey Pollack's time was Will Thompson, to whom he refers as "Big Will."

"When you evaluate our defense, you have to appreciate the play of Big Will," Pollack says. "I love Big Will. He usually stopped by my apartment each week to hang out. We just talked. Played video games. He has a big heart. He played hard and meant a lot to our defense. I'd hate to have to try to block him."

Big Will has endless praise, too, for Davey. "You know," Will smiles, "practice can sometimes get a little boring, but not for Davey. He put as much into practice as he did the games. He always wanted us to relax. He found ways to keep it interesting. He made us trip out with some of the things he would say. If people had been on the practice field with us, they might not have thought he was serious about football. They would be wrong. He played the game like it was the most important thing on earth. He never quit.

"If you have ever played football, you know that when you are scrimmaging play after play

Davey with Will Thompson, the other end

In the weight room — their goal was always to become stronger

pened. "I first thought he had batted the ball away, but when I saw all our teammates running over to congratulate him, I knew something good had happened. Just didn't know what at first. I joined in the celebration before I actually knew what he had done. The next week when I watched the play on tape, I was like everybody else. I was amazed."

There was one problem between the two defensive ends, however. "His diet," Will laughs. "I tried it, but I couldn't eat what he eats. No way. It might be healthy, but I couldn't get by on his diet."

Then Will smiles in agreement to the suggestion that a healthy relationship is more important to a team in football than a healthy meal.

███

after play it gets boring and tiring. Most of us think about quitting. Maybe not quitting the team and walking away, but we just feel like not making an effort for a play or two. Maybe try to get a little rest. Not Davey. He went all out all the time. He inspired us."

There was an interesting development during Pollack's sophomore year when his legend gained traction. "The upperclassmen," Will says, "looked up to him. That doesn't happen to an underclassman unless you are special. Davey was special. He tried to inspire everybody to do his best, and he brought out the best in his teammates—even the older guys."

When Pollack made his big touchdown in the South Carolina game, Will was on the field, but away from the play and wasn't sure what hap-

A COMFORTABLE FIT

David Allen took charge of Bulldog equipment in 1990. He had served as assistant supervisor five years prior. He is experienced and up to date—even so, nothing is taken for granted. He always follows his checklist.

Some equipment facts:

Linemen wear receiver type gloves because such gloves are more flexible.

All gloves are gray. There was a time when the color had to correspond to the color of the jersey of the player's team. Before that, some line coaches were given to issuing gloves the color of the opposing team's jersey to better camouflage holding.

Receivers wear tactified gloves.

Mouthpieces must be in color; players cannot wear white or transparent mouthpieces.

Extra shoes are very important, especially if the weather turns foul. "Players might change shoes at the half if there is rain and mud, and we are prepared," Allen says. Then he adds, "That's for the guys on the field. I don't worry about those standing by me."

All players are required to wear hip pads. During a game in Sanford Stadium in '04, an official took Fernando Velasco to the sideline to inform Allen that the Bulldog lineman was not wearing hip pads. Extras were on hand and available for a quick replacement that would conform to the rule. Velasco missed only one snap. Players are not allowed to tape their sleeves.

When Thomas Brown (5'8", 177), one of the smallest of starting players takes the field, he weighs 15 pounds more after he dresses. Max Jean-Gilles (6'4", 340), the largest, carries equipment weighing almost 25 pounds.

The weight factor for these two Bulldawgs compares like this:

THOMAS BROWN	MAX JEAN GILLES
Helmet = 4.40	Helmet = 5.00
Shoes = 1.75	Shoes = 4.90
Pants = .90	Pants = 1.00
Jersey = 1.25	Jersey = 1.40
Shoulder Pads = 5.50	Shoulder Pads = 6.35
Pads = .65	Pads = 1.35
Game Bag = 1.15	Game Bag = 3.05
Knee Braces = None	Knee Braces = 1.90
Total = 15.60	Total = 24.70

For the record, David Greene's helmet weighs 4.05 pounds. Davey Pollack's weighs 4.30 pounds. Davey's facemask is heavier.

DAWG MATES

He doesn't have the kind of personality to allow him to say so, but you have to think that Damon Evans saw something of himself in The Davids. He, too, has a positive personality—somewhat reserved like Greenie. But, he has a little conversational mischief in his makeup. Like Pollack, but less frequently, Damon slips the needle in upon occasion.

The exit of The Davids came on the first year of his athletic director watch. They played for the Bulldogs 10 years after Damon finished his own career as a receiver, which enabled him to complete degree requirements for both undergraduate and graduate degrees.

"I appreciate them for more than what they accomplished on the field," Damon says. "They exemplified what you want in character, leadership and integrity. I hear from athletic officials around the country who are aware of what these two boys stand for. It is nice when people in the business appreciate the positive attitude they find with high-profile players in your program—even though they have never met those players.

"David Greene and David Pollack are very unassuming. If you walked up to them and began a conversation, you would never know they had

won all those awards and set all those records. You would never know they are two of the greatest players ever to wear Georgia's Red and Black."

He grins enthusiastically when he is asked if he would have enjoyed playing receiver with David Greene. "Why, yes," he said quickly. "If I had played with him, it would mean that I would have an SEC championship ring. I would have enjoyed playing with him for more than his quarterbacking ability. It would be nice to be a teammate of someone who can lead like David. He is one of the most unselfish players I have ever been around.

"With David Pollack, you appreciate his drive to improve and to find ways to play better and more effectively. He is an outstanding athlete, but he has the drive and determination to be the best he can possibly be. I have never seen a player who never takes a play off. He goes all out every play, right on up to the final whistle. A lot of linemen go hard for a few snaps and then rest a play or two. Not David Pollack. He is remarkable."

When Damon was growing up in Nebraska—first Omaha and subsequently Lincoln—the highlight of those precocious years were summer trips to visit relatives in Los Angeles.

He passionately loved California: the roiling

Athletic Director, Damon Evans, gets the word from Coach Richt prior to kickoff

Pacific surf, the balmy weather, the amusement parks and the excitement that came with life, even temporarily, on the Left Coast.

"I lived for California," he recalls. "I would go out there for the entire summer and roam around with my cousins." Not many kids from America's heartland enjoyed the opportunity to visit Disneyland. All too few could choose to skateboard in the dazzling amusement parks and swim in the Pacific, which he would not go near today. "When you are young, you have no fear of water," he laughs, "but I now know what can happen to you in the ocean." That he currently affiliates with landlubbers suggests that as he matured, he learned to avoid pitfalls, problems and high-risk circumstance.

Perhaps his most memorable California episode turned out to be a significant learning experience, albeit a frightful encounter. His relatives lived in a peaceful neighborhood, but if you ventured into

certain nearby zones, you might easily find trouble. The Crips and the Bloods, notorious and violence-prone gangs, might be cruising by.

One day, he and a cousin were shooting baskets in a city park. His cousin, wearing blue, left Damon to run an errand, and suddenly a group of toughs, wearing red bandanas, approached him. The red signaled they were members of the Bloods. "Who," they asked, "was your friend in blue?" referring to his departed cousin. The Crips, the Blood's rival gang, wore blue.

Fortunately, Damon had dressed that day in neutral colors and explained that his cousin was not affiliated with the Crips. Nothing happened, but it made a lasting impression. From then on, when he dressed in the morning and headed out for the day, Damon made certain that he never chose blue or red, even though his favorite color was the red of the Nebraska Cornhuskers, who were dominant in college football.

"At that time, when you are young and become familiar with what goes on in the street, you understandably develop into a street-smart person," he says. "But you think, 'How do those things happen?' I never experienced anything like that in Nebraska. California was exciting, but it taught me that there was a danger even in a nearby neighborhood, and that I had to make good choices and decisions."

When his father uprooted the family and returned to his native Gainesville, the chicken capital of the world, Damon landed a part time job at a Mrs. Winner's restaurant. If he wanted spending money, he had to earn it.

Life in laid-back and rural-accented Hall County was more like Nebraska, but he realized that just as there was a bad element in Los Angeles, it was the same in Gainesville.

One day at work, he looked out the window and saw the white robed Ku Klux Klan parading by in protest. Again, he was frightened, perhaps more than when he was approached by the gang in Los Angeles.

How could gangs infiltrate and disrupt neighborhoods? How was it that an organization like the Klan could disturb the peace of a small town and function to intimidate and put fear in people?

He often asked those questions, and by the time he was an adult, he came to appreciate that while America is the land of opportunity, it is not a society without problems. His goal became one of serious application to principle, homework and to invoke the philosophy of treating others with respect. He would earn his keep. He would pay his way. He would overachieve. He would make friends and treat people right.

When he was under consideration for the position of athletics director at Georgia, I'll never forget his father-in-law's comment. We were having breakfast in Boston, and Wayne

The Davids with the Evans family, from left: Kennedy, Damon, Kerri and Cameron

Budd said, "I am proud that my son-in-law is even being considered for a job at a school where I could not even have applied for admission."

Damon Evans knows about gangs and the Klan, and he has felt the sting of discrimination, but he lives his life today by underscoring principle and fair play. Even though he initially was moved to make some very tough personnel decisions, he grew up under the influence of the Golden Rule and passionately believes in its philosophy. He doesn't shout out his feelings in that regard, but if you are around him long enough, you become aware of it.

Interestingly, when he settled in Gainesville, he discovered resentment and jealousy in his own family. His Georgia relatives and new friends wondered if he felt that he was better than they. "You talk too proper," they told him.

Developing inner strength became a hallmark as he began to make decisions about his life and future. Family has always been important. Scholarship was always underscored. Friends were, perhaps, the most important of all. Those who knew him in high school point out that his circle of friends was all encompassing. His good and decent way endeared him to all of his classmates. He crossed racial lines with a natural aplomb that signaled, early on, that he possessed rare abilities as a leader and communicator.

It is not lost on him that, as a minority, he is something of a pioneer with the position he holds in intercollegiate athletics but remains conscious that others paved the way. While he knew about discrimination, he came along at a time when he was cognizant that exceptional opportunity had become a reality. He is steadfastly grateful for those he never met who influenced the societal change that brought about his good fortune.

While he has a degree of impatience in establishing his agenda, he is a man slow to anger. He is never given to outburst and reasons with maturity beyond his years. He doesn't prefer to be recognized or remembered as the first black A.D. at Georgia and the Southeastern Conference.

His preference is to render a performance that identifies him as accomplishing a goal of providing the best facilities and opportunity for student-athletes who enroll at the University of Georgia.

Winning championships has priority, but he expects Bulldog coaches to provide the kind of leadership and influence that sends athletes away from the campus with an education.

He made the right choices as a student-athlete, but he is fully aware that neither he, nor anyone on the Georgia staff, can make a kid go to class, nor make him or her into a responsible student and citizen. He often has said, however, "We can at least try our best."

While he understands the decision that football and basketball athletes with exceptional ability are likely to leave campus early, he regrets that so few of them return to complete degree requirements. He was never a hot prospect for the National Football League, but if he had been, he would have put himself in position to graduate on time. That is what he will advise any potential superstar who matriculates at Georgia.

In fact, the redshirt system allowed him not only to finish his degree by the time his eligibility ended, he earned a Masters as well. Desire and discipline count for something if you set goals, and he will always preach that to Bulldog athletes, regardless of sport.

He looks the part of a big-time college athletics director. Impeccably groomed with coat and tie, he has a distinguished bearing that befits his assignment. He is polite, courteous and is comfortable in any setting. He can converse with an accomplished Ph.D. and can review a detailed financial sheet with an experienced banker. Yet he will never lose the common touch.

In many respects, he is like The Davids, putting forth dedicated effort administratively, deflecting praise and credit, and underscoring team.

∎∎∎

Georgia fans are always asking: "Do you think Florida State will come after Mark Richt when Bobby Bowden retires?" Naturally, this is to be expected. Why would the Seminoles not seek the guy who was offensive coordinator during their greatest years? Good man, outstanding football teacher and a proven record. Plus, Tallahassee is the hometown of his wife, Katharyn. Close friends live there, and when it comes to recruiting, there is arguably more talent available in Florida than any state in the country.

Sounds like it would be attractive and alluring for Richt, right? Perhaps, but unless something develops at Georgia and his chance for success becomes questionable in his mind, I don't believe his ties to Florida State will tug his emotions when the Bowden era is over in Tallahassee. In fact, I know they won't.

One day we were riding to the Athens airport for a spring trip. As we drove through the campus, the flowers were in full bloom. Students with their backpacks and their books were strolling about. It was the time of the year when life becomes energized as the dead of winter disappears, and the fragrance and bloom of the spring gives rise to emotions and inspirations.

We were in routine conversation about the trip we were about to make when suddenly he blurted out, "To mess this thing up, we'd just have to do it to ourselves. Just have to shoot ourselves in the foot." That, to me, clearly expresses his confidence in Georgia's potential and his opportunity to succeed long term with the Bulldogs. Then in the next breath, he said, "We do need an indoor practice facility." No elaboration, no dissertation, just a fact, in his view of reality.

If he has something inside, something that nobody knows but Katharyn and him, that could be a "next move" seed waiting to sprout, I have not discovered it. He is fooling me if he would consider alighting for another school. I may be wrong, but I don't think, given favorable factors based on his first four years, that Mark Richt has any plans to leave Georgia.

In a conversation with his mother, Helen, I asked her if he ever talked about working at another school when he was a highly regarded coordinator with the Seminoles. Quickly, she replied, "Georgia."

He saw the fertile recruiting grounds, tradition, facilities and alumni base of the state university of the Empire State of the South. The FSU

Coach Richt, always generous with his signature

team spent its pre-game Friday nights in Thomasville, which allowed familiarity with the state, during Richt's time with the Seminoles. He had recruited in Georgia, and he familiarized himself with what Vince Dooley had accomplished in Athens. He never talked about it to anybody except Katharyn and Dave Van Halanger, his best friend. He did ponder, to use a Biblical term, things in his heart.

When Richt spent time with Archie and Olivia Manning during Peyton Manning's senior high school year, they were duly impressed. If Peyton had not chosen Tennessee, his next choice probably would have been Florida State, principally because of Mark Richt.

On Richt's last visit to the Manning home on First Street in New Orleans' fashionable Garden District, Olivia turned to Archie as Mark was pulling out of the driveway and said, "I like that man. He is going to make somebody a great head coach someday."

Archie had this view: "A lot of coaches take any head coaching job just to become a head coach, hoping to move on to a better job. With Mark, he chose to wait until a great opportunity came along. When I heard that he was going to take over at Georgia, I knew that it would be a perfect fit."

When Jim Donnan was fired after the 2000 season, Richt immediately called Grant Teaff, Executive Director of the American Football Coaches Association and asked for a recommendation to Athletic Director Dooley. If Richt patiently waited for the right opportunity, which he considered Georgia to be, why would he be fidgeting for a move from Athens?

On two trips returning home from Bulldog Club meetings in Augusta and Macon in the spring of '04, Richt and I had conversations about a number of topics.

In one, he asked whom I thought were the top coaches in the country. My response was, "First of all, you have to be in there. ("No. No," he said. "I'm talking about established coaches," as if he weren't established.) Like everybody else, I am a fan who starts with results. On top of that, I can't ignore personal relationships. Lloyd Carr at Michigan, for example, I consider a very good friend; I have visited his home on a game weekend at Ann Arbor and have had many conversations about football philosophy. He is a consistent winner, and he is good for college football.

"Who else?" he asked. "Bob Stoops, obviously," I said. "And Frank Beamer at Virginia Tech. I don't know Pete Carroll, but he is off to a sensational start at Southern Cal. He has talent access and tradition. Phillip Fulmer has won 80 percent of his

games. He's doing something right."

"Nick Saban?" he said. "How can you have it better than LSU?" was my response. "State university, terrific fan support and facilities, but no competition for the best players in the state of Louisiana which has outstanding talent." Then we both agreed that Saban would not stay long. He seemed to be inclined to return to the NFL, which is what happened at the end of the season.

"What about Larry Coker at Miami?" he asked.

"For an unknown assistant to take over a program which, arguably, has had the most consistent success at playing for the national championship, he has to be exceptional. On top of that, he is, perhaps, the nicest guy in coaching other than you. ("We're not talking about nice guys," he cracked.)."

He said more: "Lou Holtz is a nice man. I am impressed with what Chan Gailey is doing at

Coach Mark Richt flanked by his celebrated Dawgs, Greenie and Davey

TEN THINGS YOU MAY NOT KNOW ABOUT MARK RICHT

+ He is not superstitious. After a victory, he doesn't wear any of the victory apparel the next week.

+ His favorite hymn is "Amazing Grace."

+ He does not enjoy wearing baseball caps. A floppy straw hat will do.

+ He is better at ironing than his wife, Katharyn.

+ He likes to cook and is good with the grill. His favorite dish is one he originated —beans and franks—which he calls "hot dog delight." Katharyn is certain he could bake a cake.

+ He has never shot a gun.

+ He's handy around the house. If something breaks, he usually can fix it. "One day," Katharyn says, "after our kids are grown, I think he would like to build us a house."

+ He doesn't like seafood.

+ His favorite movie is "Christmas Vacation."

+ He once quarterbacked Miami to victory over Florida, the beginning of his distaste for the color orange.

Georgia Tech. Tommy Tuberville and Auburn are always tough for us." He didn't exclude his former coach Bobby Bowden. "I learned so much from Coach Bowden. To be the guy who wins the most games of any coach in history. I admire what he has done."

At the annual College Football Hall of Fame dinner, Penn State's Joe Paterno stopped by the Georgia table and said to Richt, "You're doing a nice job." The handshake was warm and firm, and the look in Paterno's eye reflected respect. Older coaches appreciate young coaches who not only win, but place the right emphasis on the philosophy of trying to fit in with the university community and to do right by the kids they coach and teach.

We talked about purpose in life ("If you don't want your time on earth to be spent trying to influence kids and help others, why are you in coaching?), politics ("I'm conservative, but I could never

be a politician."), the near overwhelming demand for his autograph ("I like the Georgia people, and it is nice that they have an interest in our program and our people."), the quality of life in Athens for him and his family ("Awesome, I love it."), the campus ("So beautiful. I love the hills and the trees."), the alumni and fans ("Boy, do they love the Dawgs."), and money ("It is not the most important thing in my life. I want to take care of my family. I want to do something for others. If you coach, you do have to think about the fact that it can be short term. You don't always have control of your destiny.").

We spoke of the challenge of competing in the SEC ("Man is it ever tough! Tougher than I realized, but I enjoy the competition."), Vince Dooley ("I'll always be grateful for him hiring me. I am in awe of his record. He achieved a lot. His record is something."), and his thoughts after a year on the job ("I am overwhelmed at what I didn't know about being a head coach.").

Every trip we take, every time we talk, I leave feeling proud as a Bulldog that our leader is a modest, selfless and decent human being.

WATER GIRL
NOTHING MORE, NOTHING LESS

It was a warm evening when Georgia played its first road game of the '04 season at Columbia. The first ones to arrive at the stadium are the equipment support staff, the managers, the trainers and the communications crew.

The equipment team, led by Dave Allen, arrives five hours prior to kickoff to make sure everything is in order. Larry Munson and the radio crew arrive at about the same time. Munson is the first Dawg to become antsy on game day.

An hour and a half prior to kickoff, the team unloads at the stadium, and the players walk around the field, to get a feel for the playing surface, checking out sunlight angles, if it is a late afternoon kickoff, the wind and any other factors which might affect decision making when the game gets underway.

The managers and the trainers put in place ice, POWERade, water and all accessories by the time the team arrives. As we moved closer and closer to pre-game warm-ups, I spotted Katharyn Richt in khakis, a red Georgia shirt and a baseball cap wandering over to the water station.

A new water girl had joined the support ranks. I didn't know that at first, however, but when the game got underway, I walked down the sideline in front of the water station and saw her pouring water.

"What are you doing?" I asked.

"I'm just helping out," she said, grinning.

She wanted no fuss made over her new role, which she eagerly sought. While I had no interest in

Katharyn Richt helps organize the water and POWERade station prior to kickoff

Just a water girl, nothing more, nothing less

She is an original when it comes to head coaches' wives providing refreshments for the team. I doubt, even in the olden days, if a coach's wife ever assumed any responsibility on the sideline.

This is the way it came about. After hinting to Mark for a couple of years, he finally said, "If you are that serious, go ask Ron Courson." She did, which alleviated a personnel shortage for the Georgia trainer. He prefers to assign two trainers to work the water station, but in order to carry three doctors on road trips; he had to travel with one less student trainer. Katharyn's interest in "helping out" gave Courson a significant personnel assist.

When you probe her thoughts about her sideline role, she simply says, "I'm just a water girl. Nothing more. Nothing less." Georgia fans have become aware of her presence and call out to her as they pass by. Some even ask for her autograph.

While she can't see much of the game, she knows what goes on by the crowd's reaction and by monitoring the replay video screen above the scoreboards. The highlights of her rookie season:

Winning the Florida game. "It meant so much to everybody. Coming from Florida State, we know what it's like to have contempt for the Gators."

The touchdown Jeremy Thomas scored in the Outback Bowl. "He caught a deflected pass and scampered to the end zone for his only touchdown catch as a Bulldog. He is such a fine young man." When Thomas came over to refresh himself, she said, "Jeremy, that was awesome!" He replied, "Yes ma'am. I probably won't ever get to do that again."

blowing her cover, I thought it was so unusual that she would take up a responsibility to assist on the sideline, or in her words, "help out." It is without question, the worst place in the entire stadium to watch a game, unless you watch from underneath the stands, where they park the lawn mowers.

For four quarters, she stood behind a table and kept the cups filled with water or POWERade. She was always patient and smiling. She showed no emotion but obviously was proud to be part of the team. How many head coaches' wives, or assistants' wives, for that matter, do you know with her modesty and down to earth good nature?

There is only one negative, the inevitable publicity. What about that? "I don't like it," she said after the Outback Bowl. "I don't want to be written up, and I certainly don't want any TV cameras coming around." Sorry, but until it gets to be old news, she is going to have to contend with both.

■ ■ ■

STRAIGHT AHEAD
WITH NEIL CALLAWAY

During the 192 weeks Neil Callaway watched David Greene work in his career, he never saw the Bulldog quarterback complain or make excuses. He never saw Greene point a finger at his linemen, and he never showed them up. If they made a mistake, he was there to pat them on the back and to offer encouragement.

Callaway knows the value of quarterback-O-line rapport. He's been there. He knows how a lineman feels when he makes a mistake. If he misses a block, allows a quarterback sack and, worst of all, gets flagged for holding, a lineman will hear his number announced to the full stadium and the television network covering the game. For Georgia, the TV cameras were on hand for every game last year, counting local telecasts.

Revealing who was holding is unwanted recognition. If a lineman does his job, not many know about it. The fans in the stands might see the surges of the offensive line. They may realize that the right or left side is successfully pushing forward, but to be able to recognize a pancake block or one in which the defender is buried in the middle of the line is not likely. (Unless they are watching on TV and the replay camera focuses on a proficient block, which is a different

story.) However, the replay camera also catches penalties and mistakes.

Even so, linemen are best appreciated by their teammates and coaches. A feature article in the newspaper helps, but for the most part, they toil in anonymity, which can become a badge of

Neil Callaway offers encouragement in a tight moment

Coach Callaway's O-line was up to the task in 2004

courage. Paul Fersen, a Bulldog letterman at tackle in the 70s says, "There is a special bond among linemen. You hear a lot about linemen being unsung heroes. Publicity and attention don't matter to the guys in the trenches. We consider it special to work in anonymity."

Callaway never heard David Greene say anything to a Bulldog lineman except to offer encouragement: "He always focused on the positive. He made them feel good about themselves. This quality of finding good in every situation will benefit him for the rest of his life. It will help him to be successful in whatever he does after football, just like it has helped him at Georgia and will help him as he continues his football career."

As the offensive coordinator, Callaway saw

right away that Greene was motivated to learn and improve. "He never got frustrated, and he was in control in the huddle," Callaway praises. "He missed some throws. Who doesn't? Overall, he was a very accurate passer. Even when he struggled, he still made plays. That is the mark of an outstanding quarterback. We won big because of No. 14."

As an offensive lineman at Alabama who played on a national championship team, Callaway appreciated a quarterback who appreciated his linemen.

If he had written down a synopsis of what he wanted in a quarterback, it would have included: "One who was a competitor. One who had toughness. One who knew he was going to be hit and expected that and when it happened, he would

A LETTER FROM THE BEAR

In Neil Callaway's office, there is a framed copy of a letter his coach, Paul "Bear" Bryant, wrote to him in the pre-season of 1977. Neil, as a member of the team, was given instructions on his reporting date along with a few motivational thoughts from the Bear:

Winning isn't everything, it's the only thing. You can win by using the biggest little word that I know—IF:

+ IF you believe, you can.

+ IF team victory comes first.

+ IF you put nothing but God, family and education ahead of football.

+ IF your plan is to improve everyday, every practice and each play.

+ IF you receive from me the direction, leadership, instructions, planning and help that you are entitled to.

+ IF you are eager to sacrifice, cooperate and discipline yourself both on and off the field – for the good of the team.

+ IF you display class and a winning attitude at all times.

+ IF you are anxious to work – no one is ever able to work unless in tip-top mental and physical condition.

+ IF you know you can make the big play and win in the 4th quarter.

You are very special to me. I hope you will give me reasons to compliment you, pat you on the back, pet you with the news media, hug you and love you.

P.S. Former President Eisenhower's mother was a deeply religious woman. When Ike was a boy she would say to him, 'The Lord deals the cards, but the way you play them - that's up to you'.

Setting personal goals is the surest way to keep yourself developing and moving ahead. But you have to do it, not just think about it. No one is going to do it for you.

Spoken by President Theodore Roosevelt, 'It's hard to fail, but it's worse never to have tried to succeed.'

It's not the hours you put into your work. It is the work you put into your hours.

respond with resolve, not emotion. You always want a quarterback who can make plays." He saw that in Richard Todd and Jeff Rutledge at Alabama, and he saw it in David Greene.

"He espoused unity," Callaway says. "He was friends with them in a business manner. He had the right way with them, which is what you want in a quarterback. Our linemen tried hard for David."

If a quarterback is a prima donna, and many are, he runs the risk of alienating his own linemen. If he is temperamental and points fingers, he might spend a lot of time on the seat of his pants. That happened to Greenie his junior year, but only because the offensive line was overwhelmed by injury, and the challenge was accented by youth and inexperience — not a lack of quarterback leadership skills. It was a quarterback's nightmare season, but somehow or other, Greene led the Bulldogs to the championship game. When he went down, he came back to make a big play.

"A quarterback's greatest ability is durability," Bud Grant of the Minnesota Vikings once told me. He was speaking of Fran Tarkenton. "Fran knew how to avoid hits, but he took a lot, too," said Mick Tinglehoff, Vikings' center. "Didn't matter how tough it was, he never flinched. He would never let 'em know he was hurting." David Greene had that quality.

There was a lot of resilience with Greenie, who came out for one series during his junior year at Baton Rouge, and that was it, until his final game with Tech, when he suffered a fractured thumb on his throwing hand in the first quarter. Like Tarkenton, and all the other tough-minded, durable quarterbacks, Greenie came back and moved the Dawgs downfield for the field goal that was critical to the outcome of the game.

CHAPTER TWENTY

MarTEENez not MartNEZ

St. Martin of Tours was the patron saint of France, but was popular around the world. In Spanish speaking countries, the descendants of St. Martin were called Martinez. That's "Mar-teen-ez," not "MartNez," as in the Georgia community near Augusta, whose pronunciation always brings a quizzical look from Willie Martinez, the Bulldogs' successor to Brian VanGorder as defensive coordinator.

In his first year at Georgia, I commented that he was the only member of the Mark Richt staff to have a place named for him. "They better learn how to pronounce it," he remarked.

From Barry Paschal, Editor of the *Columbia County News-Times,* comes the official explanation: "Martinez: This unincorporated area, located mostly south of Evans, is named for Antonio Martinez Y Saldivar, a Cuban who moved to the county by way of New York in the late 1800s. Instead of the traditional MarTEEnez, Columbia County residents pronounce the area's name MartNEZ- but it originally was called Lulaville, after Sadivar's daughter, until postal officials realized Georgia already had a Lulaville when they built the Martinez post office in 1915."

Many Georgia fans hope the Martinez com-

munity, where countless Bulldog partisans abound, will someday return to the pronunciation of its founder, based on invincible Bulldog defensive performances.

Aside from his considerable knowledge of defensive football, Martinez has an interesting background. While he was born in America, his family had escaped Cuba before Fidel Castro seized power. As the governmental control of the previous dictator, Fulgencio Batista, was eroding, and the rebels, led by Castro, were taking over, Oscar Martinez and most of his family emigrated to Miami. Some of Felicia Martinez's family (his mother) emigrated at the same time.

Willie was born later and has no desire to return to Cuba as long as Castro remains head of the Cuban government. In the spring of 2005, his greatest concern, however, was not the political situation in Havana, but the high-powered offense of Boise State, a team which expects to score every time it gains possession of the ball. In football terms, the opener with the Broncos was right around the corner.

If you probe into Martinez's background, he will express appreciation for his life as an American and the opportunity that football pro-

Willie Martinez, in a pre-game drill, knows the value of a football scholarship

matter. Fun and games were his life, and he developed skills that united him with the Miami Hurricanes. He played for Howard Schnellenberger and Jimmy Johnson. He owns a National Championship ring that was made possible by the University of Georgia.

New Year's Day, 1983, about the time the Miami team gathered for the pre-game meal before playing favored Nebraska in the Orange Bowl, second ranked Texas was leading Georgia 9-3. Steaks were on the Hurricanes' plate when the Longhorns fumbled a punt and the Bulldogs recovered. There was hope. Georgia could win, and if the Hurricanes upset Nebraska, Miami would likely be voted the national title.

That is exactly what happened. I remember a conversation with Howard Schnellenberger, who recalled the scene after Georgia won. He said, "Steaks were flying off the ceiling. You couldn't believe the energy that coursed through the room when we realized Georgia had won. We knew what that meant for our kids."

Miami took an early 17-0 lead on the Cornhuskers, but Nebraska rebounded before the half. What got the Cornhuskers back in the game was the "fumblerooskie." When the quarterback took the snap and put the ball on the ground, All American guard Dean Steinkuhler picked it up and scored from 19 yards out. The last Hurricane with a chance to stop him was Martinez. "We won the game, 31-30, but all my friends want to talk about Steinkuhler running over me," Martinez laughs.

What I like about Willie Martinez is that he has a sense of humor and will work hard to ensure that Georgia's defensive competence continues. He will ask more of himself than any player on the team. Most of all, in the tradition of his father, he will be appreciative of the good things that come his way.

While Willie was allowed to play sports growing up, he was expected to find odd jobs for

vided him. With his father arriving in the U.S. and starting from scratch, college would have been unthinkable for Willie without the benefit of scholarship aid.

While growing up, life was like that of most any other kid in America. His hard-working parents were bent on providing for the family. They gave considerable emphasis to education, but simply could not fathom that the game of football would pay for it. To begin with, they did not understand the game. In his time in Cuba, Oscar knew about baseball and boxing, which are big in the island nation, even today.

As a kid, Willie was better at baseball, but played all games. Backyards, playgrounds—didn't

The legendary Sanford Stadium in all its glory

Another big play by Davey — a blocked punt versus Georgia Southern

spending money. He worked as a stock boy for Publix. He was a busboy in a restaurant and a Domino's pizza deliveryman, but the best job was driving a limo.

He learned the work ethic from his enterprising father, and he applied hard work to his sports activities. Martinez figured, early on, that if he got anywhere in football, he would have to work harder than the next guy.

That has become his coaching philosophy—to work as hard or harder as those who line up against you on Saturday, but not only to work hard, but to work smart. Find a better way. Just one little twist of scheme, one key well-practiced fundamental can be the difference in the outcome of a game in the highly competitive business of college football.

After he assumed Brian VanGorder's old corner office on the northwest corner of the second floor of the Butts-Mehre Building, Martinez immediately went to work recruiting. Nothing unusual about that, but he began 2005 with a different perspective. He had a bigger title, more responsibility, and he would be in charge. The defensive buck stopped with him.

He had one particular positive thing going for him. He was Mark Richt's teammate at Miami, and they have always enjoyed a nice rapport. Richt appreciated the defensive schemes Martinez and VanGorder utilized when FSU played Central Florida, when VanGorder and Martinez ran the Golden Knights defense.

Richt knew about Willie, but VanGorder impressed him, too, and the Bulldog coach's first objective for defense was to add the two of them to his defensive staff.

On a cold January day, Martinez took time out to talk to me about football and his philosophy. "My philosophy?" he responded to my question. "As we have been in the past, we are not a sit-and-react style of defense. We expect to be aggressive. The sophisticated offenses today won't let you sit and react anymore.

"You have got to take some risks, you have to blitz, you have to accentuate aggressiveness, but you must be sound in whatever you do. The most important thing is to stress fundamentals. We are a basic 4-3 defense, but that scheme is popular across the country. It is nothing new to college football.

"We are aware that you can't win without players, and we have good players at Georgia. That has been a big plus. After that, you teach sound fundamental football. Your fundamentals and playing within the scheme will often determine whether you win or lose.

"We want to continue to keep offenses off balance. If you are fundamentally sound, you have a better opportunity to make critical plays. You must always be disciplined. If your fundamentals are in place at the critical time you should be able to make plays.

"For example, if a defensive back holds a receiver, just reaches out and grabs him when running a route, that is a fundamental failure. You should never get yourself into a position to where you have to do that. The only way to avoid that circumstance is strict adherence to fundamentals."

With that, he offered a brief treatise on the problem of penalties. He understands and is sympathetic when a player is guilty of an infraction because of aggressiveness. Like jumping offside because you are trying to get off on the snap and make a play. What he abhors are those penalties, which give the other team a first down that keeps a drive alive. "When players are guilty of foolish penalties, we do discipline them, but it is a constant effort to develop a team which is able to avoid foolish penalties," he says.

He took note of the fact that Davey Pollack was probably the least penalized player on the Georgia defense, a fact of his rare concentration and discipline on the field. Martinez loved No. 47's impact on the defense. But there was more.

"Just to be around him and watch him work. You dream about players like that on your team. It was a thrill to see him play on Saturday, but it was inspiring to watch him in practice. He simply worked harder than anybody else. He gave second effort in practice just like he did in games. He has so much passion for football. I was never surprised when he made a big play. He worked to make big plays.

"It is hard for a defensive back to cover a guy, man-to-man, for more than about three seconds. To stop a passing attack, you must have that defensive rush. The defensive line doesn't have to sack the quarterback. If a D lineman can make a quarterback rush his throw, hurry him just a little, that may enable the defensive back to make a play. We knew that David Pollack would always be doing his best to put the quarterback on the ground or make him throw off balance or mess up his rhythm. The defensive line and secondary go hand in hand to play winning defense.

"I don't believe David could have made that play against South Carolina in 2002 nor the one in the Outback Bowl—two remarkable sack and steal plays—if he had not been so fundamentally sound. His work ethic was an inspiration to us all at Georgia."

Much of Martinez's football philosophy was learned under Jimmy Johnson at Miami. Johnson coached the Dallas Cowboys to a pair of Super Bowl titles and later coached the Miami Dolphins. "He believed in hard work," Martinez says. "He had enthusiasm, he underscored fundamentals and he thought every player on the team should run to the ball. A lot of what I believe started with Coach Johnson."

You can't win championships without defensive backs that find ways to slow and hopefully shut down the opposition.

Martinez's formula for success:

Work ethic and attitude, where only your BEST is good enough.

Preparation meets opportunity. "You have to want to learn. You must gain knowledge of your opponent and yourself. Tape study is vital to success at any position."

Fundaments are critical. "Work hard on your tackling technique," he frequently advises his defensive backs. You must become efficient at making open field tackles. "Make plays in space," he stresses over and over.

You must be able to defend against the big play, which requires learning to play the angles and understanding scenarios and plans that vary from game to game.

Remember YAC (yards after catch). "So many defenses get hurt when they let receivers gain extra yards after catching the ball. We want to cut down on that as much as possible. We always say it's not the catch, but the run afterwards that breaks down a defense.

The play of the Georgia defensive backs has been a winning style of football. Nobody is happier when the team succeeds than Martinez, who understands better than most what it means to be an American and to have played the great game of college football.

■■■

THE IMPORTANCE
OF SCHEDULE GOOD LUCK

The final season of The Davids concluded with 10 victories. Not bad, but they wanted more. They expected to play in the Georgia Dome. Nonetheless, it was an enjoyable senior year. They were not ungrateful.

Because of their experience, seniors are always important to any football team. Seniors have been there, and they can lead the team with seasoned performance. They often set the emotional tone. When a team wins a championship, more than likely when the coach fingers the key ingredients for success, he will start by praising the leadership of his seniors. If you've got a David Greene and a Davey Pollack on your team, then the adrenalin and the anticipation peak early.

Such senior leadership, however, can be a factor that heightens unrealistic expectations. Players are human. For the most part, they read the paper. They hear the experts on SportsCenter, but, most of all, when they walk down the streets of their hometowns and neighborhoods or show up at any gathering at any locale, they hear how great they are going to be. That's heady stuff.

If we assess this hype, as does Mark Richt, forever the positive thinker, we can say, "It is nice that they say good things about us." However, the higher the expectations, the greater the challenge. Pre-season rankings are an inexact science. After Auburn failed to measure up to exalted pre-season forecasts in 2003, Tiger coach Tommy Tuberville was asked about the results at a pre-season press conference in 2004. "You guys picked us No.1," he said. "You didn't do such a good job yourselves." With no pre-season hype and ranking expectations and with an excellent talent base, Auburn enjoyed a banner year in '04. It is best not to get carried away with the hype.

Prior to every season, those who follow football sit down and peruse the schedule, trying to figure wins and losses. Most Bulldog fans I am familiar with estimated it this way for the Greene-Pollack senior season. Beat South Carolina on the road, LSU and Tennessee at home and, at last, whip Florida in Jacksonville. The momentum from all that would be enough to carry Georgia past Auburn, which had to be down after a disappointing season in '03. Hence, this could be a national championship contender.

Didn't work out that way as we know. Before the season, if you are up on your football, you likely would have concluded that to defeat LSU and Tennessee back-to-back, in addition to

HAIRY DAWG

You know Uga, Georgia's renowned mascot. You see him cavorting about in living color on the sideline. There is little about Uga that hasn't been disclosed in print. He has been celebrated in a book and a 2-hour DVD. You also know Hairy Dawg. Well, perhaps. You see his mascot uniform, the distinctive head and the non-wagging short tail protruding from the rear. You see him on the ESPN mascot promos, but you don't see the man inside—Matthew Perkins. He works diligently to enhance the Bulldog spirit. In his words:

"There are actually two of us who play the role of Hairy Dawg on gamedays, myself [Matthew Perkins] and Josh Whitlock. We switch off at halftime of every game. Fans can tell the distinction of who is dressed up in the suit by Hairy's socks. I wear red socks and Josh wears black socks. No matter where we are, before the game starts, Josh and I always take a warm-up lap around the field. I then go to the locker room to get ready and put on all my gear.

"As you've probably noticed, Hairy is always dressed in the same red uniform that the team wears. That is one thing that sets him apart. For most schools, the mascot's costumes are dif-

ferent from their team's, but Hairy dresses like his players. He looks like he is ready to run out on the field and catch a pass! During pregame, Hairy interacts with the fans by taking pictures and signing autographs (anything to pump up the crowd). The closer it gets to game time, Hairy gets into position to run out and lead his team onto the field. During the game, whether it is through dancing around or playing with Uga, Hairy's sole job is to keep the fans up and show his support of the team."

Florida and Auburn on the road, would require superior and seasoned personnel across the board and plenty of luck to boot—such as avoiding injuries and turnovers. The fact was, Georgia was good, but it didn't have enough experienced personnel on defense, which was thin in the D line. Linebacker Tony Taylor, a quarterback on defense, was lost for the season in the spring game. That was a critical loss. Never have I seen Brian VanGorder, the defensive coordinator, more frustrated. Publicly, he kept a stiff upper lip; privately he growled in head shaking frustration. "No. 3 in the nation," he said with marked contempt of the

Bulldogs' pre-season ranking. "The people who rate teams don't know anything about ball."

Aside from the high expectations, the biggest problem for Georgia in '04 was, unquestionably, schedule alignment. Schedules are made years in advance, and the football coach has no control over alignment.

It broke just right for Auburn. The Tigers hosted Louisiana-Monroe to start the season, then Mississippi State, a slam-dunk in '04, followed by LSU at home. This game was close. It could have gone either way. But the biggest advantage was that the Tigers' next game was The Citadel at

There's an All-American David...

...on both sides of the ball

home. Oh, what a difference it would have made if Georgia had played a team like The Citadel between LSU and Tennessee.

After waxing The Citadel 33-3, Auburn went on the road to Knoxville for a 34-10 thumping of a Tennessee team struggling to get established with rookie quarterbacks. That same weekend Georgia was dismantling LSU, 45-16, elevating Athens to a memorable high that was difficult for the coaches to deal with. Tennessee, though losing to Auburn big at home, was stabilizing, and Georgia was psychologically off. We know the results.

After defeating Tennessee in Knoxville, Auburn had, as it turned out, one real challenge left, Georgia at home on November 13th, with an open date the week prior.

The schedule won for Auburn in '04 as much as anything. Put a lesser opponent on Georgia's schedule between LSU and Tennessee, and there is no telling what this team might have accomplished. The Bulldogs play six home games every year, but in 2004, Georgia hit the road four straight weekends at a time when a championship team ought to be peaking with a big game at home. This is what happened for Auburn.

Historically, the winningest coaches were those who had schedule control. General Neyland, the great Tennessee coach who won 82.9 percent of his games, would have never scheduled two tough opponents back-to-back. Bear Bryant, at Alabama, managed his schedule with the same objective. Coaches don't control schedules anymore, and to win a championship today, the schedule must be favorable, not so much with quality of competition but with the alignment and home field advantage for the big games. Georgia, perhaps, has never had a more unfavor-

2004 SCHEDULE / RESULTS

DAY	DATE	OPPONENT	LOCATION	OUTCOME
SAT	09/04/2004	GEORGIA SOUTHERN	ATHENS, GA.	W, 48-28
SAT	09/11/2004	SOUTH CAROLINA	COLUMBIA, SC	W, 20-16
SAT	09/18/2004	MARSHALL	ATHENS, GA.	W, 13-3
SAT	10/02/2004	LSU	ATHENS, GA.	W, 45-16
SAT	10/09/2004	TENNESSEE	ATHENS, GA.	L, 19-14
SAT	10/16/2004	VANDERBILT	ATHENS, GA.	W, 33-3
SAT	10/23/2004	ARKANSAS	FAYETTEVILLE, ARK.	W, 20-14
SAT	10/30/2004	FLORIDA	JACKSONVILLE, FLA.	W, 31-24
SAT	11/06/2004	KENTUCKY	LEXINGTON, KY.	W, 62-17
SAT	11/13/2004	AUBURN	AUBURN, ALA.	L, 24-6
SAT	11/27/2004	GEORGIA TECH	ATHENS, GA.	W, 19-13
SAT	01/01/2005	WISCONSIN OUTBACK BOWL	TAMPA, FLA.	W, 24-21

able schedule alignment than in 2004.

One of the greatest performances in Georgia history had to be Vince Dooley's 1980 team, leaving everything on the field to defeat South Carolina in Athens, 13-10, and then going to Jacksonville the next weekend to post a 26-21 victory over Florida in the last minute. The Bulldogs were a championship team and championship teams find a way to win critical games, but how many times will a Buck Belue find a Lindsay Scott for a 93-yard touchdown completion to pull a game out?

When the '04 season ended, Mark Richt had completed four seasons as the Bulldog head coach. His winning percentage was 80.7. Only one other SEC coach, Phillip Fulmer, at 79.7, is close to 80% success, but in '04 Fulmer finished his 13th season at Tennessee.

Nick Saban, whose reputation was flaunted favorably by the national media, jumped to the NFL after five seasons. He was 48-16 at LSU with a winning percentage of 75.0. His run at LSU, however, was accented by a national championship.

When Mark Richt hit the recruiting trail in early January '05, his staff had much to sell. When they sang the praises of their head coach, they began by noting that he not only owned the best winning percentage of active head coaches in the SEC, but also he had set a pattern of winning consistently.

The most successful three-year period in Georgia history, in terms of total victories, concluded in 2004. Richt's first four teams finished one behind the 1980-83 teams for the most wins with 42. However, Richt's past three teams experienced victory 34 times, the most of any three consecutive Bulldog teams. The 1980-82 teams won 33 times, but, as Richt is quick to point out, his last three squads played more games. For the record, 34-6 versus 33-3 for the Herschel Walker teams. The best winning percentage for any Bulldog teams belongs to those of the early 80s.

What this suggests is that Richt's last three teams have something in common with Dooley's Dawgs of 1980-83. There is a consistency of winning. When you average 10 wins a year, you have something to boast about. Richt pointed this out to his players in the locker room pre-game of the Outback Bowl in Tampa: "Nine wins is a good season. 10 is a great season. It is not, however, perfection, which is our goal."

Perfection in college football is difficult to come by. Not many coaches ever achieve that distinction. Bear Bryant pulled it off three times, when there were fewer games played, and he had schedule control. Bobby Bowden has had only one undefeated team in his illustrious career during which he has won the most games of any coach in Division I-A history.

If you are going to reach perfection, you need that consistency of success. Some day it may happen to Richt, who has maintained excellence from the start. His first team, which was adjusting to a new staff and a new system, lost three games by 26 points, four by 30, if you include the Music City Bowl loss to Boston College.

When Richt arrived, he patterned his program after what he experienced under Bowden at FSU.

Greenie celebrates after a big play

It was a good model for him to follow. The Seminoles won the ACC seemingly forever and were perennially ranked in the top five.

There is a telling difference by comparison.

The ACC did not offer the same challenge Richt has faced and will continue to face at Georgia. It is tougher to win the SEC East than most entire conferences. Bowden, in truth, had it somewhat easy, which is why he was reluctant to join the SEC when FSU was invited. Southern Cal, for example, has had, with cross-town rival UCLA being down, in 2004, only two tough games, California, which has not been a perennial power in college football lately and Washington, also down. When Oklahoma beats Texas, it has conquered the only real threat in its division. Georgia has three high-powered opponents in Tennessee, Florida and Auburn on its annual schedule. South Carolina had designs on a title under Lou Holtz and will see its lofty ambition intensify under Steve Spurrier. Is the SEC East currently not the toughest division in college football?

Until 2004, when Southern California, Oklahoma, Utah and Auburn finished their regular seasons undefeated, more often than not, the national champion lately has lost at least one game.

Watching Mark Richt up close during his time in Athens, I have concluded that he has the making of a coach who will someday add a national championship to his resume. Even that goal is very difficult to achieve. Consider that a man highly regarded by his peers, Bo Schembechler of Michigan, never claimed the big prize.

If you hang around first place, as Richt has done, you have a chance to win it all. Jack Nicklaus has not only won more major championships in golf than any man who has ever played the game, he has finished second more than anybody else. Hang around the lead long enough, and perfection may someday become a reality.

I like Mark Richt's chances.

For Dave Van Halanger, it was serendipity wrapped in gratefulness when he got to know David Greene and Davey Pollack. They were young men after his own heart. They had the right stuff when it came to attitude.

"Greenie was so laid back as everybody knows," Van Halanger says. "But you knew that he loved the game, he wanted to learn and improve and he expected more of himself than anybody." Then he laughed and paused when he mentioned Pollack's name. "He's crazy. A crazy player working for a crazy coach, what a team!"

The common bond with the trio of Greene-Pollack-Van Halanger is attitude. Different approaches, different styles, but they all think positive.

Van Halanger, like Mark Richt, who brought him to Georgia, has a spiritual underpinning with his work as the Bulldogs' strength and conditioning Coach. He often professes his belief in God in his work, but never buttonholing a kid and giving him a lecture, admonishment or a sales job—just quietly intoning the name of God with overtones of thanksgiving and good will.

At a photo session after the Outback Bowl with the two Davids, there was a scene with the kids piling on the two players. Mike, Van Halanger's four-year-old adopted son, enjoyed that.

As Van Halanger observed, he smiled, "You know, he got beat up at the orphanage in the Ukraine a lot. He enjoyed getting in on the action when it was fun."

Then, as he looked forlornly into a fading sunset, he said softly. "I just wish I had the money to help those kids. How nice it would be to take a plane over there, pick up and load and bring them here so they could have a chance in life. You can't imagine how kids are abused in this world, and the worst thing is so many of those orphanages are selling them. How tragic, making money off of kids." You could see the hurt in his eyes.

If you know Van Halanger, he believes he should help kids. Why be involved with athletics if that is not your mission? Train them to be the best players they can be. Make tem bigger, make them stronger and give them all the tools possible to win football games. But, provide emotional and spiritual direction as well.

Winning calls attention to aspiring and deserving kids. They may repay society by helping other kids along the way. They all want to extend their careers into the National Football League

Dave Van Halanger, strength and conditioning coach, with Greenie

and rake in the big bucks but many of them wind up back home in their communities doing good works. Drugs and disappointment find many of them. Some become n'er-do-wells in business, but football and athletics offer opportunities of which many take advantage.

Dave Van Halanger is here to help those who want to better themselves and to make something of their lives. If he can help one, just one, then he will have accomplished something in his own life. Truth of the matter, he has helped many in his time at Florida State and Georgia.

Van Halanger didn't write *The Power of Positive Thinking,* but he could have. If you believe in reincarnation, you could make a case that the Georgia strength and conditioning Coach has had another life and that it was he who influenced Norman Vincent Peale to write the book by that title.

Van Halanger is a man who passionately

believes in kids. He makes them feel good about themselves. The mind, he stresses, is just as important as all those other things that athletes need to compete successfully. To begin with "you gotta have heart." Was it he who wrote that tune? Natural ability he stresses is important, but you only reach your goals by accentuating the positive.

Let's begin with the premise that Georgia has good football players. Those who line up as starters compare favorably with those who line up elsewhere in this great college football universe. He believes that with all his heart and soul. "I wouldn't trade ours for anybody's," he said with the straightest face in the summer of '04.

However, when asked about the depth of the team, he dropped his positive guard—but just a bit. "We are thin," he admits, "but the young kids have gotta step up. They can do it. I know they can. I've seen 'em work out all summer."

It is doubtful that anybody is as close to the players on the team as Van Halanger. Position coaches, naturally, have a strategic role to play, and they develop rapport with players, too. It is Van Halanger, however, who is with them the most. He's getting their minds in championship sync for the next season almost as soon as they unpack upon returning from the bowl game.

Winter workouts, mat drills, spring practice— doesn't matter—they hear his sage advice daily. They identify with his sincere spiritual preachments, his upbeat encouragement and his belief that if you start the season undefeated, there is no reason for it not to stay that way.

In his past 30 years of college football, 17 with which he worked have finished ranked in the top seven. "In the last 19 years," he says with grateful pride, "I haven't begun a preseason with a team that did not have a chance to finish ranked No. 1."

Van Halanger admits that he is, first of all, a college football fanatic. "This," he says, his voice rising like an evangelist's, "is the ideal job for me.

I love what I am doing. I believe in these kids."

When he sermonizes to the Bulldogs, he reminds them how fortunate they are. "Here's what you have men, and think how few college players have what you have:

A great, and I mean great, educational opportunity. You get to play before 93,000-plus fans. You have a chance to win a national championship.

When you go to the stadium, you get there by going through something called the DawgWalk and there are 25,000 there to let you know they are passionate about our team.

They care here at the University of Georgia."

Then he reminds them not to take all that for granted. "You have an awesome experience men. Let's take advantage of our opportunity."

Mark Richt, from the first time he met with Georgia's players, underscored the family theme. The best salesman to articulate that pitch has been Dave Van Halanger, who always sees the glass as half full, and if there is any way to fill it, he will. Winning teams have heart, and Coach Van is the Dawgs' heart doctor.

+ + +

It was Jan. 12, 2005—the start of Mark Richt's fifth year. For Dave Van Halanger it was like any other year. It was time to think championship. That was the way it was every year he was at Florida State. When he, Mark Richt and the new staff began in the winter of 2001, they didn't know what the team would be like. They didn't know if the Bulldogs would buy into the plan. Identify with the system and make the desired commitment.

The Richt plan was new. It was different. Learning his complex offensive system was a challenge for many of the players, but David Greene took to his offense right away. He was anxious to learn. At the end of the season, after winning eight games, which would excite most campuses, Richt

and his friend Van Halanger were sorely disappointed. They thought Georgia should have done better. Losing in the last seconds at home to South Carolina and Auburn disappointed them deeply. They felt things should have been better. It would be in 2002. There was an SEC Championship ring.

In 2003, the Bulldogs—side whacked by injury—made it back to the championship game, and when 2004 began, there was optimism across the board.

Not making it to the championship game again stung the pride of the coaching staff. FYWTD—First Year Without The Davids—had become reality and Van Halanger took the position that life goes on. He had been there before. He had worked with teams that had lost outstanding players, and 2005 would be no different. Just deal with it.

The first thing, as it had been since the first day on the job, is to think positive and to start building an attitude. He began working on that plan less than a fortnight after the final whistle had sounded in Tampa.

He had T-shirts printed up with messages on the front and back. The front trumpeted "Leadership Equals Enthusiasm." On the back, it said "SEC Champs. National Champs. Family."

Losing The Davids, Thomas Davis and Odell Thurman, Reggie Brown and Fred Gibson, and he's talking championship? With the parity in college football today and the successful recruiting established by the Richt team, Van Halanger says with that big wide grin of his, "Why not us?"

If you have a chance, the first thing is that you must believe you can. Coach Van believes. Coach Van preaches his belief, and when the players showed up for winter weightlifting, he passed out those T-shirts and the Bulldogs, to use an old Navy term, immediately "turned to." They went to work with optimism and a smile.

There was a buzz of excitement in the air and

Keith Gray (left) and Clay Walker display in early '05 Van Halanger's goals for the season

as the grunts and groans began to echo across the weight room. You could hear the chatter of the hard working players, the weights bounding off the weight platforms and the preferred music, which accompanies the youth of today.

There is a new theme every year with Van Halanger, who pays tribute to the members of the team enthusiastically. "We have good kids," he says, without reluctance. "Our kids have pride. They want to be starters. They want to succeed. The NFL is there, they have aspirations, but they want to do well for Georgia."

Then, in his low-key evangelical style, Van Halanger waxed optimistic, just like he had done the four winters prior. "Every January it is a different year, but the goal is always the same. Every team has a different personality, different chemistry. Our first priority is team building. We talk when we get together, and following the Outback Bowl, we asked ourselves, 'Why not us?' Why should we not think about the Rose Bowl? It fell in place for

Auburn in '04, why can't it happen for us? We have good players. What we want to achieve is in place.

"I see big, strong guys, wanting to get stronger. I see talent and attitude. We are good, but these guys want to be great. They appreciate family.

"With Coach Richt the core principles and values stay the same. Players leave but the core is there. When you have good players and young players mature, then they will step up and produce. Why not us?"

At the start of a new year, he had nothing but good thoughts. That is a Van Halanger trademark. A team cannot feel sorry for itself because it has just lost great players, and The Davids were two of the greatest in Bulldog history.

Football teams must always look to the future, and nobody would be more compatible with that premise than The Davids themselves, who expect to be interested and supportive alumni. They have already talked about coming back to a game and tailgating. They left Georgia with other fields to conquer, but they will return with substantial emotion for their favorite team.

Van Halanger kept in touch with them as they began pursuit of their professional careers. "You feel good just talking to those guys," he said. "They made us proud, didn't they?" He smiled softly, underscoring how proud he was that these two stars came Georgia's way. Then he returned to planning for '05.

Life goes on. The Davids will agree.

WEIGHT ROOM RULES

Posted throughout the weight room are Dave Van Halanger's weight room rules. He is not just the Bulldogs' strength and conditioning coach; he is the attitude coach. If you BELIEVE you can win, you are on the way to achieving your goal.

You gotta believe! Because Dave Van Halanger believes, the Dawgs believe. His rules include:

1) Watch your language
2) Be on time for every workout
3) Work a full day
4) Finish with great enthusiasm
5) Eat and sleep to win
6) See yourself making a great play
7) Ask God for help

Also the following signs appear in the weight room:

G.A.T.A.
DO YOU HAVE A BAD CASE OF THE WANTS?
THE DESIRE TO WIN WITHOUT THE
DESIRE TO PREPARE IS WORTHLESS.

BE PROUD TO BE A GEORGIA BULLDOG.

And last, my favorite is:

"DID ANYONE OUTWORK YOU TODAY?"

The players see this sign when they exit the weight room. If players take its message to heart, success on the field is enhanced considerably.

G.A.T.A. This is a long-standing term, associated with Georgia football, and is another contribution from another Beloved Dawg, former defensive coordinator, Erk Russell.

At Bulldog Club meetings, speeches and coaching clinics, he would always explain, with an appropriate pause at the end, that it meant, "Get After Their ... Anatomy."

For several years the slogan went dormant, but Jon Fabris, a great admirer of Erk's, brought it back to prominence when the Richt staff took over.

Erk came up with the slogan at halftime of the Georgia-Georgia Tech game at Grant Field in 1965. The score was 10-0 in favor of the Bulldogs, but Erk was worried and told the team, 'Men, if they don't score, we win.' In the second half, the Bulldogs, with an unbalanced line on offense and tenacious defense, defeated a favored Tech team, 17-7.

As he was talking with the defense at intermission, Erk noticed that a piece of equipment was stenciled, "Georgia Tech Athletic Association." He cleverly said, "Men let's move one of those "A's" over by the "G", make it G.A.T.A. Get After Their Ass." It brought an enthusiastic reaction from the defense, which took command of the Tech offense in the final two quarters.

It has become a catch phrase. It meant something to the team, both the defense and the offense. If you do G.A.T.A., the opportunity for success is duly enhanced. Whenever the team busses pulled into the motel for road games, often the players would see G.A.T.A. greeting them from the motel marquee.

TODD BLACKLEDGE

When CBS televised the final home game of The Davids' career, Todd Blackledge used two words to describe the Snellville Sensations. With David Greene, in Todd's opinion, the one word that best described him as a college player was "poise." For Davey Pollack, he chose the word "passion."

Blackledge, a knowledgeable and articulate former quarterback who led Penn State to a national championship, was especially appreciative of Greene's unflappable demeanor. "I don't think I've ever watched a guy who was cooler under pressure than David. You could tell that the pressure would never become too great for him to become frustrated. I really like the way he played the position.

"With David Pollack, he played every play like it was his last. For a defensive lineman to go as hard as he did all the time is remarkable. He seemed to get stronger as the game went along.

"It was fun to cover Georgia because of those guys. They seemed to always rise to the occasion. It was fun to meet with them when we were in Athens. They were very pleasant to deal with.

"Both have represented Georgia well. They are what you expect in college football players. They are well rounded. They play football with the greatest of individual effort, but they are team guys. They are not ego guys. You have to like that.

"They strike me as two players who got the most out of their college life. Other than not winning a national championship, I don't see how their careers could have been more enjoyable."

Todd and CBS worked 21 games in The Davids' careers. He saw the signature play of each—Pollack's takeaway for a TD in Columbia, and Greene's fourth-down pass to Michael Johnson to win the SEC East at Auburn—both in the 2002 season.

"When Pollack made his play against South Carolina, it was difficult to grasp what he had done immediately. It happened so fast, but then you could decipher it when you saw the replay. Verne Lundquist (play-by-play announcer) knew immediately. His spotter Joe Kasztejna had played college football at Colgate and picked up on what had happened, right away. It showed Pollack's exceptional athleticism and intensity with which he plays. It was an incredible play. I've never seen anything like it.

"When David Greene made the pass to win the Auburn game, it was one of the coolest plays under pressure that I have ever seen. To make that throw under pressure shows you what an outstanding college quarterback he was. As a quarterback, I can appreciate what he pulled off. With the adrenalin and anxiousness of the moment, it would have been easy for him to throw the ball away, but he put it to where the receiver could make a play on it. In that situation he could have thrown it too far or just a little off to the side and it becomes uncatchable. I would have understood if he had missed it. That was great quarterback execution."

On Wednesday before heading down to Shellman Bluff to fish with my longtime friend John Donaldson, I met with Coach Richt to review the game. The reaction was the same as it was before the LSU game. "We must make plays," Mark said. "Greenie has to have a big day again. Nobody has more quality athletes than Florida. They are capable of big plays too. We simply have to find a way to win." Since Florida had fired Ron Zook, for whom his players obviously had great affection, everybody in Athens was concerned that the Gators might play "lights out." After all they had nothing to lose. They could throw caution to the wind.

"When I see those guys on tape, I see great talent," Mark said. "I don't know who will get the job, but he will have an unbelievable collection of talent when he takes over in Gainesville. When it comes to talent, I don't see a dropoff at any position." He seemed more guarded, but I detected a twinkle in his eye. Not like LSU, but there was something about his demeanor that made me think that this would be the year the drought ended in Jacksonville.

One of his decisions made good sense. For years, the team headquartered at the Marriott Hotel just off J. Turner Butler freeway from I-95 to the beaches. It had become a zoo. Too many people. Too much noise. Too many distractions. Mark felt a change was in order, so the team moved down to St. Augustine to the World Golf Village Renaissance Resort. Good move. No distractions there. That may not have made the difference in the outcome of the game, but I can assure you, the Bulldogs will be going back there in the future.

A few Georgia fans checked in, but they were like the players, ready to turn in early. It was quiet, almost lonely. You need that kind of environment when you play a football game.

The radio crew arrived at Alltel Stadium at 10:00 a.m., more than five hours before kickoff. Already the tailgaters had their tents up and running, their tailgates down and their game face on. Those fans who go to the game are as loyal and dedicated as any there is anywhere. They are what college football is all about. Georgia just needs to win its share.

Since I go to bed early, I had had a good night's rest, but I immediately went to the locker room, found a corner where I could stretch out and review my game notes. I dozed off when my muscles relaxed.

All's well that ends well in Alltel Stadium

Dave Allen and the student managers and trainers were there by the time we arrived. These students work hard. It is a fun experience and a rewarding association, but demanding. They put in a lot of hours. Like the football players, they have to attend class. They must post passing grades. They are the first to arrive for the games and practice also. They are the last to leave. They put in as much time and effort as the players. The rewards are less, the tributes few and far between, but these kids love the Bulldogs. Let's hear it for the student managers and student trainers!

After a rest in the Georgia locker room, I walked on the field and could tell it was going to be a warm day. Coach Richt feels that days like that, after the temperatures have dropped in Athens, give Florida an advantage. Mainly because their quarterback, Chris Leak, gets such endless mileage out of broken plays, as much or more than any quarterback in the league.

As I looked around the stadium, I thought about the fact that the Super Bowl would be played in this stadium in February. "I bet," I thought to myself, "they won't be able to pack one more body in this place that we'll have for our game with Florida. And it is not a one-time thing.

THE DAVIDS ON THE ROAD

In the career of The Davids, the road was good to them. They only lost to LSU in 2003 and Auburn in 2004, winning all other out-of-town campus games during their four years.

Of the three games lost in Sanford Stadium (South Carolina 14-9 and Auburn 24-17 in 2001 and Tennessee 19-14 in 2004), it was a case of having an opportunity to win late, but coming up short in the closing seconds.

As a matter of fact, except for the SEC playoff in 2003 (LSU won 34-13) and the Auburn game in 2004 (the Tigers won 24-6), the Dawgs, in the career of The Davids, could have won every game.

We do it every year." The largest crowds to see games in this facility, which the city of Jacksonville built to accommodate professional football, have been for the Georgia-Florida game. In fact, a record crowd with temporary bleachers added saw the Bulldogs and the Gators: 84,753. The Super Bowl attendance in '05 was 78,125.

In the locker room pregame, there was quiet resignation with the team. The Dawgs seemed relaxed and focused. There was that look of confidence. The look that signaled, "We are ready to take care of business."

When Dave Van Halanger called the team up for Mark's pre-game thoughts, Jeremy Thomas was exiting the bathroom. I could hear his cleats scraping across the tile floor as he rushed to join the huddle.

Mark pointed out that he wanted the players to play hard, but clean. "The officials will be looking for personal fouls. Remember, men, if somebody tries to provoke you into a fight, don't let your emotions get you in trouble. If they throw you out for fighting, you will be suspended for two games. Doesn't matter what they do to you, don't retaliate. Don't hurt

YOUR team.

"Offense, make Florida stop us. Don't stop ourselves. Defense, be disciplined first, then hit like a ton of bricks. Remember discipline first, but then hit with all you've got. Men, you are well prepared. Go out there, and play like it."

There was a rush of emotion at that point. You could tell these Dawgs were ready to play. They were ready to hit somebody. It had been a week of

Two Dawgs with two bulldogs

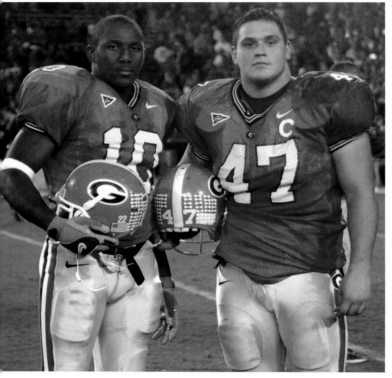

Davey with Thomas Davis

intense practice. With the University taking a holiday, the coaches were allowed by NCAA rules to spend more time on the field and in the classroom. An effort was made to pack as much into the practice sessions as possible.

As the half neared, Georgia lost a fumble at the Florida goal line that stunted the momentum. A touchdown there would have given the Bulldogs a 28-7 lead. On top of that, Des Williams, the fullback who shared playing time with Jeremy Thomas, went out with a shoulder sprain. More debilitating than that, Thomas Davis was lost with a knee sprain.

"Two warriors have gone down," Mark told the team. "We have to come together and play smart and tough. You need to give your best effort. Leaders, step up. We don't want this game to get away. Offense, what did we say? Don't stop ourselves. Get ready for an emotional second half."

VanGorder was the most disturbed coach in the room. He told the defensive players they were not playing well. "Our pursuit angles are poor. Our tackling is not crisp. If you want to win the game, you've got to activate a pass rush." (Little did any of us know that the next time he would talk to defensive players in this stadium, he would be coaching the Jacksonville Jaguars' linebackers.)

Florida pressed the tired Bulldog defense in the second half. I never felt the game was slipping away, but I was worried. When we needed a big play, we got not one, but two. Greenie, on first and 10 from his own 15-yard line, scrambled under pressure and connected with Reggie Brown for 51 yards and a first down. Six plays later, he hit Fred Gibson on the slant for 15 yards and a touchdown to make it 31-21. It reminded us again, that for four years David Greene had made big plays often when Georgia needed it most. "Scoring on that drive was big," Mark sighed as we began his post-game locker room show. "I'll sleep well tonight."

The team flew home. We drove to St. Simons Island on Sunday to spend the night with Anne and Jim Minter. Jim, a former sportswriter and former editor of the Atlanta Journal-Constitution, has a condominium at the King and Prince. He is one of those traditionalists who does not want the game moved. If we keep the game in Jacksonville, we would make one of Georgia's greatest Bulldog couples mighty happy. I do think about that.

Long-suffering Georgia fans vented their pent-up emotions after the game from North Florida to Savannah, mindful that a few Bulldog victories might prolong the existing venue for the annual match-up with Florida.

On the beach at St. Simons on Sunday, practically every sunbather wore something red and black although temperatures were such that it was a day to dress with less. Bicyclists rode the beach with flags of their favorite team flapping in the breeze, and nobody flashed any orange even though Halloween had just ended.

No more would they pack up late in the day and head home with their heads hanging low. All was right with the world. They could wave and honk their horns on the way back to their respective haunts with love and laughter reigning supreme. The hated Gators had been subdued and pride restored.

In this business of football, it is good to establish positive results for your constituency. Bragging rights must come with the purchase of season tickets. While that is not anything anybody can guarantee, it is something that comes to be expected over a period of time.

The challenge, however, intensifies. College football has become so big and popular; everybody wants the big prize and works daily to get it. If you reside in the SEC East, you have the greatest challenge in college football of reaching the top.

∎∎∎

OCTOBER 29TH – NOVEMBER 1ST 2004 ITINERARY

FIRDAY OCTOBER 29

8:00-11:00	Pick up travel sweats in equipment room
11:45	Buses depart from ECVwith players who live there
Noon	TEAM WALK THRU AT SOCCER/SOFTBALL COMPLEX (ALL TRAVEL PLAYERS)
12:05	DEPART Athens—Soccer/Softball complex
1:30	Arrive Atlanta Hartsfield Airport
2:30	Depart on Delta flight #9796
3:35	Arrive St. Augustine
4:25	Arrive at Hotel (World Golf Village Renaissance Resort)
5:00	Team Dinner (room C)
5:45	Coach Richt (room B)
6:15-6:45	Kicking Meetings (room B)
6:45-7:45	Offensive Meetings (room A) Defensive Meetings (B)
7:45-8	Snacks (pre-con area)
8-8:30	Devotion—Optional (room B)
11:00	LIGHTS OUT and quiet!

SATURDAY OCTOBER 30

8:00	Wake Up Call
8:30	Breakfast (room C)
9:05-9:45	Kicking meetings (room B)
9:45- 10:30	Offensive meetings (A) Defensive meetings (B)
11:30	Team Meal (room C)
11:45	Taping immediately after meal (room D)
12:30	Chapel—Optional (room B)
12:40	Motivational Tape (room B)
12:55	Depart Hotel
1:40	Arrive Alltel Stadium
3:35	KICKOFF—BEAT FLORIDA
	Turn back clocks when you get back!

SUNDAY OCTOBER 31

2:00	Treatment
7:15-8	Study Hall (Freshmen) Assigned tutor sessions

MONDAY NOVEMBER 1

7-8:30	Study Hall at Rankin Smith Center
Weightlifting	Frosh-2:30, char. Ed./3:00-Off/3:30-Def
4-4:30	Kicking meetings
4:30-4:45	Offense/Defense scouting reports
4:45-5:45	Segment meetings
5:50	Honor Roll (field)
7:30	Dinner at Butts-Mehre

CHAPTER TWENTY-FOUR
SELL A PLAYER. SELL YOURSELF.

In January, Mark Richt had planned a coaching vacation to Hawaii, but—"Bam! Bam!"—just like a double barrel shotgun going off with a covey of quail taking flight, two coaches left and a third, Rodney Garner, was being courted by LSU. It was too much. He had to take care of business. Richt stayed home.

The Bulldog coach had begun interviewing replacement coaches for Brian VanGorder, the defensive coordinator, who bolted for the Jacksonville Jaguars. Right on his heels, running backs Coach Ken Rucker lit out for the University of Texas. That was bad enough, but as a critical recruiting weekend was nigh, LSU approached Garner.

Garner wants to be a head coach, so nobody could blame him for moving up, but he experienced some soul-searching trepidation. He wasn't unhappy at Georgia. That weighed heavily on his mind. He kept reminding himself the program remains headed in the right direction. "If it were going in the wrong direction that would be another matter," he noted. Furthermore, he thought about the bird in hand, how secure and comfortable he was in Athens.

Then, he began to reflect on what he had been telling prospective high school athletes since he

became a member of the Bulldog coaching staff. His favorable-for-Athens emotions wouldn't allow him to make a knee-jerk decision.

If he left, he would be leaving a group of capable defensive linemen. He had recruited them; he had talked to them about loyalty and opportunity. It didn't seem like the right thing to do—to up and leave.

After reflecting on a number of reasons to stay, he reminded himself of what was great about Athens and the University of Georgia. "This is one of the top 10 places in the country to play football and get a quality education. The students love this place, and you can sense it. People come on our campus and get a special feeling. It is genuine. There are a lot of places where it is manufactured. I know what kind of man Mark Richt is and what he represents. Our staff works well together. There are no unknowns here. To tell you the truth, Georgia sells itself to a large degree. It is a great place to be."

Even so, he never pulls any punches, neither with the players he recruits nor their parents. "Parents know if a kid comes to Georgia, he'll be disciplined, he'll be required to go to class and study hall," Rodney says. He'll be counseled to stay

Rodney Garner: "The University of Georgia sells itself."

on course for a degree. Some won't achieve that goal, but we will do our best to make it happen. We will work him hard, but we will be honest with him and try to assist him."

Recruiting is about building relationships, and Garner is one of the best. Players are always welcome at his home, where Rodney, Kim and their six daughters will invite them to pull up a chair at his dining room table. "It won't be a five-course meal; it may be hotdogs, but they will always be welcome," Rodney says. His players know that and they appreciate it.

A little-known fact of recruiting is that a school like Oklahoma may send a recruiter to Georgia and offer scholarships to a dozen to two dozen kids in the state. The Sooners may not sign any of those players, but they might pick up a couple of prep stars who are taken by the attention.

Georgia can't get away with that. "Just like our

other coaches, I have to live in this state," Rodney points out. "We have to walk the hallways of those schools year after year, and we have to make good on any offer.

"I happen to agree with Coach Richt's policy. We never offer a player a scholarship and pull the offer off the table. That makes it harder to recruit, and we have to work hard at making the smart decision on who we think can play for us," Garner says.

In any conversation with Rodney Garner about coaching, the topic of recruiting surfaces. If the subject is recruiting, coaching comes into play. Garner's life revolves around both, as with all coaches. With him there is, perhaps, a little more priority when it comes to recruiting, since he is the point man for the Bulldogs.

When he talks to parents, Garner tells them what most all parents want to hear, but it is an honest presentation. He would never lie to a kid and his parents to sell them on Georgia. He is always up front with parents. If their son signs with Georgia, the rules will not be ignored.

Garner's philosophy is to be firm, fair and have fun playing on Saturday. "We tell them we will teach fundamentals and that will involve hard work. Football is not easy, but it can be rewarding if you give it the right emphasis."

Garner has always been an advocate of fundamental football. "It is has been said many times, but it is true. The game boils down to blocking and tackling. Everybody wants to try something different. There are a lot of gurus out there, but whatever twist you give the game, it won't amount to much without an emphasis on fundamentals. I want my players to be the most fundamentally sound players on the field."

Recognized as an outstanding recruiter, Garner says his success at Georgia is based on many factors, first and foremost, an impressive product to sell and the working cohesiveness of the Bulldog staff. "I may have the title as head recruiter, but you don't succeed at recruiting unless you worked together effectively as a staff." Other points Garner makes:

We work hard at all phases of recruiting. We spend a lot of time evaluating prospects and visiting in their schools. Identifying the best players in the state is your first priority. Then selling them comes next.

We have the best product to sell. There is no better football opportunity than the University of Georgia, in my opinion. Obviously, there are other outstanding programs, but none better than UGA.

We have a good captain of our ship. Coach Richt stands for the right thing, and we realize he is easy to sell, both to kids and their parents.

We tell kids there will be bad days. That's life, and life is not always fair. So go to a place where you feel comfortable and be with people you like. We have great compatibility in our program with

Davey Pollack, always around the ball

our players and our staff.

We communicate with parents. They know we will call if there is a problem. They know, too, that they can pick up the phone and call us. We underscore family at Georgia. We take kids to church, for example, which we think is important, and we have a meal with them afterward.

We want them to leave happy and know that we will remain interested in their careers. You can't imagine how happy I was when I saw Richard Seymour celebrating in Jacksonville. He earned his third Super Bowl ring. We are proud of him. I think he knows how we feel about him. I love him like a son and felt like a proud father when his team won the Super Bowl in Jacksonville.

When Kenny Veal was a sophomore and cut a class, Garner, with Richt's approval, would not let Veal dress out for an early season game. He had to sit in the stands. When Garner called Veal's mother to explain what he had done, she became mad. Really mad. Not at Rodney, but at her son. "I was wrong," Veal said later. "He did what was best for me. He was thinking about my best interest. It made me a better person. I learned real quick you have got to be a team player and follow the rules."

Garner coached Davey Pollack, who played a down lineman position his first year. He concurred with the idea that Pollack would function best on the outside. Each year the Georgia staff goes through a self-scouting session before spring practice. It is at that time they engage in second-guessing themselves. Should certain personnel be evaluated in terms of moving some players to another position? The coaches try to take a critical stance, making decisions that best benefit the team.

"We felt that Pollack, with his speed and quickness, would be able to make more plays at end. Obviously, it was a good decision. Both he and David Greene have been the greatest ambassadors for our program. They are the type of men who would be the first to tell you that they couldn't do it without the help of their teammates.

"We have no prima donnas on our team, and certainly Greene and Pollack were not prima donnas. You could never predict that Pollack would play as successfully as he did, but you know good things will happen to players who play like they practice. He did that, and you see the results.

"David Greene's leadership skills are remarkable. I don't think there was anybody on the team who truly didn't like and respect him. That is unusual this day and age when players are more selfish and self-centered. We'll benefit in recruiting because of the reputation of those guys and what they have meant to the University of Georgia. When we call on them to help us sell our program, I see them responding with the same commitment and enthusiasm that characterized their play as Bulldogs."

CHAPTER TWENTY-FIVE

DAWG RECEIVERS' FAVORITE BANKER

My favorite banker is John Eason.

You may know him, but not for any banking relationship. In all probability you are aware that he is the Georgia receivers coach, but he teaches his players by utilizing a banking concept.

Do something good and you get a "banker." Make a mistake and your balance sheet gets a check in the block marked "gasser."

In case gasser is an unfamiliar term, here's how it works. If you are required to run a gasser, for whatever reason, you start at one goal line, sprint to the other, touch the yard marker, turn around and sprint back. This explains why the receivers work diligently to maintain a positive balance sheet.

If you drop a pass, you run after practice. If you miss a block, you run. Make a penalty and you run a gasser. If you bust an assignment, there's a gasser waiting for you. On the other hand, you do something good, and you are the recipient of a banker. Things like a proficient block, extra effort on a catch, score after you catch the ball—even in practice—and you get a banker.

Receivers must settle their account daily. If there are more gassers than bankers, you run gassers until the balance sheet is even.

Good citizenship warrants a banker. Bring Eason an A from class, and you'll be credited with a banker. And get this—if you finish the season with extra bankers left over from quality performance during the fall, you are allowed to bequeath bankers to your teammates who are underclassmen.

At least that was the case until the fall of '03. Eason became so discouraged with mistakes by his receiving corps, he closed the bank. It reopened for business in '04. He doesn't dwell on any past disappointments, but he is never reluctant to resort to foreclosure.

Dropped balls make his blood pressure soar. I remember a game one year when his receivers had trouble hanging on to the ball. He lectured them with an emphatic declaration at the half. "The bottom line is catch the ball. You are a receiver, aren't you? Don't ask for a second chance. If you drop the ball, find yourself a spot on the bench."

He didn't raise his voice. It was a matter-of-fact style, but it was an unmistakable message for his receivers. They understood. They are aware he will sit the best of them down.

It is difficult to imagine a coach who is more caring than Doc Eason, but he has a simple philosophy. If you want to play football, you must

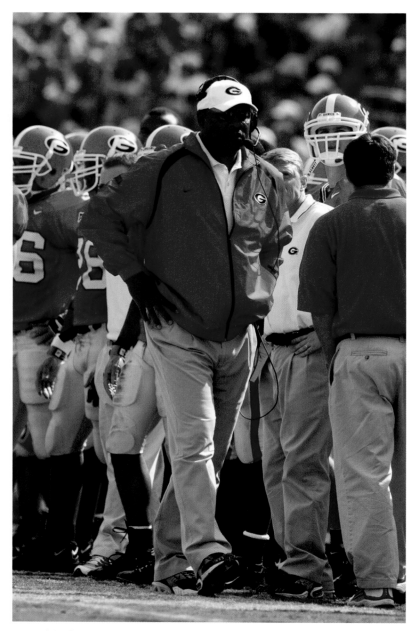

John Eason, known as Doc because of his advanced degree

that," Doc Eason says. "What we must do is constantly improve. You let up; you lose your job. All receivers want to catch the ball, which is natural, but we expect them to block and to run their routes sharply and efficiently."

A sloppily run route gets Eason's dander up. A capacity crowd sees dropped balls, but Eason, like a cogent safetyman, picks up on a poorly run route. If you are guilty, the coach lets you know. It is called teaching. Eason, with three degrees, is called "Doc" for good reason.

You learn to do it right and when you do, you are rewarded. That is why Eason's banker system makes pass receiving fun at Georgia. The last thing he wants is for a receiver to run gassers. But if it's deserved, that is what he gets.

I like the way John Eason goes about his business. He has an even pace. He is erect, confident, relaxed and straightforward. He is reserved and always under control. His emotions are in check. In conversations with him, you quickly gain confidence that he has positive and generous values. He has no agenda except for motivating young men to make something out of themselves. "There is more to life than the NFL," he tells his receivers.

In many respects his demeanor and that of David Greene are very similar. Both men are always calm and under control. "He worked well with our receivers," Eason begins in recalling the career of the Bulldog quarterback. "He made it a point to understand our receivers, how they ran their routes and how they would react to defensive pressure."

underscore discipline. If you honor the rules, you are rewarded. Football must be fun. That's why there are bankers for positive performances and gassers for mistakes.

His receivers are impressive—a capable, creative bunch with a chance for the spectacular if good health prevails. "We've got size, speed, and I like

The quarterbacks and the receivers are allowed 10 minutes together in pre-practice. That is all the time they can devote since NCAA rules restrict the number of hours a team can practice each week.

Compare that to Fran Tarkenton under Wallace Butts in the late 50s. "We had 30 minutes of passing drills pre-practice," the Hall of Famer quarterback says. "It was live. The defense was not allowed to hit the quarterback but it was live contact, full pads." Tarkenton considers that pre-practice routine significant in his development as a passer. David Greene did not have that luxury, but he made the best of the time available.

"Our receivers had confidence in David. Early in his career he did well in pressure situations, which was good for him. And the team, too," Eason notes. "The quarterback has to have confidence, and the team has to have confidence in him. It was at a high level with David during his career. He could handle the pressure, and I think the record shows that."

Ron Courson is an organized, informed, creative and dedicated sports medicine professional. No matter the circumstances, the athlete comes first.

While his first mission is to care for Bulldog athletes, he is an industry spokesman and advocate of athletic training methods and education for all levels of athletic competition. He has recommended to education officials that all athletic programs on the high school level be staffed with a certified trainer.

In his view, there should forever be the objective of improving techniques, seeking innovative ideas and finding new opportunities to provide the best assistance possible for athletes.

He lives by a simple but enlightening two-line mission statement. Courson is always reminding his staff, daily, that athletes want to "know how much you care before they care how much you know."

Courson is frequently spicing his conversations with quotes and homilies like "The rule breakers are always a step ahead of the rule makers."

Courson and Coach Richt agree on these policies:

+ Players must wear knee, thigh, hip and buttock pads.
+ Ankles must be taped or braced.
+ All linemen wear knee braces.
+ All linemen wear high top shoes.
+ Any player with a history of "stingers" must wear a neck collar.
+ Rib pads are optional for quarterbacks and receivers.
+ Eye visors are optional for anybody who has had any sort of eye complication.

The NCAA allows players to wear a hand cast if padded and covered. The officials consult with the athletic trainer of each team about casts and padding before kickoff.

Mouthpieces, which are mandatory, not only have cut down on tooth injuries, they have significantly reduced concussions. Dr. Glenn Alex, Georgia team dentist, makes an interesting point:

"The use of mouthpieces has virtually elimi-

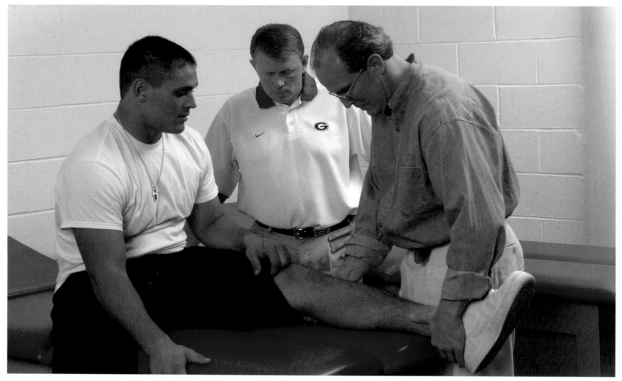

Trainer, Ron Courson (center), and Dr. Robert Hancock check Davey's knee

nated tooth injury," he says, "but there has been a great bonus in regard to reducing concussions. The mouthpiece cushions the teeth and the lower jaw from the skull if the player receives a blow to the chin.

"The NCAA mandated mouthpieces in 1989, but Georgia was ahead of the game and already required them. It's a pleasure to work with Ron Courson, who is one of those athletic trainers who always puts the care of the athlete first. He is highly respected in his profession, and Bulldog athletes are in the care of an outstanding athletic trainer."

IT'S A STRETCH

Harris Patel, a certified athletic trainer, was hired by the Indianapolis Colts to serve as an intern during the summer of 1998, which led to an association with Hunter Smith, the Colts' head athlet-ic trainer. After graduating from the University of Alabama with his Master's, Patel was recommend-ed by Hunter Smith for a seasonal internship with the New York Jets.

The Jets' head athletic trainer, David Price, realizes the importance and value of a stretching program, which contributes greatly to maintaining the overall health of football players. The extensive stretching knowledge Patel acquired from the Jets has been made available to the Bulldogs. During his daily training regimen, David Pollack was introduced to this program and is now a firm believer and advocate of it as well as its positive results. David Greene took advantage of Patel's thorough knowledge as well. Both players were eager to take advantage of what Patel provided in the way of improving their flex-ibility and endurance. The nature of Pollack's defensive position on the field and his fanaticism about fitness made him the most devoted stretching disciple on the team.

"Pollack was always asking questions. He was very eager to learn anything that would keep him healthy and overall a better athlete," Patel says. "He would stretch 25 minutes a day, including Sunday afternoons, which included treatment time in the hot and cold whirlpools. With Greenie as our quarterback we focused more on his shoulder and arm to ensure that muscles were relaxed, and there was no tension and soreness before each game."

Some stretching points from Harris Patel:

Stretching can be preventative when it comes to football injuries.

Stretching enhances performance and can be a deterrent to injury.

Stretching decreases soreness. Football contact work causes a natural buildup of soreness that means that a player will compensate and may hurt some other part of the body.

Pollack's dedication to stretching influenced younger players to take note and utilize stretching in their routine.

There is only one Harris Patel; however, there are dozens of stretching advocates. Patel, along with his fellow athletic trainer, Lenny Navitskis, and Ron Courson have developed a plan to accommodate the athletes who have become advocates of the stretching program.

SOUTHEASTERN CONFERENCE
GAME DAY CAST REPORT

HOME TEAM _Georgia_

VISITING TEAM _LSU_

DATE _October 2, 2004_

UMPIRE _____

The following players are wearing protective casts:

NUMBER		BODY PART
Marqus Elmore	#19	R wrist
Ray Gant	#90	R thumb
Dan Inman	#72	R wrist
Kelin Johnson	#30	R thumb
James Lee	#71	R thumb
David Pollack	#47	L thumb
Jamario Smith	#37	R wrist

Ron Courson, ATC, PT, NREMT-I
Head Athletic Trainer

MOTIVATIN' JOE

You work hard all week, practicing with intensity, editing game tapes and focusing on the game at hand. Finally, it is Friday. The grind is over. Meetings and last-minute reviews remain but by Friday, as Bear Bryant once said, "the hay should be in the barn."

To loosen the players up, Coach Joe Tereshinski works with Marc Klempf and Steve Graham, who produce the Mark Richt Show, and develop a weekly motivational theme on video.

It is a theme that is fashioned in concert with the coaches. In staff meetings early in the week, they talk about points and ideas that should help motivate the players. Tereshinski first meets with Coach Richt for review and ideas. He then researches the history of past games with the next opponent.

Kids love music, and Coach Joe T does, too. Additionally, he is a movie advocate. After determining the theme, he and Graham-Klempf put together a videotape underscoring the chosen

theme with messages and titles to create a customized video. The tape is shown to the team just before boarding the bus to Sanford Stadium for the DawgWalk. For road games, it is the last visual in their pre-game routine before taking the bus for the opponent's playing field.

The music and the carefully crafted video help motivate the team to a high emotional plateau for kickoff. Tereshinski and the coaches want the theme to be the last thing on the players' minds as they head to the playing field.

CHAPTER TWENTY-SEVEN

MARK CHRISTENSEN: EVERYBODY'S HERO

Mark Christensen has cerebral palsy, and is wheelchair bound, but his spirit is boundless. In many respects he epitomized the spirit of the Dawgs during The Davids' time in Athens.

"You have to believe you can succeed in life, no matter your challenge," Mark says. "I like being around these guys. They inspire me." The Davids send it right back Mark's way. It is, they say, Mark who inspires them.

"Oh, the grief they gave me," Mark says, "after the ESPN broadcast." For those unfamiliar, the network was taken by Mark's presence and his relationship with the Bulldogs. The network aired a story chronicling Mark's management of a personal challenge. The eight-minute broadcast highlighted his special relationship with the players and the response he receives from the Bulldogs he literally adores.

Yet, they play jokes on him. They will drive his wheelchair in a corner where he can't reverse out. They tape his head, and are forever kidding him. Young athletes are masters of the putdown. Mark gets his share. He gives it right back.

One day he threw Pollack's shoe in a trash can. "Okay, Big Time, I am not speaking to you for a year," Davey scowled. For several days, Pollack would see Mark in the training room and would walk by him, looking straight ahead, never acknowledging his friend. One day when there was a misting rain, Pollack laughed energetically as a teammate pushed Mark into the rain and left him. "They really mess with Mark," laughs Ron Courson, "but they love the guy."

Another day Mark hid Greenie's shoes under his wheelchair. Greene complained with a deadpan look. "What a friend. You will make me late for practice, and I'll have to run laps." All the while Mark is grinning broadly.

It is a fun-loving, healthy relationship with a group of college football players with the objective of welcoming a young man into their midst and making him feel rewarded by being associated with the game.

Mark, who has always dreamed of coaching, is a rehabilitation assistant for the Athletic Association. "He is always eager to assist us," Courson says. "Any assignment."

Pollack's first comment about Mark was predictable. "He gets more sleep than anybody in the training room," referring to catching Mark dozing off during a slow period. Then he compliments Mark for his outgoing personality. "He is always

Mark Christensen with his mother, Mary Beth, and The Davids

happy, and we all admire his friendly disposition."

Greene says, "Mark is such a neat guy. He often sits in our QB meetings. He will throw out a thought that we never think about. He is very sharp; he's thinking when he is quiet. He may look like he is not alert, but that is when he'll say something that gets your attention. We mess around with each other, but all in fun. What a wonderful person!"

One of the highlights of Mark's week is the DawgWalk. "I get there early with my mom or my dad. They let my parents roll me down the DawgWalk, and fans call out my name. I just can't believe it. The fans make a difference with our team. It was gratifying to know people are interested in me. Many of them tell me they saw the ESPN broadcast. I hear from people who tell me that it is an inspiration to them that they know someone who, even with a disability, has a reason to work to get out and enjoy life. I love my job. I love the Dawgs."

Mark does require assistance, and not only does Amy Gaines, a native of Athens and a State Rehabilitation Agency staff member who is assigned to work with Mark, provide professional aid, she has become an admiring friend. "When Mark's parents, Mary Beth and Paul, brought him to the coliseum where we met," Amy says, "I was quickly charmed by his smile and upbeat personality. We hit it off right away, and our friendship has grown. He is a lot of fun. He loves it when the players pick at him. Mark has a wonderful attitude that should inspire us all. He has accepted the fact that the wheelchair is part of his life. His attitude is so remarkable. Nobody feels sorry for him because of his remarkable attitude."

■■■

CHAPTER TWENTY-EIGHT

MEMORIES OF A WALK-ON PLAYER

You may not know Jake Hooten, one of those unheralded walk-ons who put his heart into helping make the Bulldogs championship contenders. A bright and articulate young man, he knows what it is like to suffer through long seasons as cannon fodder. He understood when there was the unlikelihood of playing time, but wearing the red and black and being a member of the Bulldog football team were still important to him.

He wrote the following essay for this book:

If you could take a walk around the UGA locker room during the 2004 season, you would have walked past the lockers of Greene, Pollack, Pope, Ware—all names that are familiar to everyone in the Bulldog Nation. However, if you were to take a short stroll over to the other side of the locker room, you would see names like Koehler, Lady, DeGenova, and Abbott, among many others—names familiar to only a few friends and loving families. The common thread that runs through all those names is this: we are all Georgia Bulldogs. We all put on the same silver britches, we all had the same Gs on our helmets, we all shared in our (few) defeats, and we all rejoiced in our many victories.

For many walk-ons, the chance to live out their dream begins in the UGA football office, where they meet Coach Joe Tereshinski, who sizes them up and decides whether or not they would be football material. I can still remember the day over four years ago when I had that meeting with Coach T. During two-a-days in 2001, several offensive linemen had injuries. There was such a shortage of bodies that Coach Richt put a notice in The Red & Black: "All students with offensive line experience, please contact the football office." I remember thinking, "Hmm, I wonder if they'll take me, I played on the offensive line in high school." The only problem was, I was lucky to have played offensive line in high school. I was not your prototypical offensive lineman. I was 6'4" and barely weighed 200 pounds soaking wet. I was sure that Coach T would see my scrawny frame and tell me "Thanks, but no thanks." To this day, I do not know what Coach T saw in me, but regardless, he gave me the paperwork I needed to fill out to sign away my free time to the Georgia football program. He then told me to meet the head equipment manager, Dave Allen, the next day to get my gear. After that meeting, I was ecstatic—I must have had a smile on my face a mile wide. I called my father at work, and he almost did not believe me. I was going to be a real, live Georgia Bulldog!

That first day of practice was an almost surreal experience. I emerged out of the locker room practically in awe of everyone around me. I had unexpectedly gone from a student fan to a student player—all in the matter of one day! The football players that seemed almost god-like to me in the past were suddenly right in front of me! One of the first players to come up to me was Jon Stinchcomb. We must have really been hurting for some offensive linemen because he went out of his way to come over to me and tell me how glad he was that we, the new walk-ons, were there.

That day was also the first day I met two of Georgia's future superstars, David Greene and David Pollack. Being an avid fan, I knew all about this Greene kid. Was he going to beat out D.J. Shockley and become our fearless leader? Was he going to lead our team to victory, or struggle under the new Mark Richt regime? Back then, he, just like me, had not proved a thing. All I can remember about David Pollack on that day was that he was this freshman kid that I was going to become awfully close to when I took my position on the scout team.

Little did I know then that I would find my niche on the scout team and spend four long years running the opposition's plays—week in and week out. The special teams, offensive, and defensive scout teams are comprised mostly of walk-ons like myself, who, simply put, do not have the same athletic gifts as the scholarship players. Every single player has a role on the team. Our role as walk-ons and scout team players is to give the most effort possible into simulating the opponent's offensive, defensive, and special teams plays so that the first and second string players will be fully prepared for the coming game. Often, I would watch film to find out the little quirks or nuances of the guy I was playing as and made sure that I mimicked them during scout team practices. As scout team players, our games are not on Saturdays—in effect, our games are on Monday through Thursday on the Woodruff

Practice Fields.

In addition, because of strict NCAA rules for dressing out, many of us watched most of the games on Saturdays in the student section along with all the other students. We cheered and screamed along with everybody else, and when Georgia won, we knew that we had something to do with that victory.

However, the chance to don the red jersey and the silver britches is a rare opportunity that must be cherished and appreciated. My first chance to suit up came on December 1, 2001 against the University of Houston. Running out of the tunnel that day was everything I had expected it to be—and then some. The energy that surges through your body is an indescribable feeling. That day was my first DawgWalk experience as well. I must have given high fives to 100 people that day. Little kids and grown men would touch my shoulder pads or slap me on the back. They had no idea who I was, but that did not matter to them, I was a Bulldog. It was during that first DawgWalk that I broke out of line and gave my mother a big hug—a tradition I continued in each subsequent DawgWalk.

Once the season comes to an end, many walk-ons decide they have had enough and go back to living their lives as students again. For the rest of us, once the season ends, we count down the days until the dreaded mat drills. I remember my first mat drills session back in the spring of 2002. We began at 5:40 that first morning, and I remember feeling a mixture of nervousness and pure horror. I had begun to really like this Van Halanger fellow during the season, but that morning he was not too high on my list. Every person on the team receives a grade after every mat drills session—I think I received a nice, big "F+" on that first day—the only "F" I received in college. I think it is safe to call mat drills a "Walk-On Elimination Chamber." On more than one occasion, I have seen a walk-on just give up in the middle of a mat drills session and walk out the door, never to be seen again. I believe it was during these mat drills sessions that I bonded with most with my teammates. It did not matter whether you were a scholarship player or a walk-on, you helped your teammate make it through the tough times, and they helped you finish the drill as well. It was at that time in 2002 that I felt I was truly a part of the team. I had become fused into this unit and would never let go. For a walk-on, making it through mat drills proves your mettle among your teammates.

Some might find it ludicrous that a walk-on would be willing to sacrifice his body on a daily basis and not receive a free education or the chance to play every Saturday. Our motivation to compete as walk-ons does not come from the potential stardom or fame we could achieve; our motivation comes from our desire to make those people who truly love us proud—our families, close friends, girlfriends, and other supporters. You will never see our faces on SportsCenter, but those who love us could not be more proud of us.

While we may not receive the monthly checks that the scholarship players receive, we are rewarded for the work that we have done. After my four years of playing football for Georgia, I take away five rings, seven watches, a TV, a stereo, an iPod, several bags, T-shirts, game jerseys, hundreds of pictures, and countless memories. Also, the four bowl trips that I have been on have been some of the best weeks of my entire life. Spending a whole week in places like New Orleans, Orlando, and Tampa with my best friends is something that I will cherish forever. The biggest reward of all is the fact that I can say that I was a member of the Georgia Bulldogs. My rings may tarnish and my jerseys may fade, but nobody will ever be able to take away from me the fact that I played with one of the finest teams in the land for four long years and received one of the finest educations, too.

I will never forget the experiences I shared with two of my favorite teammates: David Greene and David Pollack. One thing I will never forget about

Jake Hooten, lasting memories of his days with the Dawgs and The Davids

"Greenie" is when we sat next to one another for graduation in December. He and I came to Georgia with completely different expectations. He knew that he was going to be a football player, and I had no idea that I would ever play football again after my senior year of high school. Yet on that day, we both graduated with business degrees and both left the University as football lettermen. Along the way, we shared in more than 40 victories together (whether or not I was in the locker room after the game). Greenie is a great leader who is just as

SCHOLAR ATHLETES

NATIONAL FOOTBALL FOUNDATION
SCHOLAR – ATHLETE AWARDS

1966 . . . . Bobby Etter PK

1967 . . . . Tommy Lawhorne, LB

1968 . . . . Billy Payne, DE

1969 . . . . Tim Callaway, DG

1970 . . . . Tommy Lyons, C

1971 . . . . Tom Nash, OT

1977 . . . . Jeff Lewis, LB

1983 . . . . Terry Hoage, ROV

1998 . . . . Matt Stinchcomb, OT

2002 . . . . Jon Stinchcomb, OT

2004 . . . . David Greene, QB

impressive off the field as he is on the field.

Pollack is another tremendous person whom I consider to be a man of great faith and great character. Because I had been assigned to "block" him for four seasons, I asked him one time if he would write me into his NFL contract to be his professional practice dummy. I mean, I had done it at Georgia. Why not do it at the next level? Recently, Pollack signed a picture for me saying, "Dear Hootie, Thanks for letting me beat you up." That's the kind of guy Pollack is—honest and appreciative. Pollack achieved so many accolades for what he did on the field, and I take pride in knowing that I was right there across the line from him four days a week helping him prepare for that week's opponent.

The pages of this text cannot even begin to describe all the wonderful experiences and the unforgettable friendships that I have developed during my tenure as a football player for the University of Georgia, but one of my most memorable moments came on November 30, 2002, against those hated nerds from North Avenue. Toward the end of the fourth quarter, when we were up by 44, Coach Callaway came over to me and told me that I was going in on the next offensive series. It did not matter to me that many fans had already left the game—the most important fans, my family, were still in their seats waiting to see if their son would have the opportunity he had always dreamed of. And then, it happened. I sprinted from the sideline to the huddle and ran six plays. I remember thinking, "Wow, this is just like practice," and it almost seemed easier than practice because I was accustomed to blocking David Pollack every day. After the clock struck zero, I had this indescribable feeling coursing through my veins. I had just played between the hedges! Before I hopped on the team bus after the game, I passed by my parents and sister, and noticed that we all had tears in our eyes. Not every walk-on has the fortune of playing on Saturdays, but each one most definitely takes something special away from his experience as a Georgia Bulldog. To have the opportunity to put on that red helmet and those silver britches and play on the same fields that Herschel Walker, Charley Trippi, Frank Sinkwich and hundreds of other Georgia greats played on is something to be treasured by all players—both walk-ons and scholarship players.

Being a walk-on at the University of Georgia is definitely not the easiest job in the world, but if you stick around long enough, put plenty of effort and determination into everything you do, and nurture as many friendships as possible, you will find that being a walk-on can be the best, most enjoyable, and most rewarding thing you ever do in your entire life.

Dave Johnson epitomizes the teacher in coaching. He is organized, efficient and prepared. He uses written material to teach his tight ends and the punt team and can verbalize his instruction effectively in a soft-spoken manner.

"You want to enjoy success," he says. "You should try to experience as many victory celebrations as possible, but there are many things you can experience other than winning and losing, especially with your players."

As tight end coach, Johnson reminds his players that it is not natural that they take to blocking like the others on the offensive line. It is a learned function. Success comes from stressing of the work ethic.

"Kids grow up with a ball in their hand," he says. "They pitch and catch in the backyard or on a playground. Nobody ever says, 'Let's go outside and do a little blocking.' A tight end's ball skills are obvious, but unless it is in the open field, a tight end's blocking accomplishments largely goes unnoticed. The game tapes reveal when he has produced. Pro scouts figure most everybody can catch the ball these days, but what they want to know is whether a tight end can handle his blocking assignments."

Johnson also coaches the punt team, which he refers to as "the Pride team." There are several goals for this team. The first one is that you avoid blocked punts. That would be obvious, even to the most uninformed observer. To enjoy that status, as Georgia did in its championship season, there are several rules, reminders and on-the-field repetitions. Everybody must pay attention; everybody must concentrate.

The goal set forth by Johnson is to hold the opposition to an average net return of four yards. But the biggest assignment is to get the punt off without hindrance. Without that depressing thud which signals that the ball has made contact with the defender before it is airborne. For this to happen, every player on the line must know his blocking assignment.

The snap should reach the punter's hands in 1.99 seconds or less. It has to be direct, crisp and on target. Timing is extremely important, and the punter should be able to begin his punting motion a fraction of a second before the ball reaches his hands.

Georgia uses the spread punt formation, and Joe Tereshinski, III makes calls verbally and through use of hand signals. With crowd noise, he

Dave Johnson considers himself a teacher first

usually lets the gunners (the two outside guys responsible for downfield coverage) know whether it will be a directional kick (angling for the corner) or a pooch kick (high, short kick when deep in opponent's territory). He does this by patting his shoulder or his thigh. Or clinching a fist or patting his helmet.

He goes through his routine much like a third base coach in baseball. The hand signals change from week to week. Only the players know which signal is live.

■ ■ ■

CHAPTER THIRTY
A SAGE OBSERVER

It is good—damn good—for the Bulldogs that Ray Lamb is around and about the Butts-Mehre Building. His engaging good nature, which helped make him an excellent high school coach, along with his sage advice contributes significantly to the pleasant atmosphere on the second floor, the coaches' domain.

One of the reasons I like him is that he engenders limitless goodwill for the Bulldogs. His official title, Pro-Scout Liaison, doesn't adequately define his role with the Bulldogs. He is there for the defensive coaches to seek second opinions about things that make football sense. He can provide information and advice on a number of fronts; he can inform coaches whom to call when there are questions that relate to high school athletics.

His position does not allow him to recruit or scout players but he can provide information that is beneficial to the coaching staff. He has an ear to the ground, and he knows what is going on in the state. High school coaches call him often just to talk football. When they come to town as guests of the Bulldog staff to watch spring practice—or if they are just passing through—almost all of them want to have a word with their friend, Ray Lamb. Although he has no official role with recruiting,

high school coaches are always looking up their old friend when they come to the Georgia campus.

They don't just know him. They like him. When one of the players enrolls at Georgia, Lamb will greet the athlete when he reports and wish him well. He enjoys conversations with the player about his school and his family.

He manages the Georgia coaching clinic on campus, and he runs the Nike Coach-of-the Year Clinic in Atlanta. Originally, the Coach-of-the Year Clinics were founded by Bud Wilkinson of Oklahoma and Duffy Daugherty of Michigan State.

Lamb's easygoing style and general knowledge of athletics serves the University of Georgia well. He coached for 35 years and won three state championships at two schools.

Ray Lamb always trumpets the decency of the coaching fraternity. "By and large, particularly with those coaches I have known, they want the best for their kids. I have been in coaching in some capacity for almost four decades. There is nothing I enjoy more than sitting down over a meal with a group of coaches and just talking. We talk about football and our families. We always talk about our kids, and all of us are in agreement that there are a lot of good kids playing high

Ray Lamb, a friend of coaches everywhere

school and college football.

"One of the things that the high school coaches in this state understand is that if one of their players comes to Georgia, Mark Richt is going to take care of him. Mark is going to demand discipline and respect, but he will do the best for every kid who comes through this program."

Coaching at Commerce was a family affair for Lamb. Literally. His son, Bobby, was the quarterback and his second son, Hal, was a wide receiver. His daughter, Lynn, was a cheerleader.

That only leaves Linda, Ray's wife of 40 plus years. And if you ever sat near her for a Commerce game, you would know that she was nothing if she wasn't involved.

In 1981, Commerce won the state Class AA

title. While the boys and Ray played and coached, Lynn led the cheering from the sideline. She was not the only one cheering. Linda was a ball of energy and never stopped yelling from the stands. She really got into the game.

That family experience made the championship at Commerce the highlight of Ray's high school coaching career. To win a title with family contributing is the ultimate reward in coaching. To have Bobby running his offense, Hal making big plays and Lynn cheering them on gave Ray and Linda memories that will last forever.

Growing up, all Bobby, head coach at Furman, and Hal, head coach at Calhoun High School, ever wanted to do was coach. "That is all they ever talked about," Ray says. "It's all they ever wanted to do." "Bobby," he says, "was the hardest-working player I ever had. He and Hal, who was the better athlete, both really loved the game, but when we left the fieldhouse that was it. We never got into dinner table discussions about football." (Lynn is married to Hal's offensive coordinator, Michael Davis.)

Ray became involved with the Georgia Athletic Coaches Association (GACA) during his time at Commerce and rose to the organization's presidency. He also coached in the GACA all-star game and provided key leadership for the association.

Lamb was a key contributor to a group of coaches who brought the Georgia High School All-Star games back after a brief absence. "The coaches wanted to continue the All-Star games," he says, "and worked hard to get the games organized and running again. I was greatly pleased to be a part of that effort."

WEEKENDS AT HOME

Football weekends at our house are quite involved and active. Many friends stop by, and seldom is there a time when a bed is unoccupied. We have family and friends staying overnight with us every weekend, which we enjoy.

Our menu, most often, is tenderloin from the grill, with appropriate side dishes and accoutrements, accented by wines shipped in from Mat Garretson, whose Paso Robles, California, winery is gaining an exalted reputation across the country.

Often the CBS announcers, Verne Lundquist, Todd Blackledge, Tracy Wolfson, and producer Craig Silver drop by. Bowl people sometimes are on the guest list. Myrna and I like it, but the most fun we have is when our children, Camille and Kent, and their respective spouses, Chris and Stephanie, join the fun. When Kent returns home, it means our grandson, Alex, comes along.

For the LSU game in '04, the party was bigger than ever, the mood so upbeat, just like it was all over town. I don't think the excitement has ever been greater for a Mark Richt era weekend. In fact, I'm sure of it.

Georgia won, and when Kent met me at the game with glassy eyes, our conversation became purely emotional. He made me reflect in print on our past:

He's not a little boy anymore, but the flashback to those times, when he was, surfaces often. Now he's the one with a little boy. When the third generation son does something cute or impressionable, you recall his father's past with warm affection. As you reflect, humility hovers tightly.

Since picking up his diploma at the University of Georgia, the son-turned-father has lived out of state. There was the typical yearning for adventure by experiencing other landscapes. Temporary work at a ski slope in Colorado was the initial anchor away from home. Then came the California fling for which he had had a longing since his skateboard and MTV days.

All the while he sorely missed Athens. Most of all he missed his friends. Now, when he returns, he truly savors the moment. It is a tonic for the soul. He eagerly

The ball was always in good hands with Greenie

awaits limited fall weekends for action between the hedges which make him recall his days of hanging around the Dogs—traveling with the team to bowl games, cheering with his SAE pals on Saturday afternoon, partying into the night, sleeping late on Sunday and coming home for mealtime fulfillment.

In addition to those meals made with a loving

mother's touch, a college kid, matriculating in Athens, realizes that a refrigerator within arm's length is a treasured security blanket.

Having the Rocky Mountain ski slope and California experiences was meaningful, but as maturity began to set in, it was home for which he often pined. "I just miss the Dogs so much," he would say. The Southeastern Conference's affiliation with the CBS network has helped fill the void, but not every weekend. When one of the ESPN networks covers a Bulldog game that provides another option.

The hardest times have been when there was no TV or the regional package was not available in Dallas. Technology provides some relief in that when the Dogs are not on television, there is the Internet, which connects him with the Munson broadcast.

"I just never realized how good I had it growing up and going to Georgia," he says. "You cannot believe how overwhelmed I am when I come back. To drive down Milledge and Lumpkin, to go downtown and to walk through all the tailgating in the parking lot—it brings me to tears."

He was emotional when we met just prior to the LSU kickoff. "When the team took the field," he was saying, with eyes glassing over, "I couldn't help it. I was overcome with emotion. The tears were rolling down my cheeks. I didn't care if anybody saw me. I love Athens. I love Georgia."

It was a testimony to warm the heart of an old Dawg, who subsequently experienced wet eyes. On Sunday, we played with his son and recalled highlights of the big game. He checked the Internet to see what the Baton Rouge writers were saying.

Will that two-year-old follow in his father's footsteps? Time will tell, but if it happens, my wish is that loyalty gets the emphasis that has enraptured his father.

The little one is named for a friend who took a premature earthly leave after a bout with drugs. That the father, who avoided the drug scene, would name his son after a close friend, even with regrettable com-

plications, leaves you somber and reflective.

Whatever a man achieves in life, it's not worth headlining unless he develops loyalty. If he can pass loyalty on in an imperfect world, it means that there is potential for good things in the future for those of us who remain attached emotionally to our alma mater.

Something about The Davids that warms my heart is that I know they will feel the same way about Georgia in the years ahead. The Snellville sensations are going to be great alumni.

FAREWELL

It was January 4, 2005. The Davids had returned home from Tampa on Sunday following the defeat of Wisconsin in the Outback Bowl. They had spent a relaxed day with their families on Monday and returned to Athens Tuesday.

Reality had set in. They were leaving. Permanently. The separation from the campus where they had enjoyed so much pure fun had begun. Emotionally, they realized it would be sometime before that separation would be lastingly confirmed, but it was underway.

"It just hasn't hit me," said Greene, who was signing autographs for a number of kids who had shown up for a photo session. He was in no rush to clean out his locker since the day he had made a decision to contract Pat Dye Jr. as his agent. He would take his time. His training for work in the National Football League in Atlanta would soon be underway; he was leaving Athens behind. Who would be coaching him? Another former Bulldog quarterback, Zeke Bratkowski, who played 14 years in the NFL and finished his career as an understudy to Bart Starr of the Lombardi Packers. Zeke then coached 26 years in the league, retiring in 1996.

Athens would remain nearby, and Greenie

could leisurely vacate the locker in the Butts-Mehre Building where he had dressed for five years, the last four as Georgia's starting quarterback.

With Pollack, it was different. He immediately returned to Tampa, where he would train at an operation set up by International Management Group (IMG), the Cleveland-based firm, founded by the late Mark McCormack, famous for starting his super agent business with a handshake with Arnold Palmer.

IMG is also the firm that represents Tiger Woods and Peyton Manning. The company, which is best known for its work with golfers, has working agreements with an assortment of football players, but never a lineman coming out of college with the reputation of Davey Pollack.

No sooner had he worked for a couple of days, than a call went out from Tampa with the message that Davey's enthusiasm and work ethic had become contagious.

On January 4th, life began to change for the life long friends on what turned out to be their last day together in Athens. The campus was quiet, and the winter semester was set to begin six days later. It was unseasonably warm for early January. They were on hand for a photo shoot for this book.

Young 47's learning to go for the ball, Davey Pollack style

It was vintage Greene and Pollack. The quarterback was laid back and under control. The lineman, ever the court jester, was in perpetual motion, wise cracking, and a caustic needler nonpareil. He makes fun of everything and everybody.

Pollack simply cannot be still and cannot refrain from a playful putdown. He hugs, he deadpans, he pantomimes, he insults—he appears not to possess a serious bone in his body. This has been the Davey Pollack his teammates and coaches know. Only when the ball is snapped is he serious. In interviews, he is thoughtful and introspective, always says the right thing at the right time, speaks like a sage soothsayer, wise beyond his years. The rest of the time, he is off the wall.

At Sanford Stadium, when he and Greene were photographed with a statue of Uga at the mascot cemetery at the southwest corner of the stadium, Pollack, with a rolled up piece of paper,

created a fake urinal for the mascot. When they took a position in the first row of the stands, standing in a section where they may someday sit as alumni (If Pollack ever reaches a point in life when he can sit through a game, which is doubtful), he suddenly leapt up on the one of the aisle posts, about six inches square, and created a gyrating, twisting dance that reflected what he is. The thought never crossed his mind that a misstep might void millions of dollars. It also showed that he has no fear. Furthermore, it revealed that one of his greatest assets as a defensive end is remarkable agility.

All the while, Greene is chuckling and enjoying an act he must have witnessed more times than he has called an audible in his illustrious career.

Quarterbacks coach Mike Bobo showed up at Butts-Mehre for a picture with Greene, which took place near an illuminated photo display of

No penalty for piling on The Davids

Georgia's great quarterbacks, including Fran Tarkenton and John Rauch—both College Football Hall of Fame selections. Pollack began to conversationally attack Bobo, who, like Greene, wore No. 14 in his Bulldog career.

"I wanna know," Pollack said, pointing his finger at the Bulldog assistant coach, "why Greenie's picture is not up there? The quarterback who won more games than any quarterback in Georgia history."

Bobo responded, laughing, "Give us time, we'll get it up there." That wasn't good enough for Pollack. "Ought to be up there already," he admonished. "What I want to know is—whose picture is coming down? What was your record, Coach? Was your record as good as Greenie's? Nobody up there had his record, and you, the quarterbacks coach, don't even have up there a picture of the man who kept you employed the last four years."

Finally, Pollack gave Greene a chance for a brief conversational respite with Bobo, who had brought a ball and a poster for them to sign. Greene and his coach enjoyed a quiet moment and then embraced. It was a depressing postmortem. They would never be together again as player and coach. They were signing off on their official relationship. Bobo would, the next day, move full speed into recruiting, and David Greene, No. 14, would begin his schooling for work in the NFL.

As Bobo departed, he offered a parting shot to Pollack. Someone had asked about a play that Coach Richt had named "Joker." Pollack, said with smiling glee, "Hey, that play was named for me." It was Bobo's turn to apply the needle. "It was the worst play we ever put in," he said with a laugh as he headed out the door.

Claude Felton, expert at getting the word out on the Beloved Dawgs

A touching interlude soon developed for Pollack. He would bring pause to his wisecracking as his photograph session with his position coach, Jon Fabris, took place. They, too, were saying goodbye. Pollack was introspective, whispering warm and appreciative sentiments to his coach. They were thanking each other.

When we gathered later for dinner, frivolity and nonsensical banter returned full speed. Pollack walked into his host's home, headed to the refrigerator, opened the door and spotted a container of grapes. "Hey, I love grapes! Can I have some? Where's the water? Time to eat!" It wasn't rude or offensive, and that, too, is one of his remarkable charms. He can wisecrack and put down without turning people off – at least most of the time. The grapes disappeared post-haste. The jack was out of the box, and nobody could put it back.

It was a spaghetti supper for the two boys and their families and Pollack's fiancée, Lindsey Hopkins. An extra plate had been prepared for Greene's girlfriend, Veronica Clark, who was unable to attend, due to a late work assignment. Pollack consumed the extra plate with gusto. It was the only time in the evening he was quiet or

still, albeit briefly.

It was time to watch the Orange Bowl and afterwards to say farewell. As they departed, I felt a lump gathering in my throat. I was sad. I remain sad. I will be sad when I don't see them in the Butts-Mehre Building. When Georgia kicks off in the fall, I will see new faces wearing the numbers 14 and 47, arguably the two most popular numbers in Bulldog history. Certainly with fans, that is the case.

Sadness must not remain, however. Georgia football goes on. There came a rush as I stood at my front door watching them depart my driveway. How blessed is Georgia and the Bulldog Nation that David Greene and Davey Pollack came our way? An eternal toast to these "Beloved Dawgs."

Unconventional is what these remarkable young men were during their days in red and black. They stirred so much excitement for Georgia followers in their four years as Bulldogs. Their careers were like Jack's beanstalk reaching for the stars. They were stars themselves, but the only ones to offer a disclaimer to that status are the two young men.

What you have with these roommates, teammates, and Dawgmates are two kids who have been lifelong friends with similar goals and objectives, but dissimilar habits. "Complete opposites," says Pollack's mother, Kelli, "but the best of friends."

They don't drink, smoke, or use foul language. They quietly return thanks before each meal. They are serious about schoolwork, devoid of ego and never read about themselves. Their parents do and, however, pass along the news even though The Davids are not anxious to hear from their parents about praise or rebuke.

SportsCenter they watch, and sometimes see themselves at work on Saturday but remain unimpressed with their celebrity. You tell me they aren't exceptional, and I will convince you Hawaii is not an island.

Pride in their work? They've got plenty of that,

Davey Pollack just can't say no to kids

and when their careers ended, January 1, in the year of our Lord, 2005, they now may eventually take time to peruse the voluminous scrapbooks their parents have collected since they enrolled at Georgia. They may even read the magazine articles and books printed with tribute and chronicling their days on campus, but they won't pour over the tribute with any passion.

I asked Greene this question midway through his senior year. For a quarterback who is honored with constant review, nearly all of it positive, do you not ever read the sports pages? "Never," was the polite reply. "That won't help you in the next game, will it?"

Ask Pollack if he has read *ESPN: The Magazine*'s profiling of his career, and he will tell you, "Nope, I haven't read a single word of the story. Never even seen the magazine and have no interest in reading it."

They had no desire to be celebrated above and beyond the team and their teammates. They

always knew what was important. They heard themselves reviewed, along with their teammates, by their respective coaches. If they succeeded in their game assignment, there were "good job" assessments, and that was enough. Likewise, if they missed an assignment, it was pointed out, which motivated them to correct and improve.

Polite, nice and accommodating, they are kids with high moral standards and unswerving principles. They do good works, but don't shout it from the mountaintop. They would, in every instance, yield to a teammate when a camera or a microphone found its way into their midst.

Pollack was once overheard growling in the locker room after a game, "Talk to some of these other guys." Watching them for four years, you come to the conclusion that they represented the ideal in unselfishness. Priority has always been the team.

Although he was perhaps the most egotistical general of his era, I am reminded of General McArthur's famous "team" speech at West Point in his sundown years, when he advised the cadets that greatness at the U. S. Military would always emanate from "The Corps." In a fading voice, he repeated, that it will always be, "The Corps. The Corps. The Corps."

A similar refrain can be heard from the actions, deeds and attitudes of David Greene and Davey Pollack. "The Team. The Team. The Team."

Most of us have the same basic qualities as these two kids, but we get tripped up by ego, arrogance, selfishness and insecurity. These are young men of altruism. They are confident, but give way to others. I can't imagine raw arrogance visiting their personalities. In sports, that is quite unusual. They are not for self but put others first, especially their teammates. This comes naturally. It is also hard to believe.

While they don't appreciate, philosophically, an entrepreneur with eBay intent bugging them for their signatures, they will go out of their way to sign for a kid. Drive miles to a hospital and pay a visit. Hang with them in the locker room after a game.

When Greene learned that a fellow lefty, Kim King of Georgia Tech, had experienced a downturn in a bout with cancer, which eventually took his life, the Bulldog quarterback sat down and wrote King a letter of encouragement.

The letter began, "Dear Mr. King. You don't know me..." King was quite taken by the heartfelt overture and told friends, "How can that young man say I don't know who he is? He has to be a special person."

How do I know about David's letter to Kim King? A friend of Kim's told me. Greenie would never bring that up just like he, along with Pollack, would never volunteer information about any of their charitable deeds.

In the pre-season of 2004 my wife, Myrna, and I hosted them for supper. They insisted on helping set the table. When dinner was over, they cleaned the table and were ready to do the dishes. It was a challenge to successfully lobby them out of that assignment.

Fans are in awe of them, but they are never in awe of themselves. Interestingly, they are in awe of accomplished sports stars. Both enjoy golf, and you should have seen the smiles when the package of autographed pictures for them and their fathers arrived from Jack Nicklaus. "How can we meet him?" they asked, almost in unison. "He's the man."

They are what we expect of our college heroes. They came to campus to gain a degree and to play their dead level best for the Bulldogs. I don't know anybody who would suggest that they have not succeeded in their goals and objectives. Greene's degree was conferred at the end of fall semester, and Pollack is a semester shy, with plans to complete requirements after his rookie season in the National Football League.

They have been model student-athletes, model citizens, model teammates and model human beings. Surely, they have a flaw of some kind. Something has to bug them. Somebody must rub them the wrong way.

While I am certain that they are human, I not only haven't run across anything negative, I haven't heard of anything. Nobody carps and complains. From my vantage point, there was neither jealously nor contempt.

Good works, good Samaritans, good guys. We're going to miss more than big plays from these guys.

▮▮

In winter, Florida appeals to most everybody, and I've always enjoyed visiting Tampa. Lot of good Bulldogs there, and you should have seen and heard them as the game drew nigh. They are few in number, but I think the alumni group there is one of the most enthusiastic in the Bulldog Nation. They are hungry for any morsel of information. They are warmly grateful for any attention from Athens. An official Bulldog visitor there is overwhelmed with hospitality.

You can imagine how excited they were when the Outback Bowl invitation was issued to the Bulldogs and subsequently accepted.

I chose to fly so I would have more time for researching the story of The Davids. On the flight down, I thought of the remarkable career they had enjoyed and how well they had been received and affectionately appreciated by the Georgia fans.

The thought suddenly surfaced. I have never heard anybody denigrate them, even slightly. Oh, I heard from those who upon occasion called for more Shockley, but seldom do you find high-profile athletes who are high profile with such character and integrity. You might get one, but it was Georgia's good fortune to land two. Doublemint Gum should have done one of those "double your pleasure" ads with them. They aren't twins in appearance, but the two of them were a package of dual success, fulfillment, heroics, honor and class. We not only have never seen anything like it, we have never heard of anything like The Davids.

Long-time friend Bill Simpson, former public relations director for the University, has this perspective: "I think in music, it's called counter point, when two different melodies are blended into a single, even better, harmonic melody. That's what I think The Davids provided to college football, not just to Bulldog lore. They are two boyhood friends from neighboring high schools who emerged into stardom at Georgia.

"While their athletic ability, their toughness under fire and their winning achievements are what brought them to our attention what makes them so memorable is something else. Their demeanor, on and off the field, their obvious leadership and respect by teammates and their own respect for teammates, coaches, fans and the game itself, their unobtrusive but always acknowledged faith, and their love for family, friends and each other make you wish that you could clone them and populate all of the game with players—and persons—just like them.

THE TAILGATE SHOW

The Tailgate Show has become a popular segment of the Bulldog broadcast. Several years ago, I began thinking of ways to provide more sales inventory for our sold-out broadcasts and also to also provide feature information that couldn't be presented during the broadcast. That is when a lunch with the late Mike Faherty of WSB led to the origination of the Tailgate Show.

We had some troubling problems getting the show organized and running smoothly. There were some complications technically, many times the result of being too ambitious. Like hooking up two coaches long distance to talk with us from Sanford Stadium or the visitor's bench for road games. But advanced technology and better coordination of staff enabled us to work out most of the kinks.

There were three important factors that enabled us to get it down to a smoother routine:

+ WSB's commitment and involvement. Mike Faherty was a great fan of Larry Munson and eventually hired him to work at the station in addition to calling Georgia games. After Mike's death, Marc Morgan took over and sought avenues for more structured ties with the Bulldogs. Ultimately, WSB became the Georgia Network broadcast rights holder and managed the entire network. What a great day that was for Georgia! Marc, Dave Meszaros, Neil Williamson and Trey Workman teamed to make both the sales and broadcast package arguably the most attractive in the country—especially for football.

+ Larry Munson's increased presence in the TG Show.

+ The courtesy of opposing coaches, former coaches, sportswriters, alumni and sports personalities taking their time to talk with us on air. We have to do a little juggling from time to time to catch up with our guests, but most of the time they are available and generous with their time. Except, of course, for a couple of prima donna coaches.

We start putting the show together on Monday, and always seek to line up the most attractive guests possible. The hit of the Outback Bowl Tailgate Show was a telephone call to Randy McMichael, tight end for the Dolphins. He played the same position for the Bulldogs and revealed on the air that he has more than 250 pairs of shoes. "I have my own shoe closet," he laughed.

We believe in keeping the show lighthearted, loose and informative. Neil and I try to keep Munson from worrying too much, but have concluded that that is not possible.

"College football has changed a lot over the recent decades, not always for the better. The Davids reminded us of what the game can and should be like."

Bill has articulated as well as anyone what we should appreciate in The Davids. Pride in alma mater is something by which most any graduate is smitten, and to have players who make you feel they love the school as you do is simply overwhelming.

There was recall of many conversations on the flight down—their saying that would have a Bulldog Room, which they would someday buy

OUTBACK BOWL

Tailgate @ 8:00 – Kickoff @ 11:00

1)   8:01   Neil Williamson's Opening

2)   8:05   Roundtable discussion

3)   8:12   Scott Howard's Bulldog Scout Report

4)   8:20   Flashback Randy McMichael. Link up with Jim Mandich, Dolphin Radio Network

5)   8:29   Around the SEC with Neil Williamson

6)   8:38   Munson Hi-Lites from Tech game

7)   8:45   Jim McVay, CEO, Outback Bowl

8)   8:52   Neil's opponent scouting report

9)   8:57   Matthew Perkins (Hairy Dawg)

10) 9:02   Munson's picks

11) 9:08   Richt's power play

12) 9:16   Coach Barry Alvarez, Wisconsin

13) 9:26   Damon Evans/A.D.'s report

14) 9:34   Bob Davie, former Notre Dame head coach

15) 9:43   Richt's Inside Skinny

16) 9:52   Player Interview

17) 9:59   Charles Bloom, Associate Commissioner, Southeastern Conference

18) 10:05 Richt's scouting report

19) 10:12 Roundtable #2

20) 10:20 Wrap-Up

- - - - - - - -

Munson's guest: Andy Johnston, Sports Editor, Athens Banner Herald

season tickets and tailgate. I can see that happening with both of them, but when you belly up to the bar; you might have to order Diet Coke. At least with Pollack. I bet no two celebrated athletes ever went through Georgia and drank less than this pair. Davey consumed none and David had only an occasional beer or glass or two of wine in his stay on campus.

Furthermore, I bet no two star athletes ever went through college without offending less people: fellow students, professors, teammates, interviewers, coaches and passersby.

All the while in Tampa, I am wishing passionately for them to go out as winners. Ten wins would be nice, but the main thing was for them to exit with a victory. I felt that they deserved as much. Ten wins! That would have a nice ring to it.

On the bus to practice one morning, Jon

Fabris talked about the fun of the bowl week being the closeness that the team experiences. "We do everything for over a week as a team. We work together, we attend bowl social events together, and we eat together as a team. After this game, the players scatter, especially the seniors. Some of them may go for years without seeing one another. Many of my teammates at Ole Miss, I haven't seen since we left the campus. Of course, it is hard for me to get back to reunions, but I often think of them. Where are they now? What are they doing?

Are any of them down on their luck? How many of them are successful and happy?"

The news hit early in the week that Vanderbilt running back Kwane Doster had been murdered in Tampa, his hometown. The Bulldogs had played against him earlier in the season, and they were shocked. There was the thought that it could have happened to one of them.

The coaches talked about it. They always remind players to watch where they go. Don't go where it's unsafe. Be aware of what is going on around you. If trouble starts, walk way. Don't be too proud to move on. Just like on the field. If somebody hits you, don't retaliate. The official may only see the last blow, which might cost your team 15 yards and in the worst of developments, cost your team the game. Let even tempers prevail. Sometimes such preachment falls on deaf ears.

I was reminded about the death of Brice Hunter, one of Georgia's outstanding receivers. A neighbor in his apartment building in Chicago was playing his music too loud to suit Brice. He went to quiet down the volume but was shot. Dead. A life wasted. Gone. How tragic. Avoid confrontation. Mark Richt and his coaches preach that message often.

Doster's death made me think about the Georgia team in a good light. I often talk to the players about many things. I'm not an advisor or counselor, but I do interact with them. I feel I know many of them reasonably well. I hear what the coaches say. I know what Dave Van Halanger and Rodney Garner, perhaps the two on staff who are closest to all the players, think. Georgia does have good kids on its team. That doesn't mean that there won't ever be a time when trouble will find them, but I am encouraged by the basic good attitude I see in those on scholarship.

It made me recall, too, how deeply Mark Richt hurt after the 2002 season when players sold their rings and several were caught smoking marijuana. We had dinner one night at the Mean Bean, and I could sense the hurt in his voice when he discussed it. It was not representative of what he expected for his program. Most of all he hurt for the kids. He would be comforted if they learned from his discipline. He believes in giving a kid a second chance. He has enormous patience, and understands kids have limitless social pressures today. It is difficult for them not to yield to temptation, but his goal is to help them keep their lives safe, productive and on an upward path.

Bowl trips are a reward, but there is an emphasis on what you came for—to win the game. All the while you are aware that your opponent has the same objective. You want your seniors to exit with victory.

With The Davids, it was about as heartwarming as you could expect. After Wisconsin tightened the score with time running out, Pollack makes another one of his sensational plays, sacking the quarterback and stripping the ball away. I saw him making his move, collaring the quarterback, and saw his act taking place like it was scripted.

When he fell to the ground, I immediately looked to see if the official was in agreement with the Georgia sideline. The players knew what was happening. In the split second before it was reality, they knew it could be déjà vu. They were poised for a wild celebration, pending the call of the official. When it was confirmed, they burst forth with acclamation that overwhelmed Munson's voice in my headset.

I saw Jon Fabris take his cap off and sail it into the air. "I've never done anything like that before in my entire coaching career," he said sheepishly after the game. "I just couldn't hold back."

It didn't dawn on me until some time later. That was the last play of Davey Pollack's Bulldog career. Georgia, after Wisconsin scored on an interception, took over at its own 39 yard line and Wisconsin never touched the ball again. David Greene saw to that.

So typical of him, when it counted, when the game was on the line Davey Pollack's calm and cool quarterback roommate moved the Dawgs toward the Wisconsin goal. He just ran out the clock. A touchdown would have been likely if needed. With Mark Richt calling the plays and David executing superbly, the Bulldogs took the safe route. Just killed the clock.

With the clock winding down, it was 4th and 1 at the Badger 15 yard line. Neil Callaway, the offensive coordinator, suggested, "L-tight Over Max Tommy. We had not shown that play in a while," Neil said. "Since we are a field-oriented team in that situation, I told Coach Richt we might fool Wisconsin by running into the boundary." Thomas Brown got the first down and more, 11 yards. The celebration can now begin. The Davids, and their senior pals, can go home a winner.

With the early kickoff, I could return home after the game although there was a long wait at the airport. I had given my tickets to Melanie Ayres, the daughter of my good friends, Hilda and Agnew Peacock, and her friend, Jackie Cochran. They dropped me off at the airport where I watched Texas defeat Michigan in the Rose Bowl. Both coaches in that game are good friends, and in a situation like that, you don't know who to pull for. I did think about the fact that in Austin,

Texas, they think national championship. Mack Brown has recruited well for years, but he has not won a conference title yet. He has lost to Oklahoma five years in a row. Most Longhorns expect more, so I knew how much Mack and Sally would savor a Rose Bowl title.

It just goes to remind you that championships are so hard to come by. Mark Richt has one in four years and played for another. Not bad when you consider the competition he faces annually. He believes Georgia can contend every year, but it is a challenge every week. To average 10 wins in the SEC East, as he has done, means that you can never have an off day.

Davey Pollack was our POWERade Player of the Game for the locker room post game show. He thanked Georgia, and he thanked God. He also said that the key to the sack and strip was that the official, Jack R. Childress of the Atlantic Coast Conference, was in position to see the play.

On the Delta flight home, I thought about a lot of things. I sat beside the wife of a Wisconsin fan, who sat across the aisle. He had moved his family business to Atlanta, and his younger brother had attended Georgia. The younger brother had obviously visited the beer cooler frequently during the long day. He was hoarse, and he was wildly happy. He didn't put down his brother's team; he just celebrated the Bulldog victory. The Wisconsin brother seemed amused at his Georgia brother. "It really means a lot to him," he smiled. "He has the Bulldog fever. Folks down here are passionate about their football."

The Davids had something to do about that passion during their four years. I thought about Davey coming back for his final year of football. That was a great statement for the game. When he was making his decision, I thought of what Norm Pollack said about going out early for money. "That," he said about the dollars that come with high-profile draftees, "takes care of wants, not needs."

Take LeBron James, for example. With a stroke of the pen and bypassing college, he became an instant multi-millionaire with the NBA's Cleveland Cavaliers. He is rich, but he never had, nor will he ever have, the college experience. What is that worth?

The Davids enjoyed success as collegiate stars. They expect to continue in the NFL, but no matter how that journey goes, they will have the opportunity to look back on their days on campus with the fondest of memories. They not only were successful, they enjoyed their college experience as much as any two boys who ever played the game.

I landed in Atlanta a little tired and sleepy. With no checked luggage, I went right to my car and was in Athens in less than an hour and a half. It was well past my bedtime, but I was not the least bit sleepy.

The entire trip, the thought kept recurring. As an alumnus, I will be indelibly proud The Davids came our way. I thought about what Ralph Waldo Emerson once wrote:

To laugh often and much;
To win the respect of intelligent people
and the affection of children;
To earn the appreciation of honest critics
and endure the betrayal of false friends;
To appreciate beauty, to find the best in others;
To leave the world a bit better,
whether by a healthy child, a garden patch
or a redeemed social condition;
To know even one life has breathed easier
because you have lived.
This is to the meaning of success.

I wish I had said that—about the Beloved Dogs.

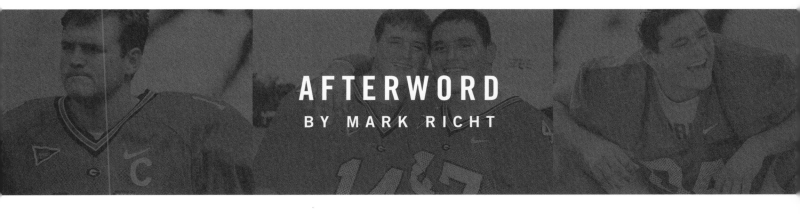

AFTERWORD
BY MARK RICHT

Coaches and teachers find their reward in seeing young people grow and develop, mature and succeed. We want them to aspire to reach a high station in life, but all the while embracing good and shunning evil. We want them to display feelings and compassion for others, to do kindness unto others, to set goals and achieve them. We want them to be good role models.

While there obviously are a lot of issues, challenges, and complications in education today, there are the many coaches and teachers who are providing positive direction for young kids.

When young men show up on our campus to play football, we begin our relationship with them when they are still maturing. They are still finding their focus in life and are making decisions that will influence where they go and what they become.

At Georgia, we want the best of our kids. Wanting the best for them, however, goes beyond winning, high priority that it is. We seek to provide an opportunity for them to grow into young men who can contribute to society. It's ambitious, but we would like for each and everyone to complete degree requirements. We know many will not. They naturally seek opportunity in the NFL, which we understand.

We realize that some won't make it to graduation, but it is our responsibility to encourage and to help them all we can.

With David Greene and Davey Pollack, we found two boys who were a joy to coach, two who gave priority to education. We preach family at Georgia, but they came from close-knit family backgrounds. They were already sold on the concept when we began fall practice their first year in 2001.

Greenie was already on board when we arrived, and we didn't know at first that he and Davey were long time friends. When I went to meet Davey, riding over and having dinner with him and his parents, I realized that he was an energized and high strung type. At dinner we loved his natural enthusiasm. He made us feel good about his attitude from the start. I still have not seen his high school film. It was a matter of trusting Rodney Garner, who has a very critical eye for talent.

Since I spend most of my practice field time with the offense, I didn't see as much of Davey as I did Greenie, but I always took time to evaluate our defense. When I watched Davey on tape—even practice footage—I was so taken by his commit-

Greenie and Mark Richt enjoyed a winning Dawgs' life for four years

versus South Carolina in Columbia and again in the Outback Bowl are important plays in Georgia history. What is important to our coaching staff is that he worked diligently to prepare himself to make such big plays.

Early in Greenie's career, we realized that he would do things the right way. I liked the way he paid attention. He was conscientious and had a sincere commitment to learning our offense executing it.

It was a new system, it was a transition for him, but he was determined to devote the time necessary to master our offense. By the time he finished his career, you could say that he was an extension of the offensive coaches and our thought process. His awareness had become very astute. Once a quarterback learns the offense, he has to also learn opposing defensive tendencies. If he is practiced and well grounded, he should be able to recognize what is taking place with the defense and react to give positive results.

If a quarterback knows the offense and has a full understanding of what we are trying to do, he must then execute. I think David did an outstanding job of learning and then executing on Saturday.

Most quarterbacks have a defining moment in their careers—the time when a quarterback shows he can do it. It is a moment when everybody, including himself, knows that he can do it. The pass for a touchdown against Tennessee in Knoxville in 2001 was that moment for David, and I think it is the reason that he went on to become the winningest quarterback in NCAA history.

In that first spring practice, we tried to impress upon David and our other quarterbacks that disciplined practice habits be given priority. That was important to us. It WAS just as important to David. With his attitude, the team had a chance to succeed.

David was unflappable and handled the pres-

ment. During the game, I usually focus on our offensive objective for the next series when we will get the ball back—but I also pay attention to our defense. I marveled at the plays Davey made. His ability to get to the quarterback was so exceptional.

I always thought, "Well, Greenie is over here with me, but Davey is going to get him back on the field right away." That usually was the case.

His most outstanding plays the sack and steal

sure of the job about as well as anybody I have ever coached. There never was a game in his career when we felt that he was the reason we lost a game. And who has more opportunity to lose games than the quarterback?

There were no doubters, no second guessers on our coaching staff. You never sensed any lack of confidence on his teammates' part, and that is important with regards to quarterbacks in college football today. Your teammates must believe in the quarterback.

His touchdown pass at Auburn in 2002 is a terrific example of combining the mental part of the game with execution. We called a play—70-X Takeoff—which we hadn't called in a while. We didn't have time to remind him what to do; he knew what to do, and he made it look easy. First, he remembered the play although it could have been rusty in his mind. Then, he calmly threw the ball where the receiver could get it. He could have been just a little off, and the play wouldn't have worked. He could not have made that play without good practice habits. He could not have made it if he hadn't become a quarterback who could perform under pressure.

Fortunately, I have had an opportunity to coach several outstanding quarterbacks, like Charlie Ward and Chris Wienke. I keep in touch with them and it gives me a thrill when they call just to say hello. I know I will be hearing from David in the future. I will always want to know what he is doing and what is going on in his life.

He and Davey can't help us on the field anymore, but they will always be important to us. We will always welcome them back with the greatest of enthusiasm.

What is important is that their teammates will welcome them back at every opportunity. That is the greatest measure of your worth as an athlete—that your teammates accept you without rancor or acrimony. Unconditionally.

David and Davey experienced high honor as players, but they always extended tribute to their teammates. I don't think any two players ever had greater rapport with their teammates than those two.

We are going to miss both of them and their penchant for making big plays. But we will also miss their exceptional leadership and feelings for others.

I recently looked up the word altruism. It means, "not for self but for others." That, to me, graphically describes The Davids. I am happy to pay tribute to these "Beloved Dawgs." They will remain prominent in my scrapbook of memories.

BIG PLAYS BEHIND THE GREENE DOOR

2001

ARKANSAS STATE

1/10/G40 (1st quarter): Greene to Damien Gary for 24 yards. Set-up Musa Smith TD run.

2/7/S48 (1st quarter): Greene to Ben Watson for 27 yards. Set-up Smith TD run. (Greene 9-for-9 in the first quarter).

3/8/S25 (2nd quarter): Greene to Edwards on hitch route for 25-yard TD pass.

4/1/S38 (3rd quarter): Greene quarterback sneaks for first down. Set-up 13-yard TD connection with Gary.

SOUTH CAROLINA

3/8/S35 (1st quarter): Greene to Gary for eight yards and a first down. Set-up Billy Bennett 45-yard field goal. 7-3 South Carolina.

3/10/S49 (2nd quarter): Greene to Terrence Edwards for 24 yards. Set-up 38-yard field goal from Bennett.

ARKANSAS

1/10/A43 (2nd quarter): Greene to Edward for 33 yards. Set-up 7-yard TD pass to Edwards on slip screen. Georgia takes 17-10 lead.

1/10/G49 (2nd quarter): Greene to McMichael for 25 yards. Set-up 24-yard field goal by Bennett.

2/G/A4 (4th quarter): Greene to McMichael on play-action pass for 4-yard TD. Georgia extends lead to 34-23.

TENNESSEE

2/G/T15 (2nd quarter): Greene to Gibson for 15-yard TD pass. Georgia takes 17-14 lead.

1/10/G12 (4th quarter): Greene to Gibson for 55-yard gain. Set-up Bennett field goals. Georgia takes 20-17 lead over Volunteers.

2/10/T46 (4th quarter): Greene to McMichael for 26-yard gain. Set up Greene to Haynes. "P-44" on first and goal from the Tennessee six-yard line. Georgia earns 26-24 win over the Volunteers in Knoxville.

VANDERBILT

2/3/V24 (1st quarter): Greene to McMichael for 21 yards. Set-up Smith run.

3/19/G42 (2nd quarter): Greene to Gibson for 58 yards on a slant taken to the end zone. Georgia extends lead to 21-0 over the Commodores.

1/G/V17 (3rd quarter): Greene to Edwards for 17-yard TD score. Georgia lead extends to 30-14.

KENTUCKY

1/10/G32 (2nd quarter): Greene recovers bad snap and connects with Gibson for 66-yard score. Kentucky lead cut to 22-7.

3/10/K21 (3rd quarter): Greene scrambles for 21 yards and finds end zone. 2-point conversion to McMichael ties score at 22-22.

2/6/G44 (4th quarter): Greene connects with Gibson for 56-yard score. Georgia takes 36-29 lead.

1/G/K5 (4th quarter): Greene hits Haynes out of the backfield for 5-yard TD score. Georgia extends lead to 43-29.

FLORIDA

1/10/G19 (3rd quarter): Greene to Watson for 36 yards.

1/10/G27 (4th quarter): Greene to Gibson for 40 yards on a slant route.

AUBURN

1/10/G33 (1st quarter): Greene from the shotgun hits Gibson for 67-yard TD pass. Georgia takes early 7-0 lead.

4/2/G44 (2nd quarter): Greene play-actions for 56-yard TD pass to Edwards. Georgia takes 14-7 lead.

1/10/G40 (4th quarter): Greene to Gibson for 44 yards. Set-up 43-yard field goal by Bennett, tying score at 17-17.

1/10/A23 (4th quarter): Greene drives Georgia downfield with a 22-yard pass to Edwards. Jasper Sanks stopped on first and goal from the 1-yard line as time expires.

OLE MISS

3/4/M9 (3rd quarter): Greene to Edwards for 9-yard TD. Georgia extends lead to 21-9.

GEORGIA TECH

2/10/G41 (1st quarter): Greene to Gibson for 48 yards. Set-up field goal by Bennett. Georgia takes 3-0 lead.

2/11/G26 (3rd quarter): Greene to Gibson for 50 yards. Set-up Haynes TD run. Georgia wins 21-17.

HOUSTON

1/10/H48 (2nd quarter): Greene to LaBrone Mitchell for 31 yards. Set-up 12-yard Greene-to-Gibson fade route that results in a touchdown. Bulldogs extend lead to 14-0.

2/10/H49 (3rd quarter): Greene play-action pass to Edwards on a stop-and-go route for a 49-yard TD pass.

3/6/H49 (3rd quarter): Greene fakes right and throws to Watson for a 49-yard TD pass.

BOSTON COLLEGE

2/11/BC15 (1st quarter): Greene to Gibson in the flats for a 15-yard TD.

2002

CLEMSON

1/G/C6 (1st quarter): Greene hits Gary for a 6-yard score. Georgia takes 7-0 lead.

SOUTH CAROLINA

1/10/G36 (1st quarter): Greene to Gibson for 52 yards. Set-up Bennett field goal. Georgia takes 3-0 lead.

NORTHWESTERN STATE

3/4/N5 (1st quarter): Greene hits Brown for 5-yard TD. Georgia takes 7-0.

3/3/N5 (2nd quarter): Greene to Wall for a 5-yard TD pass.

1/10/N12 (2nd quarter): Greene to Edwards for 12 yard TD score. Georgia extends lead to 31-0.

3/25/N29 (2nd quarter): Greene to Smith for 26 yards. Set-up Greene to Edwards 3-yard TD score.

NEW MEXICO STATE

3/7/N20 (2nd quarter): Greene hits Gary for 20-yard TD score.

3/10/N29 (2nd quarter): Greene hits Edwards for 19 yards. Set-up 10-yard run by Smith. Georgia extends lead to 21-7.

2/5/N10 (2nd quarter): Greene hits Edwards for 10-yard score.

ALABAMA

1/10/A42 (2nd quarter): Greene to Gibson for 42-yard score. Georgia takes 14-0.

1/10/A37 (4th quarter): Greene completes 37-yard TD pass to Edwards. Georgia extends lead to 24-12.

TENNESSEE

3/2/T45 (2nd quarter): Greene to Edwards for 22 yards. Set-up Bennett field goal.

3/7/T11 (3rd quarter): Greene finds Brown on a fade route in the left corner of the end zone for a 11-yard score. Georgia takes 15-0.

VANDERBILT

3/6/G39 (1st quarter): Greene to Edwards for 19 yards. Set-up Greene to Edwards 35-yard score on third down and 10. Georgia takes 7-0 lead.

3/4/G35 (2nd quarter): Greene to Edwards on a play-action fake for 65-yard TD. Georgia extends lead to 14-7.

2/9/V11 (3rd quarter): Greene scrambles for 11-yard TD score. Georgia extends lead to 41-10.

KENTUCKY

3/5/UK25 (1st quarter): Greene to Gary for 25 yard TD pass. Georgia ties score 7-7.

3/10/UK12 (2nd quarter): Greene to Edwards for 12-yard TD. Georgia takes 21-17 lead.

1/10/UK41 (3rd quarter): Greene down sidelines to Edwards for 41-yard TD.

3/10/UK 12 (3rd quarter): Greene to Edwards on slant route, 12-yard TD score.

FLORIDA

1/G/F10 (1st quarter): Greene to J.T. Wall for 10 yard TD.

OLE MISS

3/10/M17 (2nd quarter): Greene connects with Gibson for 17-yard TD. Georgia 21-14 lead over the Rebels.

3/8/M33 (3rd quarter)" Greene on a step-and-go to Edwards for 33-yard TD.

AUBURN

3/6/A22 (3rd quarter): Greene to Gibson for 18 yards. Set-up Greene one-yard TD run. Georgia cuts Auburn lead to 10-14.

3/14/G30 (3rd quarter): Greene to Michael Johnson for 20 yards. Set-up John Stinchcomb one-yard fumble recovery. Georgia cuts deficit to 17-24.

2/6/G45 (4th quarter): Greene to Gibson for 41 yards. Set-up fourth-and-fifteen from the Auburn 19 yard line, where Greene connect with Johnson for 19-yard TD and game-winning score.

GEORGIA TECH

3/2/50 (1st quarter): Greene to Brown for 15 yards. Set-up Smith TD run. Georgia takes a 7-0 lead.

4/4/GT35 (1st quarter): Green to Johnson for 16 yards. Set-up Bennett field goal. Georgia extends lead to 10-0.

1/18/G20 (2nd quarter): Greene over the middle to Edwards for 31 yards.

1/10/GT49 (2nd quarter): Greene connects with Gibson down the left side for 49-yard TD pass. The Bulldogs extend lead to 24-0.

1/10/G21 (2nd quarter): Greene to Watson for 40 yards. Set-up J.T. Wall TD run. Georgia extends lead to 41-0.

ARKANSAS

2/10/A39 (1st quarter): Greene to Wall for 22 yards. Set up Smith 17-yard TD run that extended Georgia's lead 14-0.

1/10/G37 (2nd quarter): Greene connects with Gibson for 44 yards. Set-up Bennett field goal that extended Georgia lead to 17-0.

1/10/A20 (4th quarter): Greene to Watson for 20-yard TD score.

FLORIDA STATE

3/7/F27 (1st quarter): Greene to Edwards for 12 yards. Set-up Bennett field goal that gave Georgia an early 3-0 lead.

CLEMSON

3/2/G44 (1st quarter): Greene to Gibson for 56-yard TD. Georgia takes early 7-0 lead.

3/7/C3 (4th quarter): Greene scrambles for 3-yard TD run.

MIDDLE TENNESSEE STATE

2/5/MT48 (2nd quarter): Greene hits Gibson near the sideline for 23 yards. Set-up Cooper TD run, giving Georgia a 10-3 lead.

3/14/MT21 (4th quarter): Greene hits Gary for 19 yards. Set-up Bennett field goal. Georgia extends lead to 23-3.

SOUTH CAROLINA

3/11/G13 (1st quarter): Green to Gibson for 19 yards. Later that drive, Greene connects with Brown for 14 yards on third down and 10 yards from the South Carolina 33-yard line. Set up Greene to Reggie Brown 2-yard score.

3/11/SC28 (2nd Greene to Brown for 21 yards. Set up 5-yard TD pass from Greene to Brown.

3/6/SC38 (3rd quarter): Greene to Brown for 36 yards. Set-up Cooper TD run.

LSU

1/18/G27 (4th quarter): Greene to Browning for 93-yard score. Georgia ties score at 10-10.

ALABAMA

3/26/G49 (1st quarter): Greene to Watson for 25 yards. Set-up Bennett field goal. Georgia takes 6-3 lead over the Crimson Tide.

1/3/A3 (2nd quarter): Greene to Watson for 3-yard TD pass.

TENNESSEE

2/8/T11 (2nd quarter): Greene to Michael Johnson for 11-yard TD. Bulldogs extend lead to 10-0.

3/7/G50 (2nd quarter): Greene to Watson for 18 yards. Set-up Bennett field goal.

4/1/G45 (3rd Quarter): Greene one-yard set-up Cooper 6-yard TD run.

VANDERBILT

2/10/G23 (4th quarter): Greene to McClendon for 22 yards. Set-up Browning TD run, extending Georgia lead to 17-2.

UAB

1/10/UB16 (1st quarter): Greene to Gary for 16-yard TD.

3/9/G41 (3rd quarter): Greene to Raley for 26 yards down the middle of the field. Set-up Bennett field goal, knotting the score at 13-13.

FLORIDA

1/10/F39 (4th quarter): Greene to Johnson for 24 yards. Set-up Lumpkin 1-yard TD run. Georgia cuts deficit to 10-13.

3/4/G41 (4th quarter): Greene to Johnson for 18 yards. Set-up Bennett field goal, tying score at 13-13.

AUBURN

3/11/A29 (1st quarter): Greene to Brown for 21 yards. Set-up Bennett field goal. Georgia takes 3-0 lead.

3/7/A33 (1st quarter): Greene to Johnson for 24 yards. Set-up field goal. Georgia extends lead to 6-0.

2/10/A19 (2nd quarter): Greene to Johnson for 19-yard TD in the corner of the end zone. Georgia up 13-0.

3/8/A27 (3rd quarter): Greene to Watson for 20 yards. Set-up Lumpkin TD scamper to give Georgia a 19-0 lead.

KENTUCKY

1/10/G49 (1st quarter): Greene to Gibson for 41 yards. Set-up Cooper TD run to give Georgia a 7-0.

3/9/G35 (2nd quarter): Greene to Gary for 17 yards. Set-up Bennett field goal that extends Georgia lead to 17-7.

GEORGIA TECH

1/10/G37 (1st quarter): Greene to Gibson for 46 yards. Set up Greene one-yard TD run. Georgia takes 7-0 lead.

1/10/G41 (2nd quarter): Greene to Thomas for 21 yards. Set-up Bennett field goal. Georgia extends lead to 20-3.

3/7/27GT (3rd quarter): Greene to Gibson for 26 yards. Set up Thomas TD run. Georgia up 27-3.

3/6/GT11 (4th quarter): Greene to Lumpkin for 11-yard TD pass.

LSU

1/10L18 (3rd quarter): Greene to Watson for 18-yard TD.

PURDUE

3/7/G49 (1st quarter): Greene to Gary for 43 yards. Set-up Greene to Gibson 6-yard TD.

3/10/P48 (1st quarter): Greene to Thomas for 11 yards. Set-up Greene to Gibson 4-yard TD.

1/10/G39 (2nd quarter): Greene to Browning for 43 yards. Set-up field goal. Georgia up 17-0.

1/10/P11 (2nd quarter): Greene to Brown for 11-yard TD.

2004

GEORGIA SOUTHERN

3/9/G43 (3rd quarter): Greene to R. Brown for 43 yards. Georgia up 41-14.

SOUTH CAROLINA

3/9/S12 (3rd quarter): Greene to Tyson for 12-yard TD. Georgia cuts Gamecock lead to 13-16.

2/4/S22 (4th quarter): Greene to R. Brown for 22-yard TD. Georgia takes 20-16 lead.

MARSHALL

3/10/G46 (2nd quarter): Greene to A.J. Bryant for 34 yards on a screen pass. Led to 10-3 lead.

LSU

3/10/L25 (1st quarter): Greene to R. Brown for 25-yard TD. Georgia takes 7-0.

3/2/L2 (2nd quarter): Greene to Gibson for 2-yard TD. Georgia takes 17-0 lad.

1/10/L29 (2nd quarter): Greene to R. Brown for 29-yard TD. Georgia extends 24-0 lead.

3/6/L24 (3rd quarter): Greene to Gibson for 24-yard TD.

2/11/L21 (3rd quarter): Greene to S. Bailey for 21-yard TD to extend the Georgia lead to 38-10.

TENNESSEE

3/10/G34 (4th quarter): Greene to R. Brown for 21 yard. Led to Danny Ware TD run that cut the Tennessee lead to 19-14.

VANDERBILT

3/2/V2 (1st quarter): Greene sneaks for 2-yard TD run.

Georgia extends lead to 14-0.

2/1/V22 (3rd quarter): Greene to Pope for 22-yard TD.

4/2/V38 (3rd quarter): Greene to R. Brown for 38-yard TD pass. Georgia up 30-3.

ARKANSAS

2/G/A5 (2nd quarter): Greene to Gibson for 5-yard TD. Georgia takes 10-7 lead.

2/7/A10 (3rd quarter): Greene to Pope for 10-yard TD. Georgia takes 17-14 lead.

FLORIDA

1/10/F27 (1st quarter): Greene to Pope for 27-yard TD. Georgia takes 7-0 lead.

1/10/F35 (1st quarter): Greene to Pope for 35-yard TD. Georgia takes 14-7 lead.

3/9/F15 (4th quarter): Greene to Gibson for 15-yard TD. Georgia takes 31-21 lead.

KENTUCKY

2/23/UK35 (2nd quarter): Greene to R. Brown for 32-yard gain. Set-up Greene to Pope 1-yard TD.

3/3/UK45 (2nd quarter): Greene to Gibson for 37 yards. Set-up Bailey field goal. Georgia up 13-0.

1/10/G20 (3rd quarter): Greene to Gibson for 54 yards. Set-up Brown TD run. Georgia up 27-3.

AUBURN

4/5/A6 (4th quarter): Greene to Pope for 6-yard TD.

GEORGIA TECH

3/15/GT28 (1st quarter): Greene to Gibson for 28-yard TD. Georgia up 7-0.

3/9/T39 (4th quarter): Greene returns from thumb injury and lead Georgia down the field, setting up Coutu field goal. Georgia up 19-13.

WISCONSIN

3/21/W38 (2nd quarter): Greene to R. Brown for 25 yards. Set-up 19-yard TD pass to Gibson to take a10-6 lead over the Badgers.

1/10/W24 (3rd quarter): Greene's pass deflected to J. Thomas who scampers for 24-yard TD. Georgia up 17-6.

Compiled by Jared Benko

HOW 'BOUT THIS
D-LINEMAN'S BOX SCORE

NOVEMBER 10, 2001, ATHENS
GEORGIA 10 – AUBURN 24

David Pollack had 6 total tackles (4 for a loss of 17 yards), one forced fumble and 2 sacks for a loss of 12 yards.

On Auburn's fourth offensive play from scrimmage, David Pollack sacks Tiger quarterback Daniel Cobb and forces a fumble that is recovered by the Tigers for a loss of 8 yards.

At the beginning of the second quarter, on a third and 12 from the Auburn 32, Pollack again sacks Cobb, this time for a loss of 4 yards and forces the Tigers to punt.

AUGUST 31, 2002, ATHENS
GEORGIA 31 – CLEMSON 28

Late in the game, on a decisive third and ten from the Tiger 28, David Pollack chases down a scrambling Willie Simmons for a loss of 12 yards. Subsequently, Clemson punter Wynn Kopp shanks a 17-yard punt that is returned by Thomas Davis to the Clemson 15-yard line. Three plays later, quarterback DJ Shockley makes some shifty moves on a draw play and scores to put the Dogs ahead by two touchdowns.

SEPTEMBER 14, 2002, COLUMBIA, SC
GEORGIA 13 – SOUTH CAROLINA 7

David Pollack had 8 tackles, 2 for a loss of 8 yards, 1 fumble recovered and 1 interception for a touchdown.

Georgia running back Tyson Browning fumbles the ball at the USC nine giving Carolina a big momentum boost. Three plays later on a second and two from the Carolina 17, Pollack combines with Boss Bailey to stop Gamecock running back Andrew Pinnock in the backfield, forcing the USC punt.

Soon after the start of the second quarter, Carolina has a third and eight from just inside the fifty. Jonathan Sullivan and David Pollack combine to stop Carolina's Cory Jenkins for a four-yard loss, forcing the punt.

With six minutes remaining in the first half, Carolina manages to drive to the Dogs two-yard line. Carolina's Andrew Pinnock fumbles the ball and it is recovered by Pollack at the three-yard line.

Two minutes later, one a second and one from the Dogs 24-yard line, David Pollack sacks Carolina quarterback Corey Jenkins for a loss of four yards to the 28. The Gamecocks are then charged with a substitution penalty forcing them back further and finally, the Gamecocks come up one yard short on their fourth down conversion attempt, giving the Dogs the ball at their own 24.

With less than 14 minutes remaining in the game, Pollack stops Carolina running back Ryan Brewer on a short pass for gain of three yards to the Gamecock seven. On second down, Pollack appeared to sack Carolina quarterback Corey Jenkins in the end zone for a safety but the official signals touchdown. Pollack had stripped the ball from Jenkins hand as he was throwing and Pollack is credited with an interception in the end zone for a touchdown. Georgia takes a 10-0 lead.

SEPTEMBER 28, 2002, ATHENS
GEORGIA 41 – NEW MEXICO STATE 10

David Pollack has 3 sacks for a loss of 8 yards on the day.

OCTOBER 5, 2002, TUSCALOOSA, AL
GEORGIA 27 – ALABAMA 25

With just over ten minutes remaining in the first half, David Pollack blocks Alabama field goal kicker Brian Bostick's 28-yard attempt. Seven plays later, Greene hits Gibson for a 42-yard gain and a touchdown to put the Dogs ahead 14-3.

With less than five minutes remaining in the game, Pollack sacks Bama quarterback Brodie Crolye on second down from the Tide's eleven-yard line. The Dogs force the Tide to punt two plays later; the Tide would only have one more possession.

OCTOBER 12, 2002, ATHENS
GEORGIA 18 – TENNESSEE 13

David Pollack records 2 sacks on the day.

OCTOBER 19. 2002, ATHENS
GEORGIA 48 - VANDERBILT 17

David Pollack blocks a Greg Johnson punt and returns it 16 yards to the Vanderbilt 45.

NOVEMBER 2, 2002, JACKSONVILLE, FL
GEORGIA 13 – FLORIDA 20

With eight minutes remaining in the first half, David Pollack intercepts Rex Grossman's screen pass and returns it 39 yards to the Georgia 44.

NOVEMBER 16, 2002, AUBURN, AL
GEORGIA 24 – AUBURN 21

David Pollack has 7.5 tackles and 2 for a loss.

On third and five, with just over two minutes remaining in the game, David Pollack and Tony Gilbert combine to stop Auburn quarterback Jason Campbell at the Tiger 35, forcing a punt. The next possession, David Greene connects with Michael Johnson for a 19-yard touchdown on fourth down for the go-ahead score.

DECEMBER 7, 2002
SEC CHAMPIONSHIP, ATLANTA, GA
GEORGIA 30 – ARKANSAS 3

David Pollack sacks Arkansas quarterback Matt Jones for a loss of six yards on first and ten from the Razorback 11-yard line with six minutes remaining in the first half.

AUGUST 30, 2003, CLEMSON, SC
GEORGIA 30 – CLEMSON 0

On third and goal from the Dogs ten, with almost nine minutes remaining in the game, David Pollack intercepts Clemson quarterback Charlie Whitehurst at the 16 and returns it 24-yards to the Georgia 40. Pollack's interception secured the shutout for the Dogs.

SEPTEMBER 13, 2003, ATHENS
GEORGIA 31 – SOUTH CAROLINA 7

With about three minutes remaining in the first half, David Pollack chases Carolina quarterback Mike Rathe to the sideline, forcing an errant pass that ends up in the hands of Georgia safety Sean Jones.

OCTOBER 11, 2003, KNOXVILLE, TN
GEORGIA 41 – TENNESSEE 14

With about nine minutes remaining in the third quarter, David Pollack pressures quarterback Casey Clausen, hitting him just as he releases the pass. The wobbly pass is intercepted by Bulldog linebacker Odell Thurman at the Tennessee 31 and returned to the Volunteer five-yard line. Three plays later, Tyson Browning scores from eight yards out. The extra point makes it 34-7 Dogs, effectively finishing off the Vols.

NOVEMBER 29, 2003, ATLANTA, GA
GEORGIA 34 – GEORGIA TECH 7

On Tech quarterback Reggie Ball's first attempted pass against the Dogs, defensive tackle Ken Veal deflects the ball and David Pollack intercepts it at the Tech 36.

With the Bulldogs leading 27-10 at the beginning of the fourth quarter, on second and 13 from the Dogs 41, Pollack sacks the second Tech quarterback of the day, AJ Suggs, for a loss of eight-yards back to the Georgia 49.

JANUARY 1, 2004, ORLANDO, FL
CAPITAL ONE CITRUS BOWL
GEORGIA 34 – PURDUE 27

With just over three minutes remaining in regulation, David Pollack sacks Purdue quarterback Kyle Orton on third and fifteen from the Boilermaker 25 for a loss of six yards, forcing Purdue to punt.

SEPTEMBER 4, 2004, ATHENS
GEORGIA 48 – GEORGIA SOUTHERN 28

Southern's first possession of the afternoon turned out to be a slow, methodical drive which ate up over seven minutes of the first quarter but only marched 37 yards down field. The Dogs finally stopped the Eagles at the Georgia 43. On fourth down, Pollack partially blocked Eagle punter Dan Jordan's kick and the punt went only eleven yards. Georgia running back Danny Ware would go on to score the Dogs first touchdown of the season on the Dogs ensuing possession.

SEPTEMBER 11, 2004, COLUMBIA, SC
GEORGIA 20 – SOUTH CAROLINA 16

David Pollack records 7 tackles, 3.5 tackles for a loss and 1 sack.

On South Carolina's final possession of the game, Carolina quarterback Dondrell Pinkins completes a short pass to Cory Boyd who takes the ball 13 yards before Pollack, exhibiting that trademark hustle, chased down at the 50-yard line. Two plays later, Pinkins is intercepted, and the Dogs secure the win.

OCTOBER 2, 2004, ATHENS
GEORGIA 45 – LOUISIANA STATE 16

On LSU's first possession of the day, on second down with ten to go, David Pollack stops Tiger running back Alley Broussard in the backfield for a loss of one. The Dogs sack quarterback Marcus Randall on the next play forcing the Tigers to punt. Georgia goes on to score its first touchdown of the day on a 25-yard pass from David Greene to Reggie Brown.

On the Tigers next possession, David Pollack sacks Randall on second and two, for a loss of eleven yards back to the Tiger 16. LSU runs on third down settling for a punt. The Dogs take their next possession into Tiger territory and convert on a 32-yard field goal from Andy Bailey.

OCTOBER 23, 2004, FAYETTEVILLE, AR
GEORGIA 20 – ARKANSAS 14

David Pollack had 7 tackles, 3 for a loss, 1.5 sacks, 1 forced fumble and one recovered fumble.

On third and seven with a little over nine minutes remaining in the game and the Dogs leading 17-14, David Pollack sacks quarterback Matt Jones for a loss of 15-yards. Pollack forces Jones to fumble in the process and recovers the ball himself at the Razorback eight.

David Pollack's sack on Jones tied him with Georgia great Richard Tardits as the Dogs all-time sack leader with 29.

OCTOBER 30, 2004, JACKSONVILLE, FL
GEORGIA 31 – FLORIDA 24

David Pollack sacks Gator quarterback Chris Leak on first and ten from the Dogs own 24 in the closing seconds of the first half. The sack gives David Pollack sole possession of first place on Georgia's all-time sacks list. The Bulldogs stop the Gators on the next two plays forcing a field goal attempt from Gator Kicker Matt Leach with ten seconds remaining in the half. Leach misses the 39-yard attempt and the Dogs go to the locker room with a 21-14 lead.

Pollack sacks Leak again on a first and ten, this time for a loss of three-yards from the Florida 20 to the 17 with about eight minutes remaining in the game.

NOVEMBER 13, 2004, AUBURN, AL
GEORGIA 6 – AUBURN 24

Early in the second quarter, David Pollack blocks an Auburn punt by Kody Bliss at the Tiger 15.

NOVEMBER 27, 2004, ATHENS
GEORGIA 19 – GEORGIA TECH 13

David Pollack records 6 tackles, three for a loss and two sacks.

As time is winding down in the first half, David Pollack sacks Tech quarterback Reggie Ball for a loss of 13-yards to the Yellow Jacket 8.

Early in the fourth quarter on a third and eight from the Dogs 32, David Pollack sacks Damarius Bilbo for a loss of seven. Pollack's sack effectively pushed the Yellow Jackets out of field goal range.

With time winding down in the fourth quarter, the Jackets line up on fourth down and 21 from the Georgia 32. Pollack brings pressure from the outside forcing Reggie Ball out of the pocket. Ball scrambles to his right, sees no one open and inexplicably throws the ball away, turning the ball over to the Dogs, and allowing Georgia to run the clock down to zero securing the Dogs fourth straight win over the Yellow Jackets.

JANUARY 1, 2005, TAMPA, FL
THE OUTBACK BOWL
GEORGIA 24 – WISCONSIN 21

David Pollack records 4 tackles, 3 sacks, 1 forced fumble, 1 recovered fumble and one pass deflection.

David Pollack sacks Badger quarterback John Stocco for a loss of one on second down and five to go from the Dogs 19 with about a minute remaining in the first quarter. The Badgers were held to a field goal.

On third and ten from the Georgia 18 with under a minute to play in the third quarter, Pollack again sacks Stocco for a loss a loss of one-yard. The Wisconsin field goal attempt is no good.

Late in the game, the Badgers drove deep into Georgia territory, bringing up a first and goal from the Bulldogs five-yard line. David Pollack brings pressure from the outside, sacks Stocco for a loss of ten yards and, for the third time in his career, simultaneously sacks the quarterback, strips the ball and recovers the fumble at the Dogs 16.

Compiled by Jordan Posey